Banished Messiah

Banished Messiah

Violence and Nonviolence
in Matthew's Story of Jesus

ROBERT R. BECK

WIPF & STOCK · Eugene, Oregon

BANISHED MESSIAH
Violence and Nonviolence in Matthew's Story of Jesus

Wipf & Stock
An Imprint of Wipf and Stock Publishers
199 W. 8th Ave., Suite 3
Eugene, OR 97401
www.wipfandstock.com

ISBN 13: 978-1-60608-556-1

Manufactured in the U.S.A.

Contents

Acknowledgments

DISCUSSIONS WITH JIM GOODMAN about Matthew's narrative began this book. The "Redactors" writing group was a testing ground for its development. The John Cardinal O'Connor Chair provided an opportunity to design the project. The Loras College Library staff graciously provided assistance and a space to work without interruption. David Cochran and the Kucera Center were generous with a grant. Andy Auge, Amy Lorenz, and John Waldmeir contributed careful readings and helpful suggestions at different stages of the writing. One Mean Bean coffeehouse provided an environment for supposing, discussing, and writing. My friends were generally discreet and always supporting. I am grateful to all.

Preface

THIS PROJECT BEGAN AS a sequel to *Nonviolent Story*, a study of the narrative conflict resolution of Mark's Gospel. That book attempts to understand how a nonviolent Jesus is presented in a narrative that includes his violent death. I drew the conclusion that Mark's narrative takes the shape of what we today would call nonviolent confrontation, but because it takes as its subject of examination Mark's literary effort rather than the historical Jesus behind the text, it speaks only to the views of the evangelist. After I completed that study, I began to wonder if any of the other evangelists agreed. My curiosity took me to Matthew's Gospel, as being closest to that of Mark. Although that may be true, my hope of a simple comparison was quickly disabused by the complexity of Matthew's text and situation.

Then plans were interrupted by the events of September 11, 2001. It was clear, in the aftermath of the attacks on the Pentagon and the World Trade Center, that there was little public appetite for discussions of nonviolence. Retribution was the cry of the day. Likewise, there was little market for a topic that no one wished to entertain. So the project was put on indefinite hold.

Sometime later, in a context now lost, I became aware of a Jewish biblical scholar explaining the relevance of the destruction of the second Temple in 70 CE by describing it as "our 9/11." Although obvious differences separate the two events, most notably the position of empire in respect to the deed, the reach and depth of their impact on their populations was similar. This prompted a reconsideration of the present project. A massive act of violence had altered the perspective of a people, and the world was changed. No longer was it adequate to speak of the fall of Jerusalem as an academic problem, as if loss of the Temple was simply a problem of eschatological timing, delayed beyond expectations. Matthew's problem was not simply that the events of 66–70 CE failed to bring about the close of the age and called forth an attitude of retrenchment. Matthew's problem was larger than that, and it included the fact that, in the aftermath of the Roman destruction, a message of nonviolence had become even less credible. Destroying the Temple amounted to a theological statement about power and divine reality. The Jewish historian Flavius Josephus and others proposed answers to the intolerable question that the event posed. Had God's favor has passed over to Rome? Was God punishing Israel? The questions, and the answers they provoked, constituted an attempt to rescue God from the imperial implication of God's impotence. But Matthew produced his Gospel despite the unpromising conditions, adjusting it to the new circumstances. His text shows the tension of conflicting pressures, the message of Jesus on the one hand and the reality of violent retribution on the other. The antipodal terms of this gospel bear the scars of the tensions of the time, but they also are called forth by those tensions. The pieces of the subsequent puzzle do not always fit, but the evangelist's accomplishment is impressive.

In Matthew's dilemma I saw an image of ours today. And in discovering his resolve I found my own. As this is being written, America is involved in two wars, the legacy of 9/11, including such ethically problematic methods as selective assassination and the faceless mechanized weaponry of drone warfare. The aftermath of massive violence is not simply a time of disinterest in nonviolent alternatives, it is also, and for that very reason, a time for asserting such options. So this task was taken up again after a gap of some years. Matthew's Gospel not only provided an example of courage, but it also recommended a measure of humility in addressing an issue that seems intractable. Consequently, this study can be considered an essay, a contribution toward more definitive statements.

The book employs certain strategies in pursuing the issues it addresses. One is a strategy of defamiliarizing, making a familiar text strange. The hope is to move the question beyond the usual terms in which the text of Matthew's Gospel is framed. If this gospel begins to appear foreign, even unrecognizable, then the effort will have succeeded initially. It fully succeeds only when fruitful new directions open up. A second strategy is that of literary analysis. Such analysis is to be distinguished here from the "literary criticism" of historical-critical studies, for the approach taken here looks at the text as an artfully constructed work, a piece of literature. It assumes a self-conscious literary product, neither fiction nor factual report. The frequent references I make to other literary works is intended to keep before us the fact that this study is literary and not historical-critical. It can be objected that an approach of this kind is anachronistic, and of course in many ways it is. But it does nevertheless have in its favor the capability of allowing new perspectives, which then may lead to observations that can then be judged on other grounds. Finally, a third strategy is the use of the specific technique of narrative analysis in studying the text. My intent is to make use of the insights associated with this approach without relying on its arcane and often distracting vocabulary. The rationalization for using narrative analysis is simple enough. Narratives that depict conflict also require a resolution that corresponds to the essential features of that conflict. Violent narratives, for example, resolve violently. But in the case of Gospel narrative in which nonviolent action is recommended (e.g., Matt 5:39), it would seem beneficial to study how the narrative describes and dramatizes that resolution. This was the approach used in *Nonviolent Story*, and it is continued here. By using literary analysis, I do not mean to imply that I believe that Matthew was writing a work of fiction. I do not. Neither fiction nor historical report, his work makes a claim on history and was written in at least in part as an interpretation of history. However, Matthew's interpretation takes the form of story and requires tools developed for analyzing stories.

In any work dealing with matters of violence and nonviolence, the question of definitions arises. It seems reasonable for an author to announce at the outset what he or she understands by violence and non-violence. Although I sympathize with that sentiment, I also know why so many writers on the subject do not do so. Both the common and the critical usage of these terms are so rich and necessarily variable that no one set of definitions will do. As a compromise I offer a short list of the theories of violence/nonviolence that I have found helpful and are used in one way or another in the following pages.

The ideas of Reinhold Niebuhr have returned to public notice recently due to the Nobel lecture delivered by President Barack Obama, which depended strongly on them. Niebuhr was skeptical of nonviolent action, seeing it as a form of coercion, only apparently nonviolent because coercion works through threat of harm. Nonviolence for Niebuhr was nonresistance, pure and simple, as presented in the Sermon on the Mount. Although impossible in practice, it nevertheless was useful as a guide to Christian activism.

Gene Sharp has become known for his theories of nonviolent action and political power. Beginning with the practices of Gandhi, he has
developed a broad concept of nonviolent action that includes at least 198
kinds of action, including the likes of boycotts and strikes. His concept
of violence is correspondingly narrow, including only physical harm to
persons. Like Niebuhr, Sharp sees nonviolent action involving coercion,
but he understands it differently, based on his theory of power. Instead
of coming from the top down, political power emerges from the consent
of the governed for Sharp. Nonviolent action coerces by withdrawing
consent and impairing a leader's effectiveness.

The political philosopher Hannah Arendt held a theory of violence
as the instrumental inflation of individual strength. This definition
also depended on a theory of political power, which she viewed as the
creation of human individuals freely working in concert in communi-
ties. Individual coercion of populations by instrumental means such as
weapons is an act of violence in its triumph of individual strength over
communal power. For Arendt, nonviolent action was a real expression
of political power, but would not be a match for major threats of violence. She also viewed forgiveness as a powerful form of concluding or
avoiding violent reprisals.

René Girard came from the ranks of literary critics, but has found a
home among theological circles for his theory of violence. Building on a
concept of mimesis, in which we learn what to desire by observing what
others enjoy, and then fighting over what we both now want, Girard has
developed a theory of violence as a social impulse, not functionally unlike Freud's theory of the libido, but translated from the individual to the
social and from *Eros* to *Thanatos*. It cannot be eliminated or reduced,
but it can be controlled by displacement and sublimation. His theory of
the scapegoat depicts conflict resolution in terms of such displacement.
Disputing parties spontaneously blame a third party for their troubles,
a scapegoat too weak to strike back and continue the discord, but irra-
tionally attributed with the strength to be the cause of their dissension.
For Girard, the Gospel unmasks belief in scapegoats by showing us the
victim's side, causing us to realize that it is a lie. There is little discernible
place for nonviolent action in Girard's theory, though it seems implied
in his view of Jesus.

The celebrated Trappist monk Thomas Merton also drew on Gandhi
for his understanding of nonviolent resistance. He frames it as love of

enemy in times of conflict, with emphasis on retaining a full sense of the humanity of one's opponent, even in the heat of the struggle. Merton also has contributed the notion of structural violence to the discussion, subverting the distinction between justice and nonviolence because injustice can be construed as a form of violence.

The philosopher Joan Bondurant developed her theory of nonviolence based on Gandhi's *satyagraha*. In contrast to Sharp, her definition of nonviolence is narrow, and her notion of violence is broad. She has elaborated a theory of spiritual violence (*duragraha*), which allows her to insist on including inner motives as well as outer actions for nonviolence to be authentic. She has worked out a careful set of definitions, which I will reproduce here:

- "Violence is the willful application of force in such a way that it is intentionally injurious to the person or group against whom it is applied."

- "Force is the exercise of physical or intangible power or influence to affect change." Injury includes "psychological as well as physical harm."

- Nonviolence "means the exercise of power or influence to effect change without injury to the opponent."[1]

These serve well as a foundation for the larger discussion that unfolds in this study. As I try to build on them, I will feel free to employ the different approaches as needed, indicating which I am using at any given time.

The book is separated into three parts. Because this is primarily a literary study of the plot of Matthew's narrative, the three chapters of the first part work to establish the story line of that gospel. I propose that a significant difference separates Matthew's story from the one he derived from Mark. Matthew's is a homecoming story, and as such it incorporates a number of features into a pattern or formula. Together, these comprise a familiar tale, the story of the banished and returning prince. Continual reference to literary works, both classic and popular, serve not only to illustrate the leading qualities of this story, but also to maintain awareness of the literary traits that define the gospel and this story of it. The second part of the book takes up the story of the ban-

1. Bondurant, *Conflict*, 9.

ished and returning prince as an interpretive lens to examine aspects of violence and nonviolence in Matthew's narrative. What emerges at this juncture is the importance of the imperium in shaping the narrative, and how current postcolonial criticism can provide clues to making sense of the work. In general, imperial military force provides a cultural model for what makes a difference, what constitutes reality, the way the world works. It is in opposition to this cultural model that Matthew makes his statement. And with his statement of an alternative reality and an alternative mode of managing conflict, he confronts the power of the empire. The final section, one chapter concerning the "Nostos" or homecoming itself, looks more closely at the end of the Gospel to propose a theory of Matthew's nonviolent resolution of conflict.

PART ONE

Constructing a Narrative

ONE WAY TO ASSESS a story's stand on violence is to see how it handles conflict in its narrative plot. Violent stories tend to resolve their problems through further violence. So it is that the gunslinger is shot, the hostage-taker targeted, and the terrorist eliminated with extreme prejudice. And yet there seems to be a contradiction lurking here in the failure to reduce the sum total of violence in the realm of the story. The Gospels present an interesting alternative. Because Jesus is determinedly not violent and yet suffers a violent death, a narrative analysis seems to offer insight into the teaching of the Gospels. The question arises as to how this apparent dichotomy is resolved satisfactorily. Matthew's Gospel in particular promises significant results, given its explicit language about nonretaliation and love of enemies (5:38–48) along with, in considerable tension with this, sayings that promise final and violent retribution, as in the endings of certain parables (13:41–42, 49–50). But if we go beyond the sayings of Jesus to the story itself, beyond the teachings to the plot, what does Matthew's narrative have to tell us?

A critical truism holds that Matthew came to the common synoptic narrative second-hand, with Mark's Gospel as his source. This can be put more directly: Mark's Gospel provided Matthew's work with its story line. Mark is the narrative source, whereas supplementary sources added teachings and sayings of Jesus. Although the source relationships have been established on philological grounds, narrative analysis makes an even more convincing impression. Matthew's account parallels Mark's, but with significant elaborations that both extend the reach of the narrative even while flattening it. Given these circumstances, Mark's text appears in Matthew's as an intertext, borrowed and revised to other purposes. In the second chapter we will look briefly at the story line of Mark with an eye to comparing that Gospel with Matthew's intertext—Mark-

1

in-Matthew, in effect. For the moment we will simply note that although this is a literary study, it does not ignore the legacy of historical criticism, just as it will not avoid consideration of archeological and social studies contributions to our understanding of the world in which Matthew wrote and his original readers interpreted.

Matthew's story is "flattened" in that it loses some of the dramatic intensity that is found in Mark's original. Pageantry replaces dramatic tension. Mark's effort was focused on producing a narrative with dramatic qualities of suspense, conflict, building, peaking, and eventually coming to a denouement. This difficult work having been done, Matthew could borrow it to use for other purposes. Principal among those purposes was teaching. In this Gospel Jesus is preeminently a teacher, as the evangelist is himself a scribe, bringing from his treasure the new and the old. In Matthew's hands the synoptic narrative becomes a showpiece, a pedagogical display that downplays Mark's incessant "immediately" with the more Matthean "behold."

But if pedagogical interests dictate a different treatment of the story for Matthew, that is not the only reason for the decrease in dramatic impact. For Matthew, Mark's story is only one part of the narrative. Indeed, Matthew has embarked on his own narrative development by framing the synoptic narrative with another narrative element, an itinerary circuit described later as a homecoming story. This in turn is recognized as an ancient and still familiar story pattern, sometimes known technically as the formula story of the Banished and Returning Prince. Much of the first part of this book will be devoted to explaining and defending this proposal for Matthew's narrative. Before we analyze a narrative, we need first to establish it.

Although an interest in Matthew's narrative has produced a number of significant studies in recent years, the legacy of source criticism has made it difficult to move past the sense that Matthew's story, apart from a few minor details, simply borrows that of Mark. As a result, the infancy narrative of Matthew has been difficult to place. Some tend to view the first two chapters as prologue, preliminary foreshadowing of later developments. Others recognize that the first two chapters are part of the story, without agreeing on their relationship to the larger plot. The view taken here is that the entry of the Magi (2:1–5) initiates the conflict. Coming from outside the world of the story, they are the catalyst that interrupts the false stillness that prevails where a new king is born, while an old, paranoid king has yet to learn of it. Which is not to say that the first chapter is unrelated to the narrative. The genealogy (Matt 1:2–17) makes claims for Jesus that define the terms of conflict. As such we will have occasion to return to it repeatedly. The subsequent episode of Joseph's dream gives the story its narrative program, or mandate, in the angel's message: "He shall save his people from their sins" (1:21). The rest of the story is the mandate's fulfillment.

1

The Homecoming Story

HOME IS NOT "HOME" until you leave it. It is the name of the place of departure and earns its name by way of the departure. The act of leaving "here where I am," or "here where I have always been," or even "here where I feel stifled," establishes it in the mind as "home."

And Home names the end of the wandering. It is Leopold Bloom at the end of the day in Joyce's *Ulysses*, and Odysseus at the end of his life in the foundational epic. It is Cavafy's "Ithaca" and Tarwater's shack in Flannery O'Connor's novel, *The Violent Bear It Away*, borrowing its title from a verse in Matthew. For in these accounts the truth about "home" comes home. *The Odyssey* has given to the moment of homecoming the name "Nostos," and that epic describes particularly well the deep need to return home that drives certain narratives. It is a longing that is typically increased by being continually deferred. In delaying the return, the sense of need heightens, sometimes to the degree of being barely tolerable, and so the story holds us.

The biblical expression of the pattern is inscribed in large over the entire book, as the need propels the larger narrative of Israel's history—from the promises made to Abraham, to the belated and incomplete return from the exile. It continues in the experience of diaspora, is prominent in the letters of Paul, and underlies the surface narrative of the Gospels. Yet, as we will see, Matthew's account has its own explicit expression of the homecoming story. It appears in smaller form in certain narratives, such as the Book of Ruth, which can be read as a parable of the major narrative of Israel's longing.

CONSPICUOUS ENTRANCES

What sets Matthew's narrative apart from the other gospels is its story of homecoming. In an abstract way, of course, most stories tell a tale that finds its way home in the end. After a struggle with adversity the characters finally arrive at a place they can permanently inhabit. They return to the condition of bliss from which they were roughly evicted when the story with its troubles began. "Once upon a time" becomes "happily ever after." The warrior returns from the wars; the hero returns with the prize. The lovers marry and settle down, and we never hear from them again. In this general way, most stories come home.

But some stories go out of their way to make a particular point of homecoming, naming places and, as a central feature of their plots, returning to those places. Ithaca, Elsinore, and Eccles Street, Dublin, would be on any list of such places. As we will see, the popularity of this kind of plot means that it provides a favorite story formula for animated films by Disney and its competitors.

Some of these stories are in the Bible. One of them is the story of Naomi, in the Book of Ruth. Another is the story of Jesus, Son of David, as told in the Gospel of Matthew.

Ruth

This short biblical masterpiece is about many things, but certainly one of them is the pull of physical place on human beings and the changes that being in place or out of place can work on them. After ten years away from her home in Bethlehem, her husband and her sons now dead, Naomi sees no reason to stay in the land of Moab. Of course, home means more than a physical place. Naomi wishes to return to a place she can find the network of family relationships and the security they traditionally provide. But that solace does not come quickly, for considerable damage needs to be repaired. The townsfolk realize the change in Naomi. When she entered Bethlehem after the ten long years away, her daughter-in-law Ruth coming with her, the two of them did not arrive unnoticed. Like the chorus in a Greek drama, the townspeople assess the action.

> On their arrival there, the whole city was astir over them, and the women asked, "Can this be Naomi?" But she said to them, "Do not call me Naomi. Call me Mara, for the Almighty has made it very bitter for me. (Ruth 1:19–20)

In its narrative context the vignette registers the decline in Naomi's fortunes. This is less than a welcome home. She returns bitter and unblessed, bereft of any signs of the favor she once enjoyed. In case we hadn't been paying attention to her own strident complaints, the townsfolk are putting the matter on record: Things have changed for Naomi. With this small scene of arrival, the narrative sets a stylistic marker, emphasizing the very fact of the homecoming as well as its forlorn nature.

So it is. But as the story unfolds, we discover matters to be not as obvious as they first seemed. Certainly part of her motivation is the deep comfort offered by one's traditional physical place, the pull of roots. We first see her debating with her daughters-in-law, who struggle with meeting their obligations to the older woman. And, as we know, the intrepid one named Ruth refuses to be left behind. However, in joining Naomi's homeward journey, Ruth herself is carried away from her homeland; she too becomes a sojourner among strangers, among the "alien corn," exchanging her own homeland for Naomi's—albeit with a better chance of finding a new one. Simple return to place is not a sufficient experience of homecoming. Although Naomi and Ruth arrive in Bethlehem before the end of the first chapter, all three of the remaining chapters of the book will be needed for Naomi, and Ruth for that matter, truly to arrive home. The story turns on themes of emptiness seeking fullness, blight seeking blessing. It also moves on the theme of physical place, present and absent.

Then, in an ingenious set of cartographical figures, the raw, unhealed distance between Bethlehem and Moab closes gradually with each successive chapter. Whereas the first chapter travels to Moab and back, the second chapter makes a shorter trip. It repeats the motif of the journey in a reduced and manageable way, as Ruth goes out from the city to the gleaning fields and returns at the chapter's end. An even shorter excursion, to the threshing floor just outside the city gate and back again, preoccupies the third chapter. In what structuralist critics call a mediating series, the distance progressively reduces, to be resolved in the final chapter in that site where all such business was accomplished in the ancient world—at the city gate. Bringing together the inside and the outside, the negotiations in the gate resolve the rupture between home and away from home. Once again the chorus gathers at the gate, putting the new situation on public record, revising their earlier judgment. The elders and townspeople bless the marriage of Ruth and Boaz, and the women of the town confirm the fruitfulness that has entered the life of Naomi. The painful distance has been annulled and the emptiness filled, the banns announced and the bane removed. The two women are declared to be, in the fullest sense, home.

Matthew

We know that the Matthew's Gospel indicates an awareness of the book of Ruth. It includes Ruth among the women in the genealogy that opens the Gospel (Matt 1:5). And although it draws largely on I Chronicles, the genealogy itself includes and is modeled after that found in the concluding verses of Ruth.[1]

In the Gospel of Matthew, a pair of moments echoes the scene of Naomi's homecoming entrance into Bethlehem. The first comes at the beginning of the Gospel. In chapter 2 we are told about the Magi, these exotic strangers from the east entering the world of Matthew's story, asking King Herod where they might find the newborn Messiah. The reaction to their questioning is memorable:

> When Jesus was born in Bethlehem of Judea, in the days of King Herod, behold, magi from the east arrived in Jerusalem, saying, "Where is the newborn king of the Jews? We saw his star at its rising and have come to do him homage." When King Herod heard this, he was greatly troubled, and all Jerusalem with him. Assembling all the chief priests and the scribes of the people, he inquired of them where the Messiah was to be born. They said to him, "In Bethlehem of Judea, for thus it has been written through the prophet. . . . (Matt 2:1–5)

Any entry scene is a decisive moment for a narrative. Entrances cross thresholds; entry scenes move stories into new phases of development. In this case, the arrival of the Magi nudges the plot of Matthew's Gospel into motion, and then the familiar account follows. The Magi, sent on to Bethlehem, make an offering of gifts and homage to the royal child. Unaware of Herod's animus, they need to be directed by a dream toward a different route home. Jerusalem is not yet to be a destination of return. That will come later. Joseph, for his part, is told to flee with his family. They leave for Egypt. Summarily, Herod exterminates the chil-

---

1. See Carter, *Matthew and the Margins*, 57. Carter is among those who suggest that the genealogy in Ruth 4:18–22 was a model for Matthew's genealogy, along with 1 Chr 2:10–15.

dren of Bethlehem in a futile attempt to bring an early end to the story of the Messiah, now beginning.

The Magi's arrival scene does not stand alone in the Gospel. Much later in the story we come upon a similar moment.

> And when he entered Jerusalem the whole city was shaken and asked, "Who is this?" And the crowds replied, "This is Jesus the prophet, from Nazareth in Galilee."(Matt 21:10–11)

This is, of course, the triumphal entry of Jesus into Jerusalem, amid hosannas and the waving of branches. This scene brings the Gospel narrative into its final phase. Once again, a widely noticed entry disturbs the entire city, prompting pointed questions and answers concerning Jesus, alarming authorities, and generating concerted efforts to contain an unwelcome development for the *status quo ante*. We know the story—the authorities will concentrate their efforts in opposition to Jesus, and this opposition will eventuate in the arrest, trial, and death of Jesus. But this time, too, their efforts, though equally appalling in their ruthlessness, will ultimately prove to be in vain.

Robert Alter, taking his cue from studies in Homeric epic, has taught us to think of repeated vignettes such as these as "type-scenes."[2] This version of the trope, which might be labeled the "Conspicuous Entrance," is characterized by at least four elements: a public arrival in the city, usually by a public personage; "all the city," usually Jerusalem, is thrown into a commotion as a result; questions are raised about identity, usually that of the new arrival; and answers are then given that move the narrative in a new, often devastating, direction.

As we've seen, two of these Old Testament type-scenes unmistakably relate to the Gospel of Matthew, whereas another is found in Naomi's return to Bethlehem (Ruth 1:19). Another, more extended, example is Solomon's victorious entry into the city of Jerusalem, riding David's mule as a sign of his father's endorsement (1 Kgs 1:38–45). Each of these relates in a particular way to Matthew's own type-scenes—something we can see, first of all, in the story of Naomi.

Solomon

Commentators have long noticed similarities between the accounts of Jesus' entrance into Jerusalem and that Jewish and Greco-Roman prac-

2. Alter, *The Art of Biblical Narrative*, 50–54.

tice of Parousia, or Arrival. Processions and other displays of honor accompanied these formal visitations of dignitaries. Warren Carter, for example, has listed six points of positive comparison.[3] In Matthew's case this would seem to be reinforced by the expansion of the role of the allusion to Zechariah, which he quotes explicitly, rather than implicitly as in his source, Mark.

Carter also noted some significant differences leading to an understanding that the entrance of Jesus is a parody of the exalted practice. There is no committee of local elites greeting the visitor, no display of power or triumph, no cultic act of sacrifice performed by the visitor in the temple, as a signal of taking possession of the city. In fact, instead of the latter Jesus "cleanses" the temple in an act of criticism. Carter devotes much of his analysis to the anomalous presence of the beast(s) on which Jesus is riding. Not only does Matthew's emphasis overinterpret Zechariah 9:9, but it draws much of its significance from Solomon's ascension to the throne of his father, David, in I Kings 1.

Although the arguments for the Parousia pattern have been deftly made, I would like to suggest that the Solomon story provides an additional, if not alternative, model for the entire narrative of Jesus' entrance in Matthew. The story of Solomon's ascension comes as a conclusion to the long struggle over finding a successor to David. The theory of the Succession Narrative,[4] which selects the text of 2 Samuel 9–20 through 1 Kgs 1–2 as a continuous narrative, by positing it as a distinct source, points to the accession of Solomon as the resolution of the building drama. In the case of Matthew's Gospel, the arrival of Jesus in Jerusalem occupies a similar place in the account, bringing to a culmination his long march toward the city, from 16:21.

But there are formal features that find a resonance as well. The story of Solomon's ascension is built around two themes. The first is the overcoming of rivals. The aging of David, exacerbating the need for determining a successor, sets the stage. When Adonijah, the eldest of the remaining sons, assumes he is the next in line, the Solomon party, namely Bathsheba and Nathan, begin to lobby David on Solomon's behalf. Their two interventions describe a repeated pattern that sets up an even more significant pattern shortly thereafter. However, this has a different structure. Instead of two dialogues it follows a pattern of instruction and implementation. David gives detailed instructions for Solomon's anoint-

3. Carter, *Margins*, 414. See also Davies and Allison, *Matthew*, Vol. III, 128–29.
4. For the classic expression of this theory, see Whybray, *The Succession Narrative*.

ing and entrance as the next king. A prominent feature of the plan is for Solomon to ride David's mule, as a clear indication of David's favor.

Here the episode reaches it narrative climax in a version of the type-scene of conspicuous entrance, though in a more elaborated version than we have yet seen. Following David's instructions, we have the action in literal response:

> So Zadok the priest, Nathan the prophet, Benaiah, son of Jehoiada, and the Cherethites and Pelethites went down, and mounting Solomon on King David's mule, escorted him to Gihon. Then Zadok the priest took the horn of oil from the tent and anointed Solomon. They blew the horn and all the people shouted, "Long live King Solomon!" Then all the people went up after him, playing flutes and rejoicing so much as to split open the earth with their shouting. (1 Kgs 1:38–40)

It is followed by the reaction of the Adonijah party:

> Adonijah and all the guests who were with him heard it, just as they ended their banquet. When Joab heard the sound of the horn, he asked, "What does this uproar in the city mean?" . . . Jonathan answered him. "Our lord, King David, has made Solomon king. The king sent with him Zadok the priest, Nathan the prophet, Benaiah, son of Jehoiada, and the Cherethites and Pelethites, and they mounted him upon the king's own mule. Zadok the priest and Nathan the prophet anointed him king at Gihon, and they went up from there rejoicing, so that the city is in an uproar. That is the noise you heard. Besides, Solomon took his seat on the royal throne, . . . (1 Kgs 1:41, 43–46)

The entry is very public because that is its purpose, and it stirs up a tumult in the city. It prompts identity questions that lead to implications for the continuation of the narrative. But in this case the type-scene is placed in service to the account of the rivalry for the title of Son of David, and it enters the account to settle the matter. It provides Solomon the seal of authenticity.

What does this preoccupation with rivalry and authenticity have to do with Matthew? Daniel Harrington speaks for many scholars when he notes that a strain of rivalry in the world of Matthew's community influenced his writing:

> Matthew's Gospel should be read as one of several Jewish responses to the destruction of the Jerusalem Temple in A. D. 70. The Matthean community still existed within the framework of

Judaism but in tension with other Jewish groups—especially the early rabbinic movement. Matthew's theological program should be viewed as an attempt to show how the Jewish tradition is best preserved in a Jewish-Christian context.[5]

Harrington's central idea for reading the Gospel of Matthew is to see it as one of many competing expressions of posttemple Jewish belief. The social setting of the Gospel is a controverted issue in today's scholarly debate. Although all commentators recognize the Jewish interests in Matthew, not all agree on what this means for Matthew's community. Nor do they agree on whether the community had broken with Judaism or not. Nonetheless, there remains a broad area of agreement that Matthew's church was in rivalry with alternative expressions of Judaism, particularly the early rabbinic, late Pharisaic, movement.[6] The situation would provide a reason for Matthew to be interested in the competitive issues in the Solomon story: Matthew himself struggled, on behalf of Jesus, against rivals who did not perceive Jesus as the true Messiah, the true son of David.

THE CIRCLE IN THE TEXT

The presence of two similar scenes of entry into the city of Jerusalem, situated at the beginning of the Gospel narrative and at the opening of its concluding phases, raises questions for us. What is the purpose of Matthew's paired type-scenes? Jack Dean Kingsbury, among the first to apply conflict categories to Matthew's plot, and perhaps influenced by the historical-critical understanding of the infancy narrative as an addition to the narrative, sees events in the infancy narrative that parallel later development in the Gospel in terms of foreshadowing—a common literary strategy for preparing a reader for subsequent, more substantive developments. Kingsbury has listed the parallels between the infancy narrative and the passion to support his idea of the relationship of the infancy narrative to the rest of the Gospel.[7]

But there are indications in the text that something more is going on here. The disturbance triggered by the arrival of the Magi on the

5. Harrington, *Matthew*, 17.

6. See, for instance, Hagner, "*Sitz im Leben*," 27–68; Senior, *What . . . Matthew?*, 7–20.

7. Kingsbury, *Matthew as Story*, 48–49.

scene has repercussions that continue on into the main narrative of the Gospel. If we pay attention to the sequence of actions in Matthew's story and remain undistracted by the apparently detachable nature of the infancy narrative, we can see that the two scenes in the Gospel constitute more than foreshadowing and a subsequent event. In fact, they register the beginning and ending in a chain of connected movements. It is a pattern that inscribes a circle in the action of the plot of the narrative. The arrival of the Magi from outside the world of the story jump-starts the action of the Gospel. After the audience with Herod, the Magi travel to Bethlehem (2:9). Their visit with the family of Jesus motivates the flight to Egypt, to remove the infant Messiah beyond the reach of Herod (2:14). Upon Herod's death, the family leaves Egypt but chooses not to return to Bethlehem because of the reign of Archelaus, who has replaced his father, Herod. Instead, they travel north to Galilee and the village of Nazareth (2:22–23), which is out of harm's way because Archelaus's administrative reach turns out to be less expansive than his father's. In this Gospel, this is the first we hear of Nazareth. Unlike Luke's account, Matthew's is focused on Bethlehem.

After Jesus grows to maturity in obscurity, he emerges on the scene again in the adult ministry, which begins with a move from Nazareth to Capernaum (4:13). Thus begins a ministry that winds its way eventually to Jerusalem, with a type-scene that echoes the entry that started the circle of movements. Throughout this itinerary it is noticeable how Judea and Jerusalem exert something like a gravitational pull on the Messiah Jesus, who comes as close as danger allows, until he finally enters the city and confronts the risk.

Stendahl's Itinerary

As an indicator of authorial purpose for this pattern, the moves are marked in the text by a set of Matthew's characteristic scriptural references. Krister Stendahl, whose redactional study of the eleven Matthean citation formulae has become a classic, authored a small monograph on a subset of those citations.[8] His monograph on Matt 1–2 takes note of the fact that the quotations in the infancy narrative are distinctive in their geographical references. Furthermore, their geography describes an itinerary, drawing attention to the movements of Jesus and his fam-

---

8. Stendahl, "Quis et Unde?" For Stendahl's classic study of the citation formulae, see *School*.

ily from Bethlehem to Egypt, and then from Egypt to Nazareth. In Stendahl's view, these citations show that the narrative serves an apologetic purpose. It establishes the reason Jesus was known as a Nazarene (2:23), although we know from the Gospel that he was actually from Bethlehem. A reconstruction of the original account of the flight and return, as Matthew found it in his sources, illustrates that Matt 2:22–23 are redactional compositions that adjust the destination of return to have the family arrive at Nazareth.[9]

The idea of an itinerary is a productive one, but we need to see that it doesn't end with chapter 2. Geographical references also appear in two more of the eleven Matthean formula quotations, at 4:15–16 and 21:5. The first, 4:15–16, citing Isa 8:23/9:1, puts on record Jesus' move from Nazareth to Capernaum at the beginning of his ministry. In this instance the notice that Jesus went to Nazareth (2:23) finds a complement in the notice of his departure from that place. In fact, there are many resemblances between 2:23 and 4:13, suggesting that, whether they are interpreted as having been entered simultaneously or sequentially with one modeled on the other, they deserve to be included together in a common reading. The arrival at Nazareth implies its completion in the departure from there.

Raymond Brown has reconstructed the source for Matthew's account of the birth, flight, and return episodes in the infancy narrative. He envisions a return to "Israel" at the end, rounding off the story.[10] In fact, in the present form of the text, the moment depicted at Matt 2:22–23 is not a return at all. It is a refusal to return. The distinct parallels between the itinerary notice at 2:22–23 and that at 4:12–13, also endorsed by a scripture citation, suggests we expand our sense of the Matthean itinerary account beyond the infancy narrative right into the Gospel "proper"—the part of the common Synoptic story that Matthew has derived from Mark.

In addition to the itinerary notice at 4:12–13, we can identify another—the arrival of Jesus in Jerusalem, in. 21:1–11. Here, too, in what we have already identified as the second type-scene (21:10–11), the counterpart in motif to the arrival of the Magi, we have a final Matthean itinerary marker.

---

9. Brown, *Birth*, 206. The overdetermined motivation for the decision to avoid Bethlehem and Judea also points to the redactional nature of this passage, as both a message in a dream and a report of Archelaus's ascension to the throne in Jerusalem are cited as the reason for Joseph's decision. More than is necessary.

10. Brown, *Birth*, 109.

Five Geographical Notices

When we look at the full set of citations related to the itinerary, we see a definite pattern, one worth looking at more closely, not only for the sake of seeing how they accomplish their work of signification in relation to the narrative that Matthew has constructed, but also to suggest how he seems to have constructed it.[11]

BETHLEHEM

> When King Herod heard this, he was greatly troubled,
>   and all Jerusalem with him.
> Assembling all the chief priests
> and the scribes of the people,
> he inquired of them
> where the Messiah was to be born.
> They said to him, "In Bethlehem of Judea,
> for thus it has been written
> through the prophet:
> *'And you, Bethlehem, land of Judah,*

11. Davies and Allison may be taken as representative of the historical critical approach for Matt 2. In their scenario, they envision three stages of composition that can be characterized as the Moses stage, the David stage, and the OT citation stage. The basic stories represent the first stage, built on popular Jewish tales about Moses now adapted to fit Jesus. They include the annunciation to Joseph in a dream, the machinations of Herod, and the attempt to kill the newborn king. The itinerary of flight and return appear, but without the scriptural citations that mark their progress. At a later stage the David materials were added, involving three elements—the virginal conception (based on Isa 7:14), the legend of the Magi and the star (based on Num 24:17), and the Bethlehem birthplace (based on Mic 5:1). According to these critics this much occurred at the pre-Matthean level. Matthew took the results, added the scripture quotations, and sealed the whole with his distinctive writing style.

Davies and Allison offer a historical account of the writing process. The narrative proposal given here differs from this in that it is a literary thesis and not a historical one. As such, it is concerned to show the presence of a literary pattern, and not the historical process that produced it. However, it can be noted that there is no essential contradiction between the two proposals.

Such a redactional theory may seem to conflict with the literary result. However, even with the homecoming story, we can discern successive levels. The second chapter of Matthew contains a homecoming story in itself. But the return to Bethlehem, which is anticipated in the formula, is frustrated, the family diverted, and the homecoming story opened up into the larger narrative. The two passages, 2:22–23 and 4:12–16, serve this purpose. With the assistance of the OT citations, added at the final redaction, and spread across the larger Gospel, including the part derived from Mark, the Gospel turns into a wider story of homecoming, and a close image of the banished prince formula discussed below.

are by no means least
among the rulers of Judah;
since from you shall come a ruler,
who is to shepherd my people Israel.'" (Matt 2:3–6)

Sharing a moment with the first of the type-scenes, the first of the five formula citations has the task of initiating the series. It is also the action that opens the Gospel narrative. When the Magi alert Herod to the new development of what he must suspect to be a royal pretender in the kingdom, his advisors answer his pointed questions about the birthplace of the Messiah by citing Mic 5:1 and 2 Sam 5:2, in a blended combination. Micah, writing during the reign of the David king Ahaz, envisions a solution to his dissatisfaction with this king by imagining he will be replaced, not simply by another member of the David family, but by returning to David's ancestral city and beginning again with a new "David," a fresh dynasty. The prophet's dissatisfaction is profound. The text from 2 Sam 5 names the moment when David became king of "all Israel." It is the first time such a thing happened in Israel. In combination with the Micah quotation this passage expresses a desire to return to the roots, back to the beginning. In effect, it identifies this moment in the narrative of Matthew as such a beginning.

The consensus among commentators is that this appeal to scripture is Christological.[12] Jesus is identified as the new David, the messianic king that Israel has long been waiting for. It is worth noting that the sheer fact that the citation is complex, combining two scriptures passages, helps to support such a conclusion. Insofar as it blends these, it scarcely serves the purpose to which the narrative would seem to claim for it. A doctored text cannot provide objective evidence, but it can express a statement of faith.

When we look at these texts as a part of the homecoming story we've discussed in Matthew, we notice the way they emphasize beginning anew. Not only do they establish the Davidic royal claim of Jesus, but also each of them does so in terms of a return to origins. Matthew's narrative declares this as a starting point. The narrative begins as a royal story.

---

12. E.g., Davies and Allison, *Matthew*, I, 242; Brown, *Birth*, 184–86; Carter, *Margins*, 79.

Egypt

> And [Joseph] rose and took the child
> and his mother by night,
> and departed for Egypt,
> and remained there until the death of Herod,
> that what the Lord had said
> through the prophet might be fulfilled,
> *"Out of Egypt I have called my son."* (Matt 2:14–15)

In contrast to the complexity of the previous scripture citation, the reference at 2:15 seems simplicity itself—a straightforward citing of Hos 11:1. The simplicity is an illusion, for the cited passage is itself an allusion, referring to Exod 4:22. This is the passage that tells of Moses receiving his commission to return to Egypt and free the Israelite slaves ("Let my people go!")—"Then tell Pharaoh that these are the words of the Lord: Israel is my firstborn son" (Exod 4:22).

The allusion to the Exodus event is more than incidental, as we discover when we notice the implicit allusion in Matt 2:20, that cites Exod 4:19. Davies and Allison have included in their commentary an elaboration of the parallels:[13]

	Matthew		Exodus
2.19	But when Herod died, behold, the angel of the Lord appeared in a dream to Joseph in Egypt	4.19	After these many days the king of Egypt died (LXX only). The Lord said to Moses in Midian,
2:20	saying, 'Rising, take the child and his mother and go to the land of Israel. For those seeking the life of the child have died.'		'Go back to Egypt, for all those seeking your life have died.'
2:21	Rising, he took the child and his mother and went unto the land of Israel.	4:20	Moses, taking his wife and his children, mounted them on asses and returned to Egypt (Matt: 'the land of Egypt')

---

13. Davies and Allison, *Matthew,* I, 271.

The theological implications link Jesus with Moses, or Israel. This makes its own statement in this text, but it also contributes to the narrative pattern we are tracing in Matthew's text. As mentioned earlier, in the infancy narrative we have a story of flight and return, with echoes of the story of Joseph, with the dreamer going down to Egypt, and the story of Moses, the massacre of the Hebrew children, and the journey back again.

The text from Hosea marks this moment, even as it literally announced the return—"Out of Egypt I have called my son." In fact, the Exodus text underlying the Hosea passage goes on to articulate a threat:

> So you shall say to Pharaoh:
> Thus says the LORD:
> Israel is my son, my first-born.
> Hence I tell you:
> Let my son go, that he may serve me.
> If you refuse to let him go, I warn you,
> I will kill your son, your first-born." (4:22–23)

While in its original context this dire text refers back to the slaughter of the Hebrew children in Exod 1:22, in relation to the infancy narrative of Matthew it alludes to the slaughter of the innocents of Bethlehem.

NAZARETH

> He [Joseph] went and dwelt
> in a town called Nazareth,
> so that what had been spoken through the prophets
> might be fulfilled,
> *"He shall be called a Nazorean."* (Matt 2:23)

The formula citation at 2:23 presents scholars with a conundrum because no Old Testament text fits the quotation. This is not surprising because the village of Nazareth is not an ancient site. It is not mentioned in the Old Testament or in any other early Jewish writing. Although commentators have suggested references to texts such as Isa 4:3:11:1 and Judg 16:17, no text makes itself available for quotation. It would seem further testimony to Matthew's program of charting the residential itinerary of Jesus, that even when he lacks a text to quote, he continues the policy of citing one.

In terms of the Matthean itinerary, this instance of place citation is perhaps the strongest if for no other reason than that it has little other reason for existing. Redactional activity here is signaled in the overdetermination of motivation for the shift in destination—as both angelic message and anticipated threat are named as reasons for Joseph's decision not to return to Bethlehem. One alone would be sufficient.

Further redactional intent is indicated by the similarity with the next example at Matt 4:12–16. Brown's chart,[14] reproduced here, illustrates their relationship:

2:22–23	4:12–16
But when he heard that Archelaus was king over Judea . . . he went off to the district of Galilee. There he went to dwell in a city called Nazareth so that what was spoken by the prophets might be fulfilled [formula citation]	But when he heard that John had been arrested. . . he went off to Galilee. There, leaving Nazareth, he went to dwell in Capernaum in order that what was spoken by Isaiah the prophet might be fulfilled [formula citation]

Together, the two passages open the itinerary Matthew received, to allow inclusion of the period of Jesus' ministry. With the first, Matthew erases the original moment of return that he found in his source and defers it. The itinerary is extended, even while the overall pattern of departure and return is maintained. The itinerary is made available for further use. With the second this potential is activated by engaging the nascent ministry of Jesus. After 2:23 the formula citations continue to be posted across the narrative that, from this point on, Matthew inherits from his main narrative source, Mark's Gospel.

CAPERNAUM

When he heard that John had been arrested,
he withdrew to Galilee.
He left Nazareth and went to live
 in Capernaum by the sea,
in the region of Zebulun and Naphtali,
that what had been said through Isaiah the prophet might be fulfilled:
"*Land of Zebulun and land of Naphtali,*

14. Brown, *Birth*, 107.

> the way to the sea, beyond the Jordan,
> Galilee of the Gentiles,
> the people who sit in darkness
> have seen a great light,
> on those dwelling in a land
> overshadowed by death
> light has arisen." (Matt 4:12–16)

The scripture quotation is a freely adapted account of Isa 8:23—9:1 (9:1–2). The prophet Isaiah, usually preoccupied with the welfare of the city of Jerusalem, uncharacteristically focuses on Galilee in this instance. The event indicated is the raid of the Assyrian, Tiglath-Pileser III, on the northern territories of Zebulon and Naphthali, in 732 BCE, which began the deportations that would lead to the eventual dissolution of the northern kingdom of Israel and begin the era of foreign domination and exile. Isaiah anticipates a return.

Matthew seems to cite the passage for similar reasons. The citation suggests that the first territory lost is the first to be regained, through the ministry of Jesus. The focus of the allusion is suitably territorial, justifying the Galilean ministry of Jesus, chosen as the starting point, despite a primary concern with Jerusalem. The strong parallels between the earlier Nazareth text (2:22–23) and the present text, with its focus on Galilee and Capernaum (4:12–13), also serves to register that we are now informed of the departure from Nazareth, just as earlier we were told of the arrival there. As in the earlier case with Nazareth, the text establishes that Jesus "dwelt" in Capernaum, as a base of operations of sorts for his opening mission in Galilee. This differs from Mark's Gospel, which notes a Capernaum beginning, but lacks the emphasis on Jesus "dwelling" there and venturing out from there.

In terms of the homecoming story, the movement toward Jerusalem begins with the ministry in Galilee, although the intention to return is not divulged to the disciples until 16:21.

Zion

> This happened so that what had been spoken
> through the prophet might be fulfilled:
> "Say to daughter Zion,
> 'Behold, your king comes to you,
> meek and riding on an ass,
> and on a colt, the foal of a beast of burden.'"
> (Matt 21:4–5)

The last week of Jesus' life is spent in Jerusalem. During this time he "lodged" nearby in Bethany (21:17). But the drama of his final days is played out in the city, where he is making a claim as the messianic king. His arrival is marked by the second of the "conspicuous entrance" type-scenes (21:10–11), as well as the formula and quotation given earlier (21:5–6).

Once again the cited scripture combines two passages from the Old Testament. Although most of it is from Zech 9:9–10, there is a bit from Isa 62:11. The first of these is a vignette of the "Prince of Peace" entering the city in the style of a conqueror, but without the army that customarily enables such an entry. Furthermore, upon securing the city, the royal figure proceeds to disarm it, abolishing both cavalry and infantry forces.

The passage from Isa 62:11 also imagines an entry, probably developed along the lines of an imperial visitation to one of the provincial cities, called a "parousia" and applied here to Yahweh. In its Isaian application, the passage is a symbol for the end of the exile, when Yahweh returns to his city after the long absence.

In terms of Matthew's homecoming story, this marks the victorious return itself, capped by the second of the type-scenes (21:10–11). As we come to the end of Jesus' ministry, we conclude with his coming home, as "Son of David," making good the royal claims of the Magi.

Stations along the Way

A notable feature is that these quotations align with the stations in the story of Jesus, as listed earlier. They are further marked by indications of habitation—that is, places that provide stopping points amid the constant peregrinations of Jesus, places that serve as residences. In the first case (Matt 2:11), the family of Jesus is said to be living in a "house" in Bethlehem, a feature that distinguishes this infancy story from that of Luke, who shows them already living in Nazareth and leaving there to come to Bethlehem. Once the family flees the territory, they remove themselves to Egypt for the duration of Herod's rule. Returning from Egypt, they do not return to Bethlehem or Judea, but rather relocate to Nazareth, where Matthew's text says they "dwelt" (2:23). Reaching adulthood and beginning his ministry, he moved to Capernaum, where again he "dwelt" (4:13). Matthew is expanding the suggestion given in the other Gospels that this is where Jesus began his ministry, by establishing it as something of a more permanent base of operations for the Galilean ministry. Finally, upon coming to Jerusalem, he "lodged" (21:17) in the place all the Gospels picture him staying when he is in the Jerusalem area—namely, Bethany. The point, of course, is that these are stops in the otherwise rather constant movement. They are to be thought of as stations along the way.

A table listing the stations mentioned here would take this form:

1. Bethlehem	2:15 (Mic 5:1; 2 Sam 5:2)	"house"—2:11
2. Egypt	2:15 (Hos 11:1; Exod 4:22)	"stayed"—2:15
3. Nazareth	2:23 (Isa 11:1?)	"dwelt"—2:23
4. Galilee	4:15–16 (Isa 8:23; 9:1)	"dwelt"—4:13
5. Zion	21:5 (Zech 9:9; Isa 62:11)	"lodged"—21:17

These are not simply stops along the way in the life of an itinerant preacher; these are habitations, residences, changes of address, if you will. The "house" in Bethlehem, rather than the inn of Luke's account, reflects Matthew's understanding of the family being from Bethlehem, with Nazareth entering the story only at the third stage. The time in Egypt is described by a verbal construction meaning "to remain." Meanwhile, the references to Nazareth and Galilee (with Capernaum) reflect the similar construction of 2:23 and 4:13–15, noted earlier. The final stop along the way concerns the village of Bethany, where Jesus "lodged" during his last week in Jerusalem, leaving the city at night and returning in the morning. The circuit of stations reinforces the circle of moves etched into the text, although the Magi cover the first leg of the journey.

A VILLAGE, A TOWN, AND A CITY

Supposing that Matthew wished to shape a homecoming story as described here, he had at least three problems to solve. They have to do with the relationships among three locations—Nazareth, Bethlehem, and Jerusalem, a village, a town, and a city. Tracing his solutions to these problems also allows us to understand the differences between his story and the other Gospels.

NAZARETH AND BETHLEHEM

The first problem facing Matthew was establishing Bethlehem as the starting point for his itinerary. Jesus is named in all the Gospels as "Jesus of Nazareth." Nazareth is the older tradition concerning the birthplace of Jesus, and Bethlehem came, for theological reasons, to displace it in the Christian memory. After all, there are no theological advantages for Nazareth to have entered the tradition on those grounds. The town is not recorded in the Hebrew Scriptures and had none of the credentials enjoyed by Bethlehem.[15] Presumably it preserves some historical truth. The argument followed here differs from Stendahl's apologetic discussed earlier. Whereas Stendahl saw Nazareth introduced at 2:23 to reconcile for readers the common appellation of "Jesus of Nazareth" with his account of the birth at Bethlehem, the argument here claims Matthew justifies his identification of Bethlehem as the place of Jesus' birth for original readers who knew of the Nazareth tradition. Stendahl would have Matthew justifying the title, "Jesus of Nazareth"; I would see the evangelist justifying the birth at Bethlehem.

Moved by similar theological motives, both Matthew and Luke make a point of locating Jesus' birth in the town of Bethlehem. But, significantly, they establish that point in different ways. Luke tells about the census-driven trip to Bethlehem, with no room for Joseph and Mary in the inn. It is Nazareth that stands at the center of Luke's account: Joseph makes his home in Nazareth (Luke 1:27); Nazareth is where the angel Gabriel visits Mary (Luke 1:26). It is from Nazareth they leave (Luke 2:4), and to Nazareth they return (Luke 2:39, 51). Bethlehem is simply the destination of a momentary excursion, a side trip, albeit one that suffices to establish Jesus as a native of Bethlehem. Luke's narrative, centered in Nazareth, with the family making a special trip to Bethlehem where the birth takes place, reflects the history of the tradition itself, in which Bethlehem comes to displace the older Nazareth tradition. In the tradition, as in Luke, Bethlehem is an insertion into a Nazareth story.

But Matthew, faced with the same need to place the family in Bethlehem for the birth of Jesus, has contrived more daringly to place Bethlehem, and not Nazareth, at the center of his infancy story. The

15. See, e.g., Theissen and Merz, *The Historical Jesus*, 164–66; Brown, *Birth*, 107— also 101, n. 8, and 180). Brown speaks of the Nazareth tradition as "a commonplace of the Gospel tradition," which any claims for Bethlehem will have to address. Whereas citing Bethlehem as the place of birth fulfills a prophecy, there is nothing in the way of prophecy or reputation to recommend Nazareth as the birthplace of Jesus, except the possibility that it is the actual historical site. For a discussion of Matthew's identifying Bethlehem as the original residence of Jesus' family, instead of Nazareth as in Luke's Gospel, see *Birth*, 177, n. 3.

family lives in Bethlehem (Matt 2:9,11), and their story begins there. At the end of the infancy narrative (Matt 2:22–23), their decision to relocate in Nazareth comes only as an afterthought, a surrogate destination to which they turn when they find it impossible to return safely to Bethlehem. In Matthew's Gospel, Nazareth is the place that represents a departure from the plan, against Luke's account in which Bethlehem has that role. Matthew's bold solution to the problem is to treat the older Nazareth tradition as if *it*, and not the Bethlehem tradition, were the innovation. As if it were the later, derived tradition, rather than the other way around.

Matthew buttresses his chosen role for Bethlehem by crowding it with scriptural allusions. Nearly every occasion from Israelite history that might contribute to the reputation of Bethlehem is given its moment in the first two chapters of the Gospel. If you gather all the Old Testament references to the town of Bethlehem, you will find that they group into five or six clusters. Most of these revolve around Bethlehem's role as the birthplace of David. In the Old Testament the clear majority of references to Bethlehem occur in the two books of Samuel, where the story of David is told. Anecdotes include the story of Samuel's discovery of David at Jesse's house and that of the young David's encounter with Goliath—both stories showing David's first emergence into public life. Other texts from these biblical books reinforce the same hometown theme. For instance, in the appendices to the David story at the end of 2 Samuel, in an account repeated in 2 Chronicles, we learn of the mature David homesick for a drink from the waters of Bethlehem.[16]

The theme of David's birthplace can be presumed to be at the center of Matthew's interest in Bethlehem as well because it supports the Gospel's claim that Jesus was the messianic son of David. In the genealogy that begins his Gospel, Matthew makes that point explicit more than once (Matt 1:1, 17). Furthermore, the citation of Micah's prophecy (Mic 5:1–2; Matt 2:6), brought to bear on the case by Herod's advisors, repeats the idea. Micah's prophecy also trades on the significance of David's birthplace: The prophet looks to a time when a just ruler will deliver Israel from misrule, and the prophet clothes that imagined scenario in

---

16. Bethlehem references in the account of the visit to Jesse's house appear at 1 Sam 16: 1, 4, 15. References to the Goliath story are found at 1 Sam 17: 12, 15, 58. The story of David's desire for a drink from the waters of Bethlehem are found at 1 Sam 20:6, 28; 2 Chr 11:16, 17, 18, 26.

the particulars of the David story. For his part, Matthew is doing something similar: Jesus is his candidate for Micah's anticipated king.

Then there is the case of Rachel's tomb, alluded to at Matt 2:18. Genesis reports that Rachel died giving birth to her youngest son, Benjamin, and was buried on the road to Bethlehem. Of course, the tradition that connects the tomb with Bethlehem may be another instance of David's influence because apparently an earlier tradition put her tomb elsewhere, at Ramah, a few miles north of Jerusalem.[17] Jeremiah poetically exploited the fact that the Babylonians chose Ramah as the gathering station for rounding up the exiles to be transported to Babylon (Jer 40:1), and he imagined Rachel's grief expanding to include all her subsequent offspring. As the wife of Jacob, or Israel, she is pictured mourning the conscription of the family of Israel for its long march into exile. With Jeremiah, Rachel's tomb came to be associated with the Babylonian Exile—a theme of some importance to Matthew. Although Jeremiah explicitly names Ramah as the site of the tomb and the later exilic gathering, it would seem that subsequent readers would connect this with Rachel's tomb thought to be at Bethlehem, as Matthew apparently does. For Matthew this is a part of Bethlehem's sadder history, now repeating itself in the cruelty of Herod (Jer 31:15; Matt 2:18).

And finally there is the story of Naomi and Ruth, one of the more engaging narratives concerning Bethlehem, and one we have already seen to maintain a quiet presence in Matthew's document. The book of Ruth, of course, is also associated with the David theme that preoccupies Matthew in his infancy narrative. In a concluding genealogy (Ruth 4:18–22), the book itself makes a point of David's descent from Ruth's line, a genealogy that Matthew may well have used as a model for his introductory genealogy. As we know, it includes Ruth as well (Matt 1:5).

With this flurry of allusions brought to bear on the matter, we see Matthew reinforcing his placement of Bethlehem at the beginning of

17. Bethlehem, south of Jerusalem, is identified as the site of Rachel's tomb at Gen 35:19; 48:7. The early tradition that placed the tomb north of Jerusalem is reflected at 1 Sam 10:2. Ramah, also north, echoes this idea, as in Jer 31:15 (cited in Matt 2:18). In Jer 40:1 Ramah is where the exiles are rounded up for deportation. Are these influenced by the David traditions? It would make sense that the birth of Benjamin would be located in the tribal holdings of Benjamin. Memorial sites have a strange propensity to cluster and, like oral traditions, gravitate toward the more famous names. So it seems plausible that the earlier site was Ramah and later moved to Bethlehem because of the prominence of David. However, this is inconclusive because it is also possible that attention shifted to Ramah due to its association with Benjamin.

Jesus' story. Not only does he name the town as the location of Jesus' birth, as does Luke, but he also identifies it as their place of residence when we first come upon the family in his narrative. By beginning the story of Jesus and his family at Bethlehem rather than Nazareth, the evangelist begins his circle of stages not in the northern territory of Galilee, but rather in the south, in the territory of Judea, where he will stage the homecoming scene in the city of Jerusalem. This relocation makes room for the circular itinerary that he has planned for the Gospel.

JERUSALEM AND NAZARETH

There is yet another, more basic problem. We have seen how the choice of Bethlehem over Nazareth has been at least provisionally resolved, enabling a homecoming story that begins and ends in the southern territory of Judea. But how does Matthew account for that older and stronger tradition that places Jesus' home in Nazareth, a tradition that is encapsulated by the title, "Jesus of Nazareth," found in all the Gospels, and still allow the narrative to be a coming "home"? And especially, how can the arrival in Jerusalem be called a homecoming, if in the very scene of arrival—in fact, in the very type-scene that we have used to ground the notion of a return—the crowd identifies the one entering as "Jesus of Nazareth" (Matt 21:11)? How can Jerusalem be "home," if Nazareth is, if not his birthplace, still his home?

First of all, it is worth noting that John's Gospel also seems to make a case for Jerusalem being the "home" of Jesus, even while he is named "Jesus of Nazareth." Matthew's idea is not unique. In Jesus' first flight from Jerusalem, in John 4:43–45, we see that he went to Galilee, where they welcomed him, "For Jesus himself testified that a prophet has no honor in his native place." Here John gives Jerusalem the status of Jesus' "native place." So there is something of a precedent, or second example, for the idea of Jerusalem as home of Jesus. Of course, John is not describing a homecoming built over the major arch of the narrative in Matthew's manner, for John tells of departures and returns many times over. In John's Gospel, Jesus is a fugitive Messiah, who is at home in Jerusalem, but never allowed to settle there long. And yet John's Gospel uses the title "Jesus of Nazareth" freely (John 1:45; 18:5, 6; 19:19). There is a tension in the text of the Gospel between Nazareth and Jerusalem, each of which can claim the title of "home." So it is with Matthew. He too has inherited a tradition that puts Nazareth in place as Jesus' hometown. The tradition certainly reaches deeper and further than Mark's account, but Mark is Matthew's source.

In a later passage Matthew adopts, with revisions, Mark's account of Jesus' visit to Nazareth, described as "his own country" (Mark 6:1–6; Matt 13:54–58). Among the revisions Matthew introduces in his account of this episode is the omission of the phrase concerning kinship in Mark's string: "A prophet is not without honor, except in his own country, and among his own kin, and in his own house." It would suggest that Matthew does not want us to be thinking of Nazareth as the ancestral home place of Jesus, but rather a place where he lived for a time—in this case, the duration of his coming to adulthood.

But it is with Matthean dramatic irony that the evangelist makes his main points with the Nazareth theme. It is ironic in the sense that it uses the narrative voice to impart special knowledge, divulged to readers but not to the characters in the story. Typically, dramatic irony allows the reader to understand what is happening to the characters before the characters themselves know. The narrative voice telling the story imparts this special knowledge, without divulging it to the characters. It is the narrator of Matthew's Gospel who explains to us why and how Nazareth enters the story, as if it needed explanation: . . . and he went and lived in a town called Nazareth. So was fulfilled what was said through the prophets: "He will be called a Nazarene." (Matt 2:23)

Of the four instances in which the name of Nazareth is given in Matthew's text, three (2:23; 4:13; 21:11—but not 26:71) are moments in the circling life journey of Jesus, listed among the citations we have looked at earlier. The narrator, who has disclosed to us the circling journey in the first place, has a different assessment of Jesus' Nazareth roots than that voiced by the characters in the narrative. In these instances Jesus will be identified as "from Nazareth," but *only* by characters within the narrative—the crowd (21:11) and the woman in the high priest's courtyard (26:71).

Meanwhile, the narrator informs the reader otherwise. The narration not only allows us to learn of Matthew's geographical candidate for the actual birth, Bethlehem, but the narrative voice even identifies for the reader's benefit the moments of travel to and departure from Nazareth (2:23; 4:13), thereby suggesting a rationale for the popular report of Jesus' Nazareth origins echoed by the characters: the move to Nazareth will fulfill the prophecy, "He will be called a Nazarene" (2:23). And thus later in the story, as we have just seen, he is so called.

In other words, Matthew is divulging something like insider knowledge through his use of the narrative voice. Even though the wider world,
represented here by the characters in the story, name Jesus as being "of
Nazareth" and presume that to be his place of origin, we who share the
knowledge of Bethlehem are in a position to know the inside "truth,"
and access the common title for Jesus for what it is really worth.

BETHLEHEM AND JERUSALEM

However, there remains one more large issue, one that may have troubled even sympathetic readers from the first part of this chapter: How
can this circuit of locations add up to a homecoming? Although the
sequence of stages describes a circle from Jerusalem back to Jerusalem,
Jesus joins the procession only at the second stage, Bethlehem. So how
can the triumphal entry of Jesus in Matt 21 be treated as a homecoming?
It would seem obvious enough that a person cannot return to a place he's
never been. So is it possible to close the gap between the beginning and
the end, between Bethlehem and Jerusalem? It seems that Matthew's text
would want us to do that.

We might notice first of all, the circle of moves that are framed by
the two type-scenes and connected by stages. This is hardwired right
into the plot. The redaction of the text indicates Matthew's interest in
describing a circuit that begins and ends in Jerusalem. The presence in
this text of a closed circle in the plot is not at issue. The problem is not
whether the action circles through the story from type-scene to type-
scene, from chapter 2 to chapter 21. The problem, rather, is whether this
circle can be called the itinerary of a homecoming because the Magi
travel the first leg, from Jerusalem to Bethlehem, and Jesus joins the
circle only then. However that is determined, the circle of events shows
that Matthew has departure and return in mind.

Geographically, Jerusalem and Bethlehem are neighbors. Bethlehem
lies a mere six miles south of the old city walls. So this is a quite different
problem than that presented by Nazareth, which is at the other end of
the land. The proximity of Bethlehem and Jerusalem is so close that the
difference, in terms of distance, is negligible. And Matthew's text, in fact,
tends to finesse the difference, not only in distance, but in significance. It
does not encourage a distinction between the two sites and even tends to
blur them in respect to their significance. Each serves as a city of David
(Matt 2:6; 21:9), although this isn't made as explicit as Luke's naming

Bethlehem the "City of David" (Luke 2:4, 11). Yet the relationship of both towns to the story of David is made unmistakably clear. One is the ancestral royal point of origin; the other the capital city that serves as the only conceivable site of royal arrival, whether of visiting Magi or of the returning Messiah.

How the text blurs the two locations can also be seen in another instance in the allusions to Isa 60 and Ps 72 in the Magi story.[18] Both the Isaian passage and the Psalm depict the kings of the earth bringing gold and incense for tribute to Jerusalem. The psalm seems especially influential, with its emphasis on the visitors' acts of homage —a word that appears three times in the Magi story (Matt 2:2, 8, 11). But although the destination envisioned by both of these Old Testament texts is the city of Jerusalem, Matthew has no difficulty shifting the destination to Bethlehem.

The more substantial issue behind this textual identification is that the ground of dispute vis-à-vis the new Messiah is not any particular town, but rather the territory in which those towns are located. Judea, the realm controlled by Herod and afterward by Archelaus, is the territory from which Jesus is banished and to which he will return. It is the kingdom of Judea that Herod guards jealously, and which the family must leave for reasons of safety. And it is outside of the territory that they must settle for the same reason.

Jerusalem, the city, is Judea's traditional capital, its religious and cultural hub, and figures in the story as the only appropriate site of reentry to the territory for one who is presented as bringing claims of Messiah and king. In sum, given the banishment of Jesus as Herod's perceived rival, the narrative logic of the Gospel demands an understanding of Jesus' entry into Jerusalem as of one returning home with kingly claims. This is the real meaning of Matthew's homecoming.

Once we see how the meaning of homecoming is presented here, then we can see that the series of stages is defined by their relationship to Jerusalem. The initial departure from Bethlehem is taken in lieu of a move toward Jerusalem. Given the information imparted by the Magi, the proper move for Jesus and the family would be to go to Jerusalem. This is what Herod fears. A move in this direction does not, of course, occur. Because of Herod, the family travels in the other direction, reversing the move to Jerusalem—and deferring it. Bethlehem lies within the

18. See, for instance, Brown, *Birth*, 187f.

territory of Judea, where Herod's power and authority can be felt. For this reason the family must leave. Distant Egypt provides a safe haven until Jerusalem is once again made safe. But this news of a change is misleading, and subsequent information makes Nazareth a better option. So we see Jerusalem again repulsing the protagonist, despite efforts to return to Judea.

Upon reaching adulthood, Jesus leaves Nazareth to begin his ministry. The citation at Matt 4:15–16 that signposts the third location, Capernaum in Galilee, situates this part of Matthew's story at the beginning of his return. Like Isaiah's account of restoring territory previously conquered by foreigners, (i.e., Tiglath-Pileser III), Jesus begins his mission of retrieval. He is headed toward Jerusalem, though this is not yet explicit. He begins his program in Galilee and ultimately (Matt 16:21) discloses the Jerusalem destination to his disciples, as he begins a more concerted move in that direction.

At the end of this drive toward the city, the city's sustained rejection of the Messiah is about to come to an end. The final scriptural notice in the pattern accompanies the entry into Jerusalem. This is the moment deferred for so many years. Altogether, the structure as a whole transforms the entry into a return and converts Jesus' confrontation in Jerusalem into something quite different from Mark's straightforward challenge.

Back to the Homecoming Story

When we draw back and look at the narrative program of Matthew's Gospel, we see then two entry scenes that are connected by a series of moves. The picture that results is one of an attempt on Jesus' life that is deferred, until he returns to Judea and enters the city of Jerusalem, at which time the threat is renewed. In effect, to use drama categories for describing phases of the plot, this would describe the rising action of the plot.

In addition, we see that the arrival in Jerusalem has the character of a response, rather than an initiative, as in Mark's Gospel. This will become significant when we compare the story to others of a similar nature, in which the return is a time for settling scores. In this work it happens differently.

As for the type-scenes of Conspicuous Entry, they open to our view two other connections with the Old Testament, one with the book of Ruth and another with the ascension of Solomon to the throne, in I Kgs 1. Although the story of Naomi, from the book of Ruth, has more prominent connections with the first of Matthew's type-scenes in Matt 2, not least due to the emphasis on Bethlehem, it in fact has relevance for Matt 21 as well, insofar as it reports a homecoming, providing a hermeneutical signal for interpreting Matthew's story. Likewise, although Solomon's story provides an antecedent for the entry of Jesus into the city, Solomon's presence is also felt in the early chapters, influencing the story of the Magi.

The interpretive guides these Old Testament examples provide help us understand aspects less conspicuous (for modern readers) of Matthew's account. If Naomi points to a story of homecoming, it must be added that it is a delayed homecoming, with resonances in the experience of Israel returning from exile. It alerts us to make use of Empire Studies for our investigation of the role of violence in Matthew. And if the ascension of Solomon to the throne is a guide for understanding the story of Jesus' entry, it alerts us not simply to the claim being made about the Son of David, from the first to the last. It also reminds us that this claim is contested, and this is another aspect of Matthew's experience as his community surveys the wreckage of Judaism after the destruction of the temple, with its central role. The rivalry between the Jesus movement and the Pharisees is the more prominent of these rivalries and requires our attention.

There are many dimensions to the experience of violence in the posttemple era and multiple arenas in which the proposal of nonviolence would seem absurd. The homecoming story begins to open a blind on these vistas.

2

Discourses in Conflict

MATTHEW'S HOMECOMING STORY IS an interpretation of a story already in place. The scholarly consensus of source criticism, reinforced in a close comparison of their narratives, is that Matthew reworked Mark. Of the sources that Matthew is said to have available to his project, it is Mark's Gospel that provided him with the story line. Matthew adopted the dynamics of conflict development and resolution developed by Mark, even while adjusting them to new purposes. To see Mark's influence on Matthew, we can compare the two. But first that means drawing a picture of Mark's story line. We will begin with a description of the plot.[1] The description makes use of geographic indicators in the text, coupled with a version of the discourse theory of Michel Foucault, to sketch the conflict development in Mark. The resolution of narrative conflict is illuminated by a comparison to Gene Sharp's analysis of nonviolent conflict resolution. In the final part of the chapter, these findings will be used to characterize Matthew's adjustments in a narrative now appearing as the Markan intertext of Matthew, or Mark-in-Matthew. Although a somewhat graphic image of the Markan plot is reductive, it will help us visualize Matthew's use of it in his own work.

A CLASH OF DISCOURSES

It is not difficult to sketch a summary of Mark's story. We are aware of moving between two major sites—the territory of Galilee and the city of Jerusalem. These correspond to actual places, identifiable on maps. Galilee is in the north, by the Sea of Galilee; south of there, Jerusalem is the capital of the province of Judea and the site of the Temple. But in the

---

1. This description of conflict development and resolution in Mark abbreviates my more complete presentation in Beck, *Nonviolent Story*, Chapters. 3–7.

narrative they are virtual places that take on specific functions. Galilee is the site of developing the ministry; Jerusalem is the site of opposition and attempted destruction of that ministry. Beginning in Galilee, Jesus gradually widens his mission until it reaches beyond the borders of the Galilean province to include the gentile lands adjacent. Shortly after the ministry is engaged, scribes arrive from Jerusalem to assess it and confront Jesus (Mark 3:22). Their arrival foreshadows the second primary setting of the action. The dramatic tension, which increases through the Galilean mission, reaches an early crisis in Mark 8:27–30, when Peter identifies Jesus as the expected Messiah.

At this point he and his disciples turn south, toward Jerusalem. The holy city of Jerusalem, the traditional capital of Judea, is then the other primary setting for the action. Here the story arrives at its conclusion. Here he will return the challenge of the religious authorities by prophetic activity in the temple (Mark 11:15–19); here he will consequently be killed for his presumption. Turning this dire ending to the story around, the gospel concludes with a message of "a man in white" speaking from the empty tomb: The disciples are to return to Galilee, where they will find the risen Messiah.

This is the familiar shape of Mark's story, played out on a map of Galilee and Judea. But the two territorial areas do more than simply provide settings for the action. They also take on certain narrative functions. In particular, each provides a home base for the contending parties—the protagonist and antagonists of the plot. Galilee is the home territory of Jesus; the Jerusalem temple is the corresponding center for his opposition.

The gospels, of course, are more than engaging stories. They teach; they make a case. Although traditional exegesis has a successful history of extracting the theology from the words of Jesus, we can remember that the stories themselves are theological, intended to teach and persuade, and we can read them in that way, paying attention to the issues contested in the conflict of the plot—the central conflict is also a struggle of ideas. A useful way to engage with the ideological struggle at the heart of Mark's plot is to read it as a clash of discourses—in the rich sense of "discourse" posited by Michel Foucault.[2] On the one side, Jesus and his movement can be presented under the heading of the "Galilee Discourse"; on the other side, his opponents allow presentation in terms of the "Jerusalem Discourse." Each of these can be examined in terms that have become somewhat traditional in employing Foucault's idea. We will, then, consider each of the discourses through three categories: (1) as a set of characteristic statements, (2) as certain representative practices, and (3) in terms of a social or institutional setting.

The Galilee Discourse

The Galilee Discourse configures the narrative position of the protagonist occupying one side of the narrative conflict of Mark's Gospel—Jesus and the Jesus movement. In this discourse, statements are couched in the vocabulary of Galilean village life, especially noticeable in the parables. The social location is a village life sustained by a Galilean agricultural economy. The Galilean cities of Sepphoris, near Nazareth, and Tiberias are excluded from Jesus' ministry. According to Mark, his mission was restricted exclusively to villages. The third element, the praxis of the Galilean discourse, consists primarily of Jesus' healings and meals with his followers.

1. *A Family of Statements*: Village culture is reflected in the *teachings* of Jesus, especially his parables. "Without parables he did not speak to them, but to his own disciples he explained everything in private" (Mark 4:34). If we are to identify a "family of related statements" that relate to the Gospel's Galilee discourse, we have to begin with the parables. In Mark four fully fleshed-out parables serve this purpose: the Sower (Mark 4:3–9), the Seed Growing of Itself (4:26–29), and the Mustard Seed (4:30–32), all three clustered in chapter 4, along with the Wicked Vineyard Tenants, in chapter 12 (Mark 12:1–12). The parables themselves reflect country life: those in chapter 4 reflect the experience of tending growing plant life. Some of the key words of the agricultural culture code are *sower, seed, soil, bushel, blade,* and *ear*. In chapter 12, terms

2. Discourse, as the idea is used here, can be described as a family group of statements that share a certain set of words and meanings. Discourses are grounded in social institutions that they also help to create, and they find expression in a characteristic set of social practices. See Michel Foucault, *Archaeology*. The relation of ideology and discourse is still under negotiation among critics. Some see ideology as a feature of discourse; others see ideology as the larger concept, embracing different discourses. See Eagleton, *Ideology*, 193–220, and Mills, *Discourse*, 29–47.

like *vineyard*, *winepress*, and *tower*, register the viniculture of the time.[3]
The agricultural parables assume listeners who are familiar with farming
life. And, of course, they are indeed parables, not farming instructions.
We know that Jesus is not teaching farmers best agricultural practices.
The language is metaphoric, in the way that parables are narrative metaphors.[4] But should there be any doubt on this score, Mark makes things
perfectly clear by including an explanation of the first parable, the Sower
(Mark 4:13–20). This interpretative moment generates an entirely different set of terms that evoke ministry and discipleship—*word, Satan,
persecution, listen, accept*, and so forth.

Furthermore, the parables of Mark intersect with the narrative plot
of the Gospel itself. If the Gospel text can be said to contain an image
of discourse, that text also gives indications that it is part of the Galilee
discourse that it sets before us. This is apparent, for instance, in the case
of the Sower (with its allegory, Mark 4:1–20). Not only is there a match
of concerns—the beginnings of the sowing are congruent with the beginning of the narrative in which we are engaged—but also the seed is,
we are assured, the word (Mark 4:14). What word? The word of Jesus
now entrusted to those "inside," the word of the disciples learning to be
apostles (Mark 6:30). Ultimately, it is the written word of Mark himself,
the word we are reading.

So, for instance, in the explanation of the Sower parable with its
world, flesh, and devil (Mark 4:13–20), we see previewed future turnings
of the plot, as when Peter is told, "Get behind me, Satan" (Mark 8:33),
after he objects to the news of the foreshadowed Passion. The rocky
ground, as interpreted as persecution, anticipates the flight of the disciples (Mark 14:50), and the thorns, interpreted as riches, prepare us for
the rich man's failed call (Mark 10:22) and Judas's venality (Mark 14:11).
The Kingdom teaching of Jesus, which has been clothed in the language
and conceptual metaphors of Galilee, is now seen to be part of a larger
discourse that would include not only the disciples of Jesus in the narrative but also the faith community of Mark, and Mark himself.

---

3. Robert Scholes tells us that basic to reading stories is learning their narrative
coding. Cultural codes are those key words that enable us, when reading, to construct,
or construe, a world—"to orient ourselves in it, to locate and understand the characters,
their situations, and their actions. See Scholes, *Textual Power*, 21–22, 27.

4. Ricoeur, "Biblical Hermeneutics," 75–106.

2. *Social Location*. In Mark, village life provides social metaphors for the Kingdom of God that Jesus announces.[5] The Galilean rural village life can be mapped onto sociological categories.[6] Village life rotated around the family. Between the family and the outside world stood the village. Frequently villages were equivalent to extended families. The village provided the primary identifiers for those from elsewhere—for example, "Jesus of Nazareth." Beyond the village stood the outside world, and the first point of contact in that larger horizon was the city. Every village connected to a city, situated within that city's circle of influence. For Nazareth this city was Sepphoris.

The first move toward organizing the Jesus movement depicted in Mark's Gospel is the naming of the Twelve, in Mark 3:13–19. Mark develops this initiative by way of a contrast with Jesus' natural family. His natural family appears at 3:21 and 3:31–35, in a paired set of passages. In the latter place Jesus is shown dismissing his natural family in favor of "those about him" in the house, gathered to hear him speak. "Here are my mother and brothers. Whoever does the will of God is my brother, and sister, and mother" (Mark 3:35). Nor is it merely incidental that Jesus is addressing them inside because the "house" is consistently the place that *his* people meet, in contrast to the synagogues of Galilee, where his opponents can be found (Mark 1:21–28; 3:1–6; 6:1–6), in a contrast announced at the very beginning in the explicit positioning of the Capernaum synagogue against the house of Simon Peter.

All these stage directions of inside and outside come into play with the parables account in chapter 4. Here we read that after Jesus delivered his initial parable, the Sower, he was invited to explain himself:

> And when he was alone, those present along with the Twelve questioned him about the parables. He answered them, "The mystery of the kingdom of God has been granted to you. But to those outside everything comes in parables, . . ." (Mark 4:10–11)

5. "Village life can replicate a metaphorical system for the Kingdom, because various aspects of that system can furnish a model of the kingdom. For these parables the kingdom is a village, and each parable works out different aspects of that implied metaphorical system derived from village life." B. Scott, *Parables*, 91.

6. "Throughout all these parables of 'family, village, city, and beyond,' the social landscape has furnished a map that is expected to replicate the Kingdom of God. Understanding that map is key to understanding the parables." Scott, *Parables*, 98.

With the twelve, the metaphor of family is brought into play with
the New Israel. Moreover, "those about him" are also "those inside" and
are distinguished from "those outside." Here the observation of Bernard
Scott is pertinent: "The family system provides a metaphorical system
for distinguishing those inside and those outside the kingdom. The social map explains who I am, where I am, and by inference who is not
with me."[7]

3. *Characteristic Praxis.* Discourse theory posits an intimate relation between the two phenomena: a characteristic set of statements, on
the one hand, and social practices that support and are supported by
those statements, on the other.[8] Commentators have long recognized
that in Mark the praxis singularly characteristic of Jesus' ministry is the
work of healing. They show the Galilee discourse of the Kingdom in
action. In this Gospel there is an unexpected and explicit convergence
between preaching and healing already in the first public action of Jesus,
the exorcism at Capernaum (Mark 1:21–28). Although an act of healing,
it is acclaimed by the crowd as an illustration of his teaching with authority, unlike the scribes (Mark 1:22, 27). Parables and healings are in some
ways equivalent dimensions of the Galilee discourse of the Kingdom.

After the initial five chapters of the Gospel, the Kingdom discourse
becomes disengaged from its setting in Galilee, beginning with the rejection by the family and native village of Jesus (Mark 6:1–6). He can do
no miracle there (Mark 6:1–6). They refuse the discourse. The failure
at Nazareth is symptomatic of the narrative conflict in this Gospel, for
it is precisely in the healings that the two discourses of Jesus and of his
opponents meet and clash.

The Jerusalem Discourse

Early in the Gospel (Mark 3:22) scribes arrive in Galilee to engage with
Jesus and his movement. Coming "from Jerusalem" they mark for the
reader the social site of the oppositions' ideological center. Although
Jesus and his growing movement is elaborated in the Galilee discourse,

7. B. Scott, *Parables*, 85.

8. See, for instance, Poster, *Foucault*, 14: "The interpenetration of discourse and
practice goes on interminably because they imply each other's existence from the beginning. In studying discourse it is not a question of perfect truth; in studying practice
it is not a question of determining discourse."

the discourse of his opponents is related to Jerusalem and its Temple. The Jerusalem discourse is also expressed in a family of statements, in this case couched in the ritual language of Judaism, which configures holiness as purity, and expresses it by contrasting the holy and the unclean. The corresponding praxis of the Jerusalem discourse consists in maintaining the boundaries it defines. In this regard, for instance, the scribes of the Pharisees challenge the behavior of Jesus and his disciples who are "eating with sinners" (Mark 2:25–27).

1. *Statements*. The ritual language of purity and pollution serves as a prominent cultural code in Mark's account. Symptomatic of this, the word *unclean* (*akathartos*) appears eleven times, always in the phrase "unclean spirits." Because Mark has available to him the alternative and more literal language of "common," or "profane," an expression he employs when he writes of the ritual washing of cups and utensil (Mark 7:2, 5), his use of "unclean" is clearly purposeful. Matthew's Gospel, by contrast, omits all but one of Mark's references to unclean spirits (Matt 10:1).[9] We see that Mark's agenda is not shared by Matthew. Although Matthew includes this language, it is minimally and casually.

We find converging evidence in the contrasting term, "holy." Mark favors the word as a modifier of "Spirit" and avoids using it of established religious institutions. This can be seen clearly by contrasting the practice of Matthew, who disregards this usage and shows other tendencies.[10] Most notably, in contradistinction to Mark, he applies the word *holy* quite freely to Judean institutions, such as the temple and city. Matthew speaks of the "holy city" (Matt 4:5; 27:53) and of the coming desolation in the "holy place" (Matt 24:15). Mark lacks these and even appears to go out of his way to avoid what is, after all, a rather normal designation of the sanctuary, when he speaks of the desolation "where it ought not to be" (Mark 13:11). In sum, Matthew applies the word where Mark would not and omits Mark's own usage. Again, it would seem that Mark has an agenda for the word *holy* that is not shared by Matthew.

For Israel, the rules of purity were derived from chapters 11–16 of the book of Leviticus. John Pilch noted: "These specific chapters [of

---

9. Matthew also includes one Q-source instance (Matt 12:43), and omits the reference to cup washing.

10. Four of Mark's seven instances of the word refer to the Holy Spirit. The situation is quite different for Matthew. Of Matthew's eleven instances of the word, only three correspond to Mark.

Leviticus] are considered to derive from the post-exilic era (after 537 BCE) or approximately contemporaneous with Ezra's determination to restore holiness to the community by dissolving marriages with foreign women (Ezra 10:10–11)."[11] Permeable boundaries represented a social threat. Points of exit or entry can portray political infiltration or dispersal. "The rule governing boundaries of the social body were replicated and reinforced on the physical body, and vice versa."[12]

In the ritual language of "holy" and "unclean," purity is a metaphor for holiness, one of many possible metaphors. Its nonliteral character is seen in the arbitrary opposition between *holy* and *unclean*. Literally, the contrary of holy is profane or secular; the normal opposite of unclean is clean. The opposition of holy and unclean, though arbitrary, is an effective metaphor, equating holiness with purity. Repentance is symbolized as washing and cleansing, removing a stain.[13]

2. *Social Location*. Jerome Neyrey has shown how the language of purity as "holy" and "unclean" provided a ritual framework to chart the full scope of Judean reality.[14] This institutional dimension adds to the metaphor of purity, in that the holy takes its norm in this discourse from the temple and its Holy Place. When early in the Gospel (Mark 3:22) Scribes come to Galilee from Jerusalem to engage with Jesus and his movement, they are signaling to readers the location of the opposition's ideological headquarters. In the latter part of the narrative, Jesus returns this favor by descending on Jerusalem and visiting their base in the temple area.

The list of places is instructive. Ten degrees of holiness, counted from the least and most general to the most important and specific, begin with the land of Israel, "holier than any other land," and gradually narrow to Jerusalem, its Temple, and finally the Holy of Holies in the Sanctuary.[15] Seen from the other direction, places range from the epicen-

11. Pilch, *Healing*, 50.

12. Pilch, *Healing*, 51.

13. Underlying the metaphor of purity is an understanding of "unclean" that has been illuminated by an influential study of Mary Douglas, *Purity and Danger*. Here she has projected an understanding of dirt as "matter out of place." Dirt is disorder; cleansing consists of restoring order. Things have their places, and to ignore that fact is to create dirt, or filth, or noise, or any of the many other names for this phenomenon.

14. Neyrey, "Idea of Purity," 91–128. Neyrey identifies in Jewish writings of the early centuries AD lists that describe the relative holiness, in graduated degrees, of food, persons, times, and places.

15. Neyrey, "Idea of Purity," 95.

ter of holiness, the Holy of Holies in the Temple, outward in concentric circles through the Temple, the courts of the Temple, the Holy City of Jerusalem, the Holy Land of Judea, with the least holy of all, the gentile lands, off the charts. Here purity intersects with geography to allow the early rabbinic writers to calculate degrees of Jewish identity, configured as holiness. In effect, the entire land was imagined as a virtual set of concentric regions, centered in the Sanctuary of the Temple, and decreasing in the intensity of holiness as it moves outward.[16]

3. *Characteristic Praxis.* The ritual discourse of holy and unclean served to identify boundaries that established what was permissible and what was not, what was proper to the community, and what was external to it. Holiness was a matter of excluding the sources of contamination. It was a process of quarantine.

John Pilch sees the story of the leper (Mark 1:40–45) as the master key. Biblical leprosy, which doesn't appear to be Hansen's disease (our notion of leprosy), was a matter of pollution rather than contagion. That is, the emphasis lay on the leper's impact on society, and not on the physical impairment caused by the disease itself.[17] Contagion concerns the individual, the locus of biomedical sickness, whereas pollution concerns the group. The leper becomes the poster child for social pollution. And what is true of the leper's illness is also true of the other illnesses in the land.

Illness does not stand alone, but is directly connected to social disorder. On the one hand, illness is a disruptive social event. "Its consequences are social and communal events. They are socially disruptive and often threaten the most essential values, behavioral norms, and conceptions of order. What is required of the healer is restoration of order by placing the threat in its proper framework, controlling the disruptive

16. In an influential series of articles the Jewish New Testament scholar Paula Fredriksen has insisted, in response to certain readings by Christian exegetes, that this temple practice was not based on ethnic, moral, nor gender discriminations, but solely on a sense of holiness, and a concern about access to the holy. Such restriction of access would reinforce the sense of reverence. However, it seems that restricted access was just the objection mounted by Mark's Jesus, along with the underlying notion of the holy as purity. See, for instance, Fredriksen, "Purity Laws?" 18–25, 42–47, (also on her home page).

17. Pilch, *Healing*, 51: "The interpretative strategy of placing this story of Jesus healing the leper into the wider context of biblical leprosy certainly shows the concern is not contagion but pollution, an integral part of the Judean social system . . ."

effect on the sick person and that person's network, and making the entire experience personally and socially meaningful."[18] On the other hand,
illness is only one of many forms of social disorder and is considered
primarily as being one of these, and not as a phenomenon in isolation,
as with modern models of medicine. If, as some say, Mark's narrative
is driven by the vision of Jesus' inauguration of a covenant renewal of
Israel,[19] we can be sure that the healings are both a primary symbol and
a cause of that social renewal.

The Conflict of Discourses Engaged: The Healings

So in Mark's story the two worlds are set at odds—the Galilee discourse
of Jesus' people and the Jerusalem discourse of his opponents. The two
discourses erupt into conflict at the point where their contrasting practices intersect: the meals and healings of Jesus.

Marcus Borg has elaborated a thesis of the role of meals in the
Pharisaic program of resistance to Gentile incursion in the land.[20] Mark's
narrative program includes this strand of dissension in some reports of
contested meals. Of these, the most elaborate is that concerning washing of utensils and hands (Mark 7:1–23). Here mutual recriminations
include charges leveled by the Pharisees that Jesus' people disrespect the
traditions (Mark 7:5), and his countercharge that their traditions reject
the commandments of God (Mark 7:9). An echo of this lively language
appears as early as chapter 2, when objections are raised to the lack of
circumspection shown by Jesus and his disciples when they share a meal
with "sinners" (Mark 2:18–20). Such behavior was inviting pollution.

In the debates in chapter 2 of Mark, the scribes and Pharisees are
responding to the sudden arrival of Jesus' ministry among the ill and
unfavored, which we have seen was presented as a case of Holy Spirit
among the unclean spirits. As a matter of fact, most—perhaps all—of the
healings involve elements of the unclean, whether spirits, leprosy, bodily
emissions, withered hands, or corpses.

But the healings are also an expression of the Galilee discourse of
the Kingdom. In Mark there is an unusual and unexpected convergence
between preaching and healing. This is signaled immediately in the first

18. Pilch, *Healing*, 28.
19. See Horsley, *Telling*, 177–201.
20. Borg, *Conflict*, 77–82.

public action of Jesus, the exorcism at Capernaum (Mark 1:21–28). Jesus expels a demon from a possessed man, but it is presented as an illustration of his teaching with authority, unlike the scribes (Mark 1:22, 27). In point of fact, it is especially in the healing episodes that the two worlds, the two discourses of Jesus and his opponents, come into most sustained conflict. In effect, he performs his healings in the face of and over the objection of the guardians of purity, who do not recognize him, though the unclean spirits do.

Not only do the two discourses stand in contrast, but they also meet in vigorous opposition. Their collision occurs immediately after Jesus begins his mission, in the episode at Capernaum. This clash begins with the works of Jesus in chapters 1 and 2 and proceeds into the debates that follow. If the healing of the leper illustrates the praxis in Mark's Galilee discourse, the story of the man with the withered hand (Mark 3:1–6) exemplifies the arena of conflict. The opposition to Jesus takes a clear view. This is the Sabbath, a day set aside for God's glory. There are traditions in place to keep the Sabbath holy, including the refusal to work. Healing is a work. It might be excused in an emergency, but this is no emergency. The man's hand has been withered for years, presumably since birth. There is no reason for the healing not to wait another day and thereby satisfy both the man's need and the Sabbath law.

Mark shows us a Jesus who sees things differently. If this is God's day, if this is God's place, what would God best want here and now for this man? Health and wholeness. It is not without significance that the withered hand is a violation of holiness understood as wholeness (and as such, prevented certain individuals from becoming priests, even though they may have been born to the role). Jesus frames the issue in terms of life and death: Is it lawful on the Sabbath to do good, or do harm? To save life, or to kill? What does God want; what is God about? The terms are extreme, escalating the conflict toward an absolute contrast: life and death. In choosing to restore the man's hand, Jesus is answering his own question. He is for restoring life to its fullness, implying that those who oppose him oppose life. As if in compliance with his terms, the Pharisees immediately depart to meet with the Herodians to plan his destruction. Mark's signals are clear: A concern for purity over compassion is an endorsement of death over life. God, it would seem, is thought to prefer suffering, if it is necessary to maintain the law.

In these two stories of outstretched hands—Jesus reaching out to the leper, Jesus enabling the maimed man to reach out—we see in small the inclusive program of Jesus' ministry in this Gospel. Here holiness as compassion has overrun barriers and prohibitions. Against it, in un-accustomed unity, is the religious establishment, protecting a common cultural discourse.

As noted earlier, the radicalizing of opposition will continue in Mark's third chapter, when the scribes arrive from Jerusalem to inter-pret Jesus' behavior as a case of demon possession (Mark 3:22). Jesus turns the tables on them with miniparables about houses and Satan, the upshot being the judgment that one or the other is indeed in posses-sion of the Holy Spirit, but whichever side is not is instead controlled by unclean spirits. Each side claims the right to speak in the name of the Holy, but the reader, guided by timely prompts from the narrator, knows that the Holy Spirit has come upon the carpenter from Nazareth from the beginning of the narrative.

TWO HILLS

The Final Week

Midway through the narrative, Jesus and his followers leave Galilee and begin a journey toward Jerusalem. As the scene of action shifts south to the city, the terms of engagement adjust. Earlier the conflict of discourses was waged among the villages of Galilee. At that time scribes came north from Jerusalem to confront Jesus on his home ground (Mark 3:22). But now the action has turned to the south, to the city at the center of his op-ponents' discourse. In the final part of the story the conflict plays itself out in Jerusalem in a rhythm of reciprocal movement that shuttles between two hills that confront one another across the Kidron valley—Mount Zion on the west and the Mount of Olives on the east. Upon his arrival in the Jerusalem area, Jesus takes up temporary residence in the village of Bethany, on the Mount of Olives just out of sight of the city. His evenings are spent in Bethany and his days in the temple, teaching and debating with various representatives of the religious establishment. In its repeti-tion, his daily commute from the village to the city and back, returning each evening to the village of Bethany, inscribes a distinct figure in the action of the narrative. The daily journey establishes the two hills as sites of opposition, different as night and day. Their opposition establishes a grid on which the final drama is played out. In an act of narrative sleight of hand, the two discourses translate into these two hills, as votive sites for the interaction in the final resolution of conflict. The two mountains are topographical surrogates for the two discourses. The relationship established by Jesus' daily commute becomes a virtual confrontation of the two discourses they represent, an arena for working out their resolution. The stone-clad urban temple mount of Zion is site and representative of the Jerusalem discourse. Zion is the center of Judaism, the center of the holy, and the place of their worship. Home of the hieratic discourse that it serves as primal ideology, it is the centerpiece of its imaginary chart of the world. Jesus has come to the city to encounter the Jerusalem discourse in its own house. The neighboring hill of the Mount of Olives with its groves and villages, including Bethany, serves the narrative as "Galilee South." When Jesus comes to the city, he stays in the village, consistent with his Galilee mission. When he prays to his Father, it is in Gethsemane on the slopes of the Mount of Olives. Site of gardens and graves,[21] the Mount of Olives stands in the narrative, by way of the village of Bethany, as Jesus' home base when he is in this part of the story. From here he makes his daily incursions into the city.

Building on the system of reciprocal movement between the two sites, the narrative steps through the resolution of the conflict between the Jerusalem authorities and the Jesus movement. In an intensified version of the daily movement, the action culminates in two "raids," from each hill to its opposite. Each of these is marked by the key term *lestes*, translated variously as bandit, thief, rebel, robber, or insurgent. Although these translations range from political violence, what we would call terrorism, to social banditry, to simple robbery, the various meanings converge in an image of violent incursion, a violation of safety and social order, undertaken for whatever reason. As much as anything, it is the knell-like recurrence of this term, *lestes*, with its associations that lends to the temple action and the garden arrest of Jesus an undercurrent of violence and suggests the term *raids*.

---

21. Although today the Mount of Olives is known for its tombs, this aspect of its reputation is not prominent in Mark's treatment. The closest the text comes to that theme is in its allusions to the book of Zechariah—Zec 14:4, 21 (Mark 11:1, 15), which imagines the Lord Yahweh coming across the Mount of Olives, and the merchants banished from the temple, in the final days.

In an initial move, Jesus' challenge takes him from Bethany to the temple. It completes his long march to the city.

> They came to Jerusalem, and on entering the temple area he began to drive out those selling and buying there. He overturned the tables of the money changers and the seats of those who were selling doves. He did not permit anyone to carry anything through the temple area. Then he taught them saying, "Is it not written:
>> 'My house shall be called a house of prayer for all peoples'?
>> But you have made it a den of *thieves.* [*lēstōn*]"
> (Mark 11:15–17)

This bold move on the part of Jesus culminates the long buildup from the beginning of the story, and it prompts an immediate response from his opponents. The authorities find this incident to be the occasion to put into action the destructive intent they've harbored since his first week in public life (Mark 3:6). They make their move:

> The chief priests and the scribes came to hear of it and were seeking a way to put him to death, yet they feared him because the whole crowd was astonished at his teaching. When evening came, they went out of the city." (Mark 11:18–19)

However, their program is stalled by public opinion because Jesus proves too popular to intercept at this time. So they bide their time for now, debating with him in the temple area, looking for the main chance to stop him. Later in the week, giving up on the possibility of a public turn of fortunes, they send a "crowd" to capture and arrest him, in what appears in the narrative as reciprocity, a counterraid, in which they invade the Olivet site of Gethsemane, where Jesus is praying. As he disrupted their site of worship, so do they his.

> Then, while he was still speaking, Judas, one of the Twelve, arrived, accompanied by a crowd with swords and clubs who had come from the chief priests, the scribes, and the elders. . . .
>
> At this they laid hands on him and arrested him. One of the bystanders drew his sword, struck the high priest's servant, and cut off his ear. Jesus said to them in reply, "Have you come out as against a *robber* [*lēstēn*] with swords and clubs, to seize me?"
> (Mark 14:43, 46–48)

The third "raid" remains stillborn. Jesus refuses it, in a most deliberate manner. He does not resist the arrest and makes that move with all deliberation. At this point the action of the narrative finally moves outside the reciprocity pattern of the two hills, to a third, unanticipated hill:

> They brought him to the place of Golgotha (which is translated Place of the Skull). They gave him wine drugged with myrrh, but he did not take it. Then they crucified him and divided his garments by casting lots for them to see what each should take. It was nine o'clock in the morning when they crucified him. The inscription of the charge against him read, "The King of the Jews." With him they crucified two *revolutionaries* [*lēstas*], one on his right and one on his left. (Mark 15:22–27)

And so the story plays out. And it is this narrative plot line that Matthew borrows for his own work, although with important adjustments. What needs emphasis, however, is that Mark's Gospel already forms a narrative whole, with conflict development and resolution. Adopted by Matthew, this narrative whole provides him with a ready-made, dramatic storyline he can use to best effect.

Gene Sharp and the Resolution of Conflict in Mark

Gandhi is recorded as saying, "Jesus was the most active resister known perhaps to history. This was non-violence par excellence."[22] We do not know what precisely Gandhi saw in the story of Jesus that prompted this statement, but one strong candidate for such a claim is the similarity between his nonviolent campaigns and the narrative conflict resolution of the Gospel, as directed by Mark. The action dramatizes what has come to be recognized in modern analyses as the threefold structure of nonviolent resistance: nonviolent confrontation; repressive response; nonresistance. This obviously is not to say that Mark saw Jesus in modern nonviolent resistance categories, but simply that the analysis illuminates a recurrent pattern in nonviolent conflict.

The threefold pattern unfolding in the resolution of conflict in Mark's plot suggests the nonviolent action model proposed by Gene Sharp, in a study based primarily on an analysis of Gandhi's campaigns. This model identifies three primary moves: the protester's initiative of *nonviolent confrontation*, the targeted party's answer of *repressive response*, and the protester's responding initiative of *nonretaliation*. The *nonviolent confrontation* represents an initiative. Typically, nonviolent confrontation addresses a situation of injustice that has been in place for some time,

---

22. Merton, *Gandhi*, 40.

growing gradually intolerable. But it takes an act of initiative to do something about it, to move from silent resentment to overt resistance. That this confrontation is conducted in nonviolent terms requires discipline and represents a further act of discipline because the "natural" thing is a violent outburst, if anything. The *repressive response* to the confrontation by the oppressor is typically violent, if for no other reason than that this is how dominance has been maintained until now. Although threat is preferred to actual damage, the upshot is a restatement of the violence-enforced control that has established the intolerable situation. Although it is often deferred, as the first two moments cycle around more than once, a third structural moment can be identified—*nonretaliation*. This too is an act of initiative, insofar as it interrupts and refuses an inclination to escalate violence with further violence, only ratcheted up a notch. Although nonretaliation superficially looks like surrender, it is not. The difference is that the nonretaliatory moment continues the resistance, even while refusing to adopt the violent methods it suffers. An example is the practice of protesters going limp during an arrest after an act of civil disobedience. Although resistance is not given, assistance is not offered either. Because Sharp's model is based on the history of nonviolent action, it offers an image of the tendencies taken by such actions. *Mutatis mutandis*, it allows us to see how Mark's plot has the characteristics of what we today would call nonviolent confrontation. It should be pointed out that nonviolent action is to be distinguished from nonresistance, in that it willingly initiates a confrontation. Nor is it to be confused with violent altercations, insofar as the nonviolent confrontation is engaged with a deliberate refusal of violent means. Again, Gandhi's campaigns are a historical example.

The convergence between Mark's gospel and nonviolent resistance can be seen by aligning the two patterns—the *lestes* pattern of Mark and Sharp's threefold model of nonviolent action.

Sharp	Mark
1. nonviolent confrontation	1. "raid" on the temple, Mark 11
2. repressive response	2. "raid" on the garden, Mark 14
3. nonretaliation	3. refusal of a third "raid," Mark 15

The nonviolent confrontation in the temple, although confrontational and disruptive of good order, is a deliberate prophetic action that is nondestructive and nonviolent, insofar as it directs its vehemence away from the killing and maiming of human beings. The repressive response begins immediately (Mark 11:18), but is finally accomplished in the second incursion, in the garden arrest of Jesus. The third moment begins here, as Jesus refuses retaliation, despite the possibility of sword-play, a ready option indicated in the narrative by the ally who severed the ear of the high priest's servant (Mark 14:47). In effect, the resolution of the conflict between Jesus and the religious authorities follows the pattern that Sharp has elicited from similar actions, which we know as nonviolent resistance.

What interests us in this study is the degree to which Matthew either retains or alters the narrative formula of Mark. We've seen so far that Matthew incorporates the basic pattern of Mark's gospel, even as he enlarges it with his narrative framing device of the homecoming. In Matthew's account, Jesus begins life and takes flight as a future king. In this Gospel, Jesus' sojourn as a Galilean peasant is only provisional. Although Matthew retains Mark's nonviolent confrontation pattern, it is now put in service of a new dynamic—that of a return. No longer initiating, Jesus is responding. We can expect changes when Mark's presentation of a nonviolent confrontation in the Jerusalem temple, orchestrated by a Galilean insurgency figure, is made a part of Matthew's homecoming pattern.

MARK-IN-MATTHEW: THE MARKAN INTERTEXT

Mark assembled from his sources a paratactic narrative in which each episode stands alone in its box, typically brought into play with a simple connective—"and." One can appreciate that the adverb "immediately" that peppers the text—especially in the opening chapters—provides a sense of urgency that helps to propel a narrative that might otherwise stall.[23] It reminds us that this evangelist's responsibility was to shape a story with dramatic movement and a mounting tension. Matthew has eliminated most instances of the word, having borrowed his primary narrative from Mark, not sharing the original author's concern to make it work, and consequently allowing the narrative momentum to relax. Symptomatic of this shift in intention is his repeated invocation of the particle, "behold," many instances of which are introduced as modifications of episodes

---

23. In Greek, *euthus.* See Mark 1:10, 12, 18, 20, 21, 22, 23, etc.—forty-two instances in Mark, as compared to seven in Matthew. The repetition of this word impresses itself on any reader who attempts to read the Gospel straight through. On narrative intensity see Drury, "Mark," 409.

found in Mark, in some cases deliberately replacing Mark's "immediately." Compare, for instance, the two accounts of the Baptism:

Mark 1:10–11:	Matthew 3:16–17:
And when he came up out of the water *immediately* he saw the heavens opened and the Spirit descending, upon him like a dove;	And Jesus was baptized, he went up *immediately* from the water, and *behold*, the heavens were opened and he saw the Spirit of God descending like a dove, and alighting on him.
and a voice came from heaven, "You are my beloved Son, with you am well pleased."	And *behold*, a voice from heaven, saying, "This is my beloved Son, with whom I am well pleased."[24]

The purpose may be similar, to punch up the narrative. But the method reveals a different sensibility at work. These are merely signals; it seems they are symptomatic of two different attitudes toward the gospel narrative. The slower pace of Matthew's account almost comes to a stop at various points and seems to say, "Here is something worth pausing to ponder." Rather than Mark's dramatic tension, Matthew has produced something paced more closely to a Gospel pageant, or even a diorama, in which Mark's narrative is only one, albeit a central, exhibit.

The Galilee Discourse

This difference in interests can be seen in the way Matthew uses Mark's clash of discourses. Compare, for instance, the opening moves in Jesus' public ministry, as handled by the two evangelists. After the call of the four disciples, Peter and Andrew, James and John (Mark 1:16–20), Mark opens the lines of conflict in the story of the demoniac in the synagogue of Capernaum. Here the characteristic statement, typical praxis, and social location converge to set up the Galilee discourse in opposition to what will emerge on the scene as the Jerusalem discourse.

---

24. Here the language is clear in the RSV translation. For another example for comparison, see Mark 7:25 and Matt 15:22 in the story of the Gentile woman with the possessed child. While in Mark she "immediately" heard of Jesus, Matthew reports, "Behold," a Canaanite woman came and cried out to him. Of 58 instances of *idou* meaning "behold" or "lo" introduced into the text by Matthew, over half (28) modify episodes found in Mark.

Jesus is said to "teach with authority, unlike the scribes"—a statement that introduces a conflict with the religious authorities. But what is praised as teaching is described as an exorcism, merging statement, and praxis. And in the description of the exorcism, Mark uses the peculiar phrase "unclean spirit" three times (Mark 1: 23, 26, 27) so as to establish it in the narrative vocabulary, in contrast to the "Holy Spirit" invested in Jesus (Mark 1:8, 1, 12), and initiating another dimension in the conflict to come. In addition, the social location of the Galilee discourse in underscored by the meticulous reports of entering and leaving the synagogue and then the house. As the Gospel unfolds, Jesus' people will meet in the "house" (and sometimes, the boat), instead of the synagogue. Tensed, condensed, and germinal, the simple yet astonishingly complex pericope of the Capernaum demoniac launches Mark's plot.

When we turn to Matthew, we find that the only part of this story that he selects for use is the refrain by the onlookers, "He teaches with authority, unlike the scribes" (Matt 7:29). And with this we see what he is doing. He dismantles the Markan Galilee discourse, which has just been described as fusing the aspects of statement, praxis, and social location, to display each part in turn through chapters 5–10 in an expansive gesture of exposition.

The three chapters of the Sermon on the Mount (Matt 5–7), as just seen, introduce us to this discourse's family of statement, presented as a manifesto. It is immediately followed by two chapters of *healing praxis*, assembled from various sections of Mark's account and supplemented with additional stories from his own sources (Matt 8–9). This in turn introduces an exposition that concludes with the call and mission of the Twelve (Matt 10), providing the *social and institutional location* for the new movement. Having set this much out, displaying the incipient movement, we come to Matthew 11 and a sense of building conflict and tension.[25]

The Jerusalem Discourse

In the adoption of the Jerusalem discourse in Mark, Matthew's changes are less visible, but just as significant. Whereas in Mark the opposition builds in a gradual manner as the story develops, in Matthew it is already in place at the beginning. Mark's first hint of opposition, in terms of human groups and institution, is at the Capernaum Demoniac, where the

---

25. Kingsbury, *Structure, Christology, Kingdom*, xiv: "In the second phase (11:1–16:20), Israel responds to Jesus' ministry by repudiating him."

scribes' teaching is compared unfavorably to that of Jesus. By the second chapter, in the story of the Paralytic, the scribes are on the scene, providing active opposition to Jesus' works and claims (Mark 2:6). In short order the Pharisees arrive as well (2:16), and by chapter 3 the Herodians have joined the Pharisees (3:6), and scribes have come north from Jerusalem (3:22). At this point the opposition is fully formed and has identified its ideological center.

In Matthew, The Baptist identifies an opposition already in place. Sadducees and Pharisees combine the early and late opposition Jesus will experience in the coming story. Through chapters 9, 12, and 14–16, in which the conflicts are depicted in the Galilee part of the story, before Jesus begins his move to Jerusalem (Matt 16:21), the opposition is labeled as the "scribes and Pharisees," either in separate groups or as joined in common purpose. With few exceptions these also appear in Mark. However, Matthew has made the theme his own, framing this strand of opposition between two texts. The first is the programmatic statement in the Sermon on the Mount: "I tell you, unless your righteousness surpasses that of the scribes and Pharisees, you will not enter into the kingdom of heaven" (Matt 5:20). The other is the much elaborated set of seven woes in chapter 23, perhaps intended to provide a parallel with the beatitudes in Matthew 5, when this conflict is brought to a climax.

But the language of *holy* and *unclean*, which Mark's text employs to characterize the Judean authorities and which he borrows to express the conflictual forces behind the plot, is mostly abandoned in Matthew, seen in his diffident use of the phrase "unclean spirit," a Markan staple.[26] Perhaps the place this comes through most prominently is in Mark's reluctance to name the Temple as a Holy Place, something that Matthew, as we have seen, has no trouble doing (Mark 13:14; Matt 23:15).

Conflict Resolution

Similar shifts can be observed in the closing chapters of the narrative, in Matthew's treatment of Mark's conflict resolution. Although Matthew retains the *lestes* pattern seen in Mark, he neglects the pattern of reciprocity that is so prominent in Mark. In Mark the moves are clearly articulated, showing deliberate, planned action. Jesus enters the city and

---

26. It is peculiar that the purity theme identified with Pharisaic Judaism, as noted by Marcus Borg (*Conflict*, 73–77), should be more pronounced in Mark than in Matthew, in which the Pharisaic opposition receives greater emphasis.

temple on the first day, then returns on the second day for the temple action. In Matthew's account the move into Jerusalem becomes one grand sweep, with the entry and the temple action in one gesture on the same day. Matthew also omits the notice in Mark 11:18, informing us that the chief priests and scribes sought to destroy him as a consequence of the action. Because in Mark this begins the period of repressive response by the opposition, the pattern is somewhat blurred in Matthew's handling.

Meanwhile, Matthew brings other elements to the story. The blind and lame are healed in the Temple. The children cry out Hosanna, as in the triumphal entry (Matt 21:13–16). The chief priests and scribes criticize this outburst, but nothing as decisive as in Mark. Matthew has edited the episode to respond to what has gone before, rather than anticipate what is to come. Matthew's emphasis is on the entry, the return of the king. The sense of arrival overwhelms the alternating pattern of "raids" so prominent in Mark. As a consequence, it is not so easy to discern what I have called a dynamic of nonviolent action in this text.

Whereas the Temple action in Mark corresponds to the moment of nonviolent confrontation, following the schema of Gene Sharp, Jesus' arrest in Gethsemane corresponds to the third move, that of nonretaliation. In Matthew, this account is expanded considerably. Elaborations would include the nonviolent sword saying (Matt 26:52), the expression of deliberate refusal of self-defense, citing the example of angels ready to come to his defense (26:53), and the scripture fulfillment formulae, redoubled in Matthew (26:54, 56) despite the lack of a specific scriptural text. As the moment of nonretaliation in the pattern of nonviolent action, its emphasis here converges with the recurring theme of response to harm done, so prominent in this Gospel, as shown in this chart, a revision of that describing Mark, earlier in this chapter.

Sharp	Matthew
1. *nonviolent confrontation*	1. Entry and temple "cleansing" as one action. *Moment emphasized as return, response to earlier harm.*
2. *repressive response*	2. Omits Mark's notice of official retaliation (Mark 11:18). *Repressive reaction de-emphasized in Matthew.*
3. *nonretaliation*	3. Garden arrest considerably elaborated. *Moment on nonviolent response emphasized.*

What we see is that Mark's back-and-forth pattern of movement is muted. The moves made by Jesus undergo considerable development. In each case the emphasis is placed on the quality of response to threat. The entry, combined with the temple action, is now construed as a return, a response to earlier threat and banishment. The nonviolent response to Jesus' arrest in Gethsemane is enhanced by other indicators that underscore its nonretaliatory meaning. Meanwhile, the move of his opponents in response to his confrontation in the temple is de-emphasized. The result of these editorial adjustments is a text that dwells more on the response to evil than the need to confront it. Even the moment of confrontation in the temple action is construed as a response to previous violence. Still, it does retain its standing as confrontation.

Displacement Scenarios

Although the pattern of the Markan conflict resolution pattern seems disrupted in Matthew's Gospel, it finds echoes in small scenarios in the teachings of Jesus in Matthew's text, as if displaced. In the Sermon on the Mount, we find a passage that recommends reconciling with your enemy before going before the magistrate (Matt 5:58–59). The series of "handings-over" evoke the similar series in Mark's Passion (Mark 14:10, 45; 15:1, 15), as if displaced from there. And later in the same chapter, the well-known text on nonresistance (5:38–43) outlines a process of conflict reconciliation that proposes a nonviolent response to harmful assault: When someone strikes you on the right cheek, turn the other. The nonretaliatory response, along with its previous attack, correspond to the second and third moments in nonviolent action pattern of Gene Sharp, which we saw in the reciprocal raid pattern in Mark's conflict resolution. That is, the initial provocation that prompted the attack is not considered—only the final response. Here we see again an emphasis on response, on the second moment in an altercation. This can also be seen in a third scenario, namely, the teaching of forgiveness in Matt 18. After Peter asks how often one must forgive, Jesus expands Peter's seven times to seventy-seven. The saying echoes Lamech's boast in Gen 4:24, in which his capacity for revenge is inflated from Cain's sevenfold to his own seventyfold. Revenge, the opposite of nonviolence, is replaced by forgiveness, as an equivalent of nonviolent response.

This attention to the second moment, the moment of response, is a feature of Matthew's text and plot, and it is consistent with his modification of the synoptic narrative by adding the homecoming story. The temple action, a deliberate initiative in Mark, has now become a second moment, a moment of return. This makes a decided difference in the meaning of violence and nonviolence in the Gospel.

An "Inclusive Story"

There is another aspect of Matthew that deserves remarking on here. It has been called Matthew's "inclusive story,"[27] referring to the way in which the evangelist has overlaid Jesus' story with certain issues of his own community, to include the worlds of both Messiah and Evangelist. This is apparent in Matthew 10:16–23. In the discussion on Matthew's treatment of the Mark's discourses, we identified the missionary sermon of Jesus as representing the institutional setting of the Galilee discourse. Jesus names twelve apostles and sends them out two by two on mission, to prepare the way for his own ministry. But in vv.16–23, Jesus speaks to the time beyond this narrative, borrowing elements from the farewell speech of Jesus in Mark 13, concerning persecutions that the disciples will experience in the period of the early church. After all, it is not likely that the disciples will be experiencing persecution in Jesus' name during his early ministry, before he himself will have experienced his passion and death. That will only come later.

If Matthew is reading his own times and circumstances into the story, it has become apparent with the rise of New Testament Empire studies in recent years that these times and circumstances involved tensions with the Roman Empire. Although it has long been axiomatic that the occasion for Matthew's writing included a reassessment of the meaning of Jesus' story after the temple was lost, and that this meant a redirection in both Judaism and the nascent Christian movement, the discussion was carried on in an irenic manner that pondered the theological crisis of a delayed Parousia, with its disappointment that the end of Jerusalem was not the close of the age, but left unnoticed the theological crisis of a destroyed Temple, with its implications of the divine dominance of violence. However, the destruction of Jerusalem and the temple, along with that of Qumran and Masada, needs to be seen as that

27. See Howell, *Inclusive Story*, 14.

massive object lesson in which Rome demonstrated that it was in charge of events. It represented a largely successful move to change the course and tone of history. Succinctly put, it deployed massive violence to make a point. It insisted that violence be recognized as the foundational reality. Under these circumstances, Matthew's adoption of Mark's drama of nonviolence required adjustments. In the aftermath of this major display of violence all the more will he need to reaffirm the ethic of Jesus. It is not fertile ground for this. We can suspect that Matthew's more violent passages are not proposals, but rather they are reflections of the world in which he found himself, and in which he needed to state the claims of the Jesus movement. We might expect that his writing does not sort things out as cleanly as we might like. But we might read his gospel in terms of a pushback against the prevailing spirit of the time. It is in this framework that we can set his story, with its attention to the second moment, the moment of response to evil and harm done.

At this juncture we have seen merely a sketch of Matthew's changes and the resulting narrative. The rest of this book will probe the implications. In the following chapter the narrative that emerges from marrying the homecoming story to the common synoptic narrative as given in Mark will be shown to fit a recurring popular story formula, available to Matthew and in some form recognizable to his readers. By way of partially accounting for the revisions, chapter 4 will consider the text in terms of the new imperial conditions under which the text was produced. What has been made of the Jerusalem discourse in Matthew will be the theme of chapter 5, whereas chapter 6 looks at the transformation of the Galilee Discourse, in some measure. The conflict development as it evolves in Matthew, with its disclosures of Matthew's dramatic use of violence and nonviolence, will be the concern of the seventh and final chapter.

3

The Return of the King

Sing and be glad, all ye children of the West,
for your King shall come again,
and he shall dwell among you
all the days of your life.

—J. R. R. Tolkien, *The Return of the King*

A RECURRING STORY, ANCIENT and yet fully contemporary for us today, tells of a privileged infant rudely sent away, only later to be welcomed back with a grand homecoming on reaching adulthood. The story can be recognized as a particular version of the homecoming story of the previous chapters. The usurpation of the kingdom and the threatened life and escape of the young hero are consistent features. A typical scenario might read like this:

The wicked brother of the king gains control of the kingdom. The royal family is executed, except for the infant prince, who escapes the massacre with the aid of faithful retainers such as an ancient nurse and a simple gardener. The child is spirited away to a distant land to be raised to adulthood by a childless peasant couple, perhaps a woodcutter and his wife. Upon reaching maturity, the prince is discovered to be the true king by means of signs and/or trials, such as pulling a sword from a stone. Prepared for his new role by a mentor, such as Merlin, he mounts a victorious campaign in which he returns to the kingdom, expels the usurper and restores the kingdom to its rightful rule and former prosperity. Marrying a princess he reestablishes the lost dynasty, and order is ensured for the foreseeable time to come, if not forever.

Of course, the story of the hero's departure and return is an old story as well as a popular one. It is not the adventure story of the hero cycle because in this story the hero fails to volunteer for the journey. Joseph Campbell popularized a species of it in his account of the hero journey.[1] Campbell's hero is an adventurer who leaves home in search of glory or the lost boon that would revive his troubled society. From Gilgamesh to Jack in the Beanstalk, this version of the hero populates both myth and popular tale. But Campbell's hero journey is not to be confused with the story of banished prince because Campbell's hero volunteers for the journey. More simply put, the action in the traditional hero story takes place between the departure and the return, and this is the part that is missing in the story of the banished and returning prince. For here the action is in the departure and return themselves.

Freud highlighted an aspect of the story that he called the Family Romance and located it in the changeling fantasy of adoption that so often accompanies the adolescent trauma of preparing to leave the parental nest.[2] Wendy Doniger is thinking of Freud when she describes a "corpus of myths" in which "a child is taken from his real, high-born parents and raised by low-born people or animals (often in the forest) until, years later, he finds his parents, establishes his noble birth and comes into his inheritance."[3] Among examples she includes are the stories of Oedipus, Krishna, Tarzan, and Mowgli. Enticing for our sake here, she also includes Jesus in her roster. But his story is told in so many ways, in creeds as well as gospels, that we need to look much more closely than this if we want to learn something about Matthew's Gospel.

The literary critic Hugh Kenner placed James Joyce's *Ulysses* in the same group of stories. Kenner's sense of the story sees it reflecting political experience more than psychological, public life more than private. Kenner enlarges the roster to include *The Odyssey*, Don Giovanni, Hamlet, and the Count of Monte Cristo. But perhaps more promising for our study, he indicates that, in addition to the plot lines, the fixed set of character roles in the story formula can offer keys to its various permutations.[4] In addition to the usurper and the avenger, other character roles remain remarkable stable through the various changes the formula allows and will further claim our attention in this study. Of surprising interest among these is the mentor figure that guides and prepares the young hero for his return.

1. E.g., Campbell, *Hero with a Thousand Faces*.
2. Freud, "Family Romances," *Papers*, V, 74–78.
3. Doniger, "Female Bandits?" p. 21.
4. Kenner, *Joyce's Ulysses*, 343.

Before we explore the meaning of the story formula for Matthew's Gospel, as we will do especially in the second part of the book, we will need to demonstrate its appropriateness in relation to the Gospel. And to do that, we will need to examine the story itself as it takes shape in its various expressions. Storytelling manifests itself in many incarnations. Animated films, less bound to the demands of realistic narrative, have fantastic features in common with folktales and myths, but with greater immediacy and intuitive apprehension for us than the ancient stories. They provide handy illustrations of some of the features of the formula story. Particular aspects that show up in these examples would include the popularity of the formula, its power to generate, shape, and even deform narratives, and its political possibilities.

One characteristic aspect of the formula, seen in the films, but worth isolating as a prominent feature of story formulae, is the ability to undergo various permutations without losing their identity. A fruitful comparison might be made with musical form. A fugue by Bach might take a melodic line, slow it, speed it up, invert it, or reverse it, and yet it is still recognizable as a variation on the theme. So it is with story formulae, and specifically with the story of the banished and returning prince. And as we will see, related to this variability, ambiguity shadows the roles of the usurper and the hero, who threatens to be an impostor.

A second group of stories that will prove useful for defining the formula and its narrative possibilities comes from the classics of Western literature. Many of these have already been mentioned. Among these, Homer's *Odyssey* and Shakespeare's *Hamlet* will prove especially useful. Aspects that these stories illustrate include, again, variation of form and the ambiguity of usurper and impostor. Primarily, these classics of literature show more clearly than elsewhere an important dimension of the formula, and that is the impulse toward revenge that feeds it. This has certain dangers for any who would make use of the formula, and that would certainly apply to the evangelist. *matthew influenced by ?*

The third group of stories that interests us is that of the ancient classic tales, older than the Gospel, and providing some warrant for the claim that Matthew would be influenced by them—or would willingly make use of the possibilities they offered him. Using these stories, we will determine how they relate to the Gospel, and what conclusions we might draw, especially in terms of the use of violence in Matthew's narrative plot. With those results in hand, we can turn to the role studies in the second part of the book. *banished/returning prince*

Lion King   THE FILMS

In our time we have added to the instances of the story's telling, in film
as well as print, demonstrating clearly the popular appeal of the formula.
Tolkien's massive novel, *The Lord of the Rings*, uses the formula to frame
its tale. Much less complex, and therefore better able to illustrate the
workings of the story formula, are the many versions it has assumed in
film, especially in the feature-length animations that come out of the
Disney studios and others, such as DreamWorks and 20th Century Fox.
Film animation shares some of the virtues of popular folk art, despite
(or perhaps because of) the dominating role that marketing plays in its
production. As Propp and others discovered in folktales, animated films
are good for discerning the ways of story. The simplified plots, which
favor traditional tales, place things clearly in mind. A small vivid cast
of characters keeps the story manageable, and the reduced expectation
of realism allows for greater narrative freedom, akin to the vagaries of
myths and dreams. Not the least among these virtues is that they allow
us to experience the impact of the story as it does its work in a living cultural situation. Hugh Kenner's term "homomorphism" may be unwieldy,
but it speaks to the way the formula is consistently changing as we move
from example to example.

My examples are drawn from four feature-length animated films.
The four films sample the field widely enough to give a sense of the
variable possibilities of the formula, while including among themselves most of the features of the formula that need to be illustrated.
The films include an original fable, a Greek myth, a historical legend,
and a religious narrative. These in turn are *The Lion King* (Disney),
Hercules (Disney), *Anastasia* (20th Century Fox), and *The Prince of
Egypt* (DreamWorks). Among them they illustrate the aspects of the
formula and also give hints of the political uses.

The Lion King

Fables are stories that feature animals. *The Lion King*, a Disney film, is a
fable that embodies the formula story of the banished prince in its nearly
full form, with the obvious alterations that are dictated by the fact that we
are dealing with animals here. It is no surprise that *The Lion King* leaves a
strong impression of déjà vu on its initial viewers. In the supplementary
material on the DVD, the producers and directors describe how they

researched traditional stories in preparing the film. They mentioned in particular the stories of Moses and *Hamlet*. They intended to mine the tradition for familiar themes and motifs. So the impression we receive of viewing a familiar story, despite having never seen it before, is fully justified.

The familiarity of the formula relates to both plot and characterization. These are intimately related of course, because the plot dictates a certain set of typical character positions: The royal family, in addition to the young prince, Simba, includes his father, the king Mufasa, his mother, queen Sarabi, along with a more distant relative, his future bride, princess Nala. Then there is his wicked uncle, Scar, usurper of the kingdom and villain of the piece. The two parties to the conflict are expanded by the addition of the king's chancellor, a hornbill named Zazu, representing the faithful retainers in the palace, and the nefarious hyenas that support Scar in his effort to overthrow the kingdom.

Filling out the needs of the story are Simba's youthful buddies, Timon, a meerkat, and Pumbaa, a warthog—scarcely suitable companions to a young lion and future monarch, not unlike Falstaff's association with Prince Hal. In addition to the traditional role of the peasant couple that adopt the young prince and raise him in obscurity, these two characters fulfill a need of the genre of popular animated films. There has to be a couple of comic characters that contrast sharply with the main story line, exploit the possibilities of animation, and offer comic relief. The last character that needs to be mentioned is the mentor figure of the witch doctor, the wise old baboon, Rafiki. It is this character that manages to get Simba's story turned around, and he sets the young prince back on the road to his royal future.

The story itself is a rather straightforward example of the formula. Mufasa is treacherously murdered by Scar, the royal cub Simba is banished, and the kingdom falls into disrepair. Simba grows up far from the kingdom in the company of a lowly meerkat and warthog. But as a young adult, Simba discovers his destiny literally in the stars, as he sees an astral vision of his slain father. The witch doctor Rafiki, a mentor figure, helps him to find his way back home, where he organizes the remainder of his father's followers and dislodges the hyenas and his wicked uncle Scar. Simba starts a family with the princess Nala, sires an heir, and the kingdom returns to its former prosperity.

The film is a clear appeal to African pride, seen in its visual styling and songs. But it derives its power primarily from the force of its story line. The satisfactions we feel with Simba's return to the kingdom and reprisals he exacts on his enemies derive from the resentment built up by our witnessing his rough treatment and banishment—that, and the subversion of the kingdom and its widespread barrenness. Light-hearted as it may be, this is essentially a revenge story, enlarged by a mythic expansion in a lost and restored society.

In sum: *The Lion King* is a fairly full expression of the formula story of the banished prince. It not only offers a model of the formula plot, but also an example of the satisfactions the formula generates in audiences. It has been adapted as a very successful Broadway musical, with numerous traveling road show versions.

Hercules

The Disney Studio's affection for this formula is particularly demonstrated in its treatment of the Hercules myth. Critics decry its many departures from the traditional story.[5]

The traditional myth is fairly well known: Hercules was a child of Zeus and the mortal Alcmene. Hera was jealous and sent snakes to kill both Hercules and his twin brother. Hercules strangled them. Later he married Megara, who bore three children. Hera afflicted Hercules with madness, which caused him to murder his family. The labors of Hercules were meant to atone for that action. In fact, atonement for rash actions is the common thread of the stories. Hercules is strong but dense. An emotional mesomorph, he is given to rash acts, which do great damage and require reparation.

This image of Hercules is entirely lost in the Disney treatment. He is converted into a typical hero of the story formula. Changes introduced to bring it into line include the following. Hera is no longer the enemy of Hercules. Rather, Dis, lord of the underworld and, in the Olympian scheme of things, younger brother to Zeus, plots to displace Zeus as

---

5. For instance Christine House, in "Hercules the hero: understanding the myth," an article published online (http://www.yale.edu/ynhti/curriculum /units/1998/2/98.02.06.x.html#n) in the Yale-New Haven Teachers Institute series, produces a long list of Disney's departures from the traditional tale, so as to be "barely recognizable as the same story." As a matter of fact, it isn't. It is another story: the formula story of the banished prince.

primary god in a "hostile takeover bid." Hercules is born to Zeus and Hera, but is targeted by Dis due to an oracle that foretells the child will be a problem for him. The comic pair, Dis' hapless helper imps, Pain and Panic (comic relief), mishandle the infant's abduction, stolen while his parents sleep, and as a result the baby is adopted by a childless couple, Amphitryon and Alcmene. In the classic myth, of course, the latter is his true mother, after a dalliance with Zeus. The mortality of the hero is here a consequence of this duplicity, not his birth.

The boy, growing up in ignorance of his origins, is troubled by his enormous strength and the difficulty he has in controlling it. The film makes much of adolescent awkwardness and insecurities. After a heart-to-heart talk with his foster father, an encounter with Philoctetes ("Call me Phil"), the trainer, allows him to channel his strength, which is strength, and prepare for the return and heroic exploits for which he was destined.

On his return to Thebes he encounters Megira ("Meg"), a damsel in distress, speaking with the same urban toughness as Phil, who is first employed to subvert him, like Delilah, but eventually is won over. Here too Megira takes a position in the story different from the classic myth. Hercules succeeds in his labors and repelling of Dis and wins the universe back for Zeus. Hercules himself chooses to reject his immortal heritage and take up mortal life with Megira. All in all, the film rearranged the story entirely, fitting it to the formula.

Two roles are emphasized in this version—those of the usurper and the mentor. The usurper is an addition to the Hercules cycle. The filmmakers devised a usurpation plot out of whole cloth, recasting Dis as the wicked uncle. The usurpation sets up the final action of the film, demoting the labors of Hercules as rehearsals for the climactic action. The usurpation is the central imbalance that is introduced into the world of the story, the imbalance that the hero is born to redress, correct, or undo.

Similarly, the virtually invented character, Phil, the prizefighter's trainer, brings out the importance of that role in the formula. The counteraction to the usurpation requires as serious a preparation as that developed by the villain in the first place. The Usurper and the Mentor represent the conspiracies of the two sides, each planning to overthrow the other. The political dimension behind this story formula, a narrative about political intrigue, is charted in these two positions.

In sum: Disney's *Hercules* is an appealing, stylized (per)version of the classic myth of Hercules, largely replacing the traditional myth with the formula story of the banished prince. This is surely strong testimony to the popular affection felt for this formula. The film highlights certain roles: the Mentor, with an elaborate character study, and the Usurper, surprisingly added to the cast of characters.

Anastasia

The legends of the lost Grand Duchess Anastasia Nikolaevna Romanova are fairly well known. The youngest daughter of Tsar Nicholas II, the last ruler of imperial Russia, she was rumored to have escaped the slaughter of the royal family during the Bolshevik revolution. In a case of life hoping to imitate art, numerous impostors appeared on the scene claiming to be the lost Duchess. The most famous of these was Anna Anderson, whose story was fictionalized in animated film.

The 20th Century Fox adaptation of the historical legend of the lost daughter of the Tsar follows the precedent of the Disney films fairly closely. We have the familiar ambience. We have the cute creature for dramatic relief, Bartok, a talking bat. In addition, we have the story form of the banished prince. There are a number of interesting transpositions. For one, this includes a female protagonist, with Anya, a young woman, in the place of the traditional hero. To fit the film to the formula, the tsar's daughter is reduced in age, closer to the infant helplessness that the form requires.

Even more interesting, the revolution of 1917 is passed over cursorily. In its place we have inserted a villain–usurper in the person of the monk Rasputin, pictured insinuating himself into the royal family, only to overturn it. In effect, the story is given a more domestic shape, disregarding the larger implications and focusing on the family crisis. In this context, homecoming takes on a very intimate shape:

> Home, love, family,
> there was once a time I must have had them too.
> Home, love, family
> I will never be complete until I find you
> . . . and bring me home at last.

The formula is fully present in the story. In addition to assigning Rasputin to the role of usurper, it walks through the stages of the formula:

childhood in the palace, the rough expulsion, assassination of the family, and escape of the royal child. The coming of age in obscurity happens in an orphanage in this case. Two journalists, the commoner Dmitri, the future love interest, and Vladimir, a person with prior experience among royals, prepare her for her return to royal life. This takes the form of surviving an interview with Sophie and the Dowager Empress, who is looking for her lost granddaughter, but has to endure the claims of countless impostors. Anastasia succeeds in convincing them that she is the authentic princess. After a surrealistic battle with Rasputin, Dmitri saves Anya, who chooses life with him as the true homecoming, instead of adopting the royal manner in a Paris apartment.

The decision to inform the historical story with the narrative formula of the banished prince(ss) is almost inevitable in this case. The stories of the Russian empire have numerous examples of impostors emerging into the light with royal claims. The most famous of these is Boris Gudonov, another instance of the story formula interpreting historical events. One wonders if the formula hasn't invested the actual legend itself, and the film simply takes it from there.

The story as it plays itself out in Russian history is a conservative one. The impostors represent a threat to the empire and the emperor, divinely ordained, in this view, to rule Russia. Any threat to this rule is a thrust at the established order and the order of creation itself. The Romanovs ruled over 300 years in Russia. It would have seemed almost an eternity to those who lived during the latter parts of that reign. Lenin objected to the "naïve monarchism" that denied the peasants the ability to imagine life without the tsar.

The historical story behind the film, the story of Anna Anderson, is also an account of disputed imposture. Though she was recognized as the authentic Anastasia at the time, subsequent investigation has shown her to be an impostor. This pattern is to be expected in a society in which a royal title, or alliance with such, was the sole ticket to power, wealth, and social standing. It spawned hanger-on figures like Rasputin and numerous impostors.

James Scott has pointed to the "naïve monarchism" that expressed itself among the peasantry of Russia in the form of a legend that the tsar occasionally traveled about the country incognito, learning about his people. The affection for the tsar took the form of attributing deleterious government actions to the officials, against the tsar's knowledge. The tsar was seen as a friend.[6]

In sum: The animated film *Anastasia* develops a persistent legend about the lost daughter of the tsar by way of a domesticated version of the formula story. Notable features include the switch from prince to princess in the leading role, along with the depoliticizing of the tsar's overthrow. This version can be enlisted to represent a staunchly conservative account of the formula story of the banished prince.

The Prince of Egypt

The first attempt at a feature-length animated film from DreamWorks was *The Prince of Egypt*, a reworking of the Moses story from Exodus, chapters 1–14. As with the Anastasia story, this film depicts a narrative that is already in the shape of the banished prince formula. However, the film does take a few liberties with the story, the boldest being the decision to make Moses and the Pharaoh Ramses virtual brothers. Although this move shifts the adoptive parent of Moses from the daughter of the reigning Pharaoh to the wife, and mother of the future Pharaoh, it also has the virtue of personalizing the dramatic quality of the original story. The dispute between Egypt and Israel evolves as a struggle between brothers. In addition, Moses is raised in the palace, with Ramses, instead of having his upbringing hired out to the natural mother of Moses. In effect, this adheres to one feature of the formula even as it eliminates another.

The most dramatic variation on the formula, one shared with the original account, is the role reversal in which the usurper is cast as the hero. We are given to see the struggle from the other side. Insofar as the usurpation is seemingly justified, we view the story as the revolutionary ousting of an unjust regime. The revolutionary story contrasts sharply with the conservative version presented by the Anastasia story, even as it is built on the same formula. The political variability of the formula story is one of its innate features. What seems at first like a naturally conservative piece of propaganda (more "naïve monarchism") emerges as a double-edged sword.

Closer to home, we need to remember that the Moses story is a prominent influence in Matthew's Gospel, not only in the story implied in the infancy narrative, with its descent and return from Egypt, with its

---

6. Scott, *Domination and the Art of Resistance*, 96–103.

slaughter of the Israelite children, but also elsewhere in Matthew, in the five discourses and the rereading of the Law in chapter 5.

In sum: 20th Century Fox's animated feature length film, *The Prince of Egypt*, is a surprisingly faithful adaptation of Ex 1–14, given certain ingenious adaptations required to honor the medium. Most notably, the decision to have Moses raised in the palace with the future Pharaoh, rather than by his real mother, allowed the producers to personalize the conflict between Moses and Egypt as a struggle between brothers. Given the fact that in this account Moses is the usurper rather than the usurped, it allows a view of the story from the perspective of the other side and offers a revolutionary model of the formula story of the banished prince.

In addition to the narrative patterns described in the story formula, certain typical roles make a constant appearance. Those that emerged in this survey of four films include, in addition to the cinematic comic characters and cute beasties, the king and the usurper, often his brother, the young prince who escapes the palace coup and is destined to return, the foster parents who raise him, and the mentor figure who prepares him for the return. The princess he marries is needed to complete the restoration of the dynasty, as well as other small parts, such as the faithful retainers who spirit the infant prince off to safety in the midst of the coup. Some of these will prove helpful as we analyze the aspects of the Gospel in the second part of this book.

THE FORMULA IN LITERATURE:
THE ODYSSEY AND HAMLET

The animated films are good for demonstrating the mechanics of the formula story through its different versions. More substantial literary examples, from the *Odyssey* to Joyce's *Ulysses*, from Sinbad the Sailor to *The Count of Monte Cristo*, demonstrate some of its implications and consequences. The roles are identifiable, and the patterns remain in view, including aspects such as the permutations. For instance the *Odyssey* exhibits the pattern in which no one recognizes the returning hero, but instead he is identified by signs; upon his return he routs the usurpers. But one significant variation alters things—it is the father who leaves home rather than the son. The story follows out the pattern adjusted to the new set of variables. Odysseus' son, Telemachus, seeking those who might know where his father might have gone, initiates the return movement under the impetus of promptings from Athena, appearing as Mentor, a friend of Ulysses. Mentor, in fact, gives his name to this role in society and in the formula pattern of the banished and returning prince.

Furthermore, here, as in the case of *Hamlet*, the role of revenge in the story demands our attention, for vengeance is comprehensive, with the goddess Athena urging the hero on. In Robert Fagles's translation:

> "Royal son of Laertes, Odysseus, old campaigner,
> now is the time, now tell your son the truth.
> Hold nothing back, so the two of you can plot
> the suitors' doom and then set out for town.
> I myself won't lag behind you long—
> I'm blazing for a battle." (16.188–93)[7]

Or, in the vivid, cinematic poetry of Christopher Logue's translation:

> Teenaged Athena jumped up and shrieked:
>   "Kill! Kill for me!
> Better to die than to live without killing!"[8]

The contrast couldn't be greater when comparing this with the divine directives of Matt 26:52–54:

> Then Jesus said to him, "Put your sword back into its sheath, for all who take the sword will perish by the sword. Do you think that I cannot call upon my Father and he will not provide me at this moment with more than twelve legions of angels? But then how would the scriptures be fulfilled which say that it must come to pass in this way?"

A similar situation prevails with *Hamlet*. Although this classic of Western literature explodes all formulaic conventions, it has its genre precedents in the tradition of the revenge play. As a variation of the returning prince formula, it restricts its action to the time of the prince's return, the earlier departure and usurpation having already taken place before the play begins. Here, too, the slaughter is comprehensive, littered with broken bodies at the end of the play. But, of course, the satisfaction anticipated here by damaged honor through recourse to retribution is inhibited by the lack of survivors. And so Shakespeare offers us a critique of the genre and practice that he pretends to present. But the missing

---

7. Also, *Odyssey* 13.215–20, 426–36, 448–53; 20.35–58.

8. Logue, *All Day Permanent Red*, 17.

highlights the
role of the usurper

satisfaction underlines the drive toward such satisfaction that the form trades on, as shown especially in the ending of the *Odyssey*.

The bent toward revenge that is so prominent in the literary examples is reflected in the animated films as well, though it is not so belabored nor so horrifying—due no doubt to the popular idiom. Here, however, the inconspicuous role that the payback of revenge offers alerts us to how the formula story provides our satisfaction without, perhaps, our even noticing the release it provides us. We just enjoy the happy ending with the villains eliminated. The experience of satisfaction, as a reward of narrative conflict resolution, is a feature we will need to return to.

As a second trait worth noting, both of these highlight the role of the usurper. In different ways the act of usurpation is presented as a problem. In the case of the *Odyssey*, as we will see later, Odysseus' disguise at his return, his various explanations of his past, and the tenuous signs that authenticate his identity all put into question (to anyone not assured by the narrator of the tale) the legitimacy of this claimant to the throne. If it were not for the fact that Odysseus was known for his ability to deceive, one might doubt it was he.

Hamlet begins with a state of affairs that echoes the formula story of the banished prince, for it is the Wicked Uncle, the brother of the king, who assassinates the king and takes the throne, and the queen as well. Here the usurpation, like the subsequent playing out of revenge, is complete. But here, too, the meaning of usurpation is rendered problematic by the dithering of Hamlet. Instead of acting like an impostor as does Odysseus, the prince of Denmark ponders the value and of revenge, which is to ask, how does this response improve the situation?

In his history plays Shakespeare has explored the problem of usurpation to exacting extent. When the pragmatic Bolingbroke deposed the king in *Richard II* to become Henry IV, competence is seen to displace misrule. But at what price? Can incompetence excuse the deposition of the divinely appointed king? The play suppresses the question of Bolingbroke's ambition to a degree sufficient to allow the question of legitimacy to be clearly examined. If efficiency of government is the proper criterion, as the charge of misrule would suggest, then what provides the stability of office that would prevent further depositions in favor of even better management? Bolingbroke's own father, John of Gaunt, repudiates Henry's move, as does his uncle, the Duke of York, and the Bishop of

Carlisle because Richard is God's anointed king.[9] Because the deposition cannot be justified, it becomes, in their view, a usurping act.

> *Gaunt.* God's is the quarrel, for God's substitute,
> His deputy anointed in His sight,
> Hath caused his death. The which if wrongfully,
> Let Heaven revenge, for I may never lift
> An angry arm against His minister. (I.2.37–41)

The play as an individual drama dwells on the lost world, the "emerald isle" of England. But in the context of the Shakespearean history plays, it names the event that triggers the Civil War between the White Rose of York and the Red Rose of Lancaster. Once the inhibition of the Divine Right of the king is removed, what is to prevent a cycle of reversals? Shakespeare employs features of the banished prince formula to manage the outworking of the history series. In his turn, Prince Hal, protagonist of his own play and hero of his own story of departure and reemergence, guided through the time of exile by his burlesque mentor, Falstaff, prepares to take over the throne as Henry V, while his father worries that his own line will in turn be deposed. The cycle of reprisals looms on the horizon and guides the actions and reactions in the days and the plays to come.

These literary examples, which can be multiplied, direct our attention to certain features in the formula story that are present in the earlier examples as well, though not emphasized to the point of attracting our notice. The usurpation or threat of usurpation sets up a crisis that demands redress—the more outrageous the usurpation, the more comprehensive the required vengeance.

On the other hand, the situation can be imagined from the side of the usurper, as we saw in the case of the animated film about Moses, *The Prince of Egypt.* In these circumstances, issues arise as to the social causes adequate to justify the deposition of a sitting ruler and whether or not to condemn it as the crime of usurpation.

Although these reflections will certainly strike many as far removed from any consideration of Matthew's Gospel, which is supposed to be the task at hand, it would nonetheless seem that if we are to claim that Matthew made use of an available story form, it is to our advantage to explore the implications of that narrative choice.

9. See Bevington, *Richard II*, xix–xxviii. Also, Forker, *King Richard II*, 16–23.

implications of narrative choice

hero
cycles

STUDIES OF THE ANCIENT CLASSICS

As early as 1876, Johann Georg von Hahn was part of a movement to discern the formula of the hero cycles of myth. He identified a variety of forms, including one, fourth on his list, that he called the Aryan Expulsion and Return Formula (*Arische Aussetzungs– und Rückkerh-Formel*).[10] He published the narrative pattern as a list of sixteen elements organized into four basic groups. With considerable success he applied the pattern to a wide array of mythic heroes. He listed seven Greek, two Teutonic, two Hindu, and two Persian heroes. Among the roster we find Hercules, Oedipus, Theseus, Siegfried, and Cyrus.

In 1881, in an article entitled "The Aryan Expulsion-and-Return Formula in the Folk and Hero Tales of the Celts," Alfred Nutt expanded the list to include Finn, Cuchulain, and Cumhall. Nutt followed von Hahn's procedure of articulating the list in four sections:

1. The birth of the hero (1–3)

2. The hero's youth of poverty, struggle, and service (4–9)   mythic heroes

3. The hero's return to home and power (10–13)

4. Supplementary incidents (14–16)   departure/return of the hero

This articulation gives welcome shape to the lists produced by the philologists. The initial section recounting information of the status of the parents and the marvelous birth stands preliminary to the action, but it is emphasized in myths. But the main action of the plot concerns the departure and return of the hero, which corresponds to our own center of interest.[11]

10. Von Hahn, *Sagwissenschaftliche Studien* (Gena, Ger., 1876). See Alan Dundes, *The Study of Folklore* (Englewood Cliffs, NJ: Prentice-Hall, 1965), 142–44.

11. Nutt, "Aryan Expulsion-and-Return Formula," 1–44. For Lord Raglan's seminal article and taxonomy, "The Hero of Tradition," along with von Hahn's list in a helpful introduction, see Dundes, *Study of Folklore*, 142–145. Von Hahn's list, grouped into four categories, is as follows: *Birth:* 1. The hero is of illegitimate birth 2. His mother is the princess of the country. 3. His father is a god or a foreigner. Youth: 4. There are signs warning of his ascendance. 5. For this reason he is abandoned. 6. He is suckled by animals. 7. He is brought up by a childless shepherd couple. 8. He is a high-spirited youth. 9. He seeks service in a foreign country. *Return:* 10. He returns victorious and goes back to the foreign land. 11. He slays his original persecutors, accedes to rule the country, and sets his mother free. 12. He founds cities. 13. The manner of his death is extraordinary *Additional Events:* 14. He is reviled because of incest and dies young. 15. He dies by an act of revenge at the hands of an insulted servant 16. He murders his younger brother.

In 1934, Richard Somerset, Lord Raglan, published another influential list. Raglan based his pattern of twenty-two elements on the Oedipus story. His expanded roster includes a Japanese hero and two prominent Hebrews—Joseph and Moses.[12] In a subsequent study he added a Welsh hero, a Javanese, and Robin Hood. Raglan's list covers the flight and return in steps six through thirteen, as follows:

6. At birth an attempt is made, often by his father, to kill him, but

7. He is spirited away, and

8. Reared by foster parents in a far country.

9. We are told nothing of his childhood, but

10. On reaching manhood he returns or goes to his future kingdom.

11. After a victory over the king and/or a giant, dragon, or wild best,

12. He marries a princess, often the daughter of his predecessor, and

13. Becomes king.[13]

Raglan's is an independent study, not a revision of the earlier lists. Nevertheless, it is in many respects comparable to von Hahn's pattern. Here, too, it breaks down into four parts. After an introductory section dedicated to the wondrous aspects of the hero's birth (1–5), two sections follow, devoted to the flight (6–9) and return (10–15) of the hero. In the fourth part, where von Hahn names "supplementary incidents," Raglan includes a secondary narrative making an account of the end of the hero's life. The heart of the pattern remains the "Banishment and Return" formula.

Alan Dundes has pushed this project further by explicitly adding the story of Jesus to the list of hero stories explored by the earlier authors.[14] Richard Horsley, among others, mounts strong objections to this application.[15] Because Dundes arrives at his conclusions by admitting into the equation all versions of the story of Jesus, from canonical to

12. As summarized in Dundes, *Study of Folklore*, 145.

13. Adjustments include the elimination of the gap in step 9 as a separate step insofar as it does not involve an action, along with combining steps 12 and 13, as being two sides of the one act of restoring the dynasty. In addition, I have brought forward the usurpation theme, which seems to be suppressed in these "Aryan" studies.

14. Dundes, *Hero Pattern and the Life of Jesus*, 1977.

15. Horsley, *Liberation of Christmas*, 162–66.

*Matthean
social location* [handwritten annotation]

apocryphal, necessary controls seem to be missing from the study. In particular, genre prescriptions would be a welcome addition in Horsley's view. When we apply those controls and narrow our attention to the canonical gospels alone, very few of the items in the taxonomy apply, and those that do are found almost exclusively in the infancy narratives. And for Horsley's set of interests, only the birth story seems viable, and not the flight and return.

However, the persistence of the pattern across genres is a significant part of its claim on our interest. If we can derive a common structure that moves across genres, we have a tool we can use to apply in candidates for the formula story. Here the studies of Lévi-Strauss can contribute toward a determination of such a structure.[16] Furthermore, in identifying a common form among diverse examples, we can learn not only from the form, but also from the variations. Consequently, the range of diverse genres does not seem an obstacle. Nevertheless, the frequency of the formula in popular settings and demotic literature seems an important clue. *birth, flight and return* [handwritten annotation]

In that regard, we notice that Raymond Brown has provided us with a Matthean social location for such a narrative in his notion of an "ethos" of *popular narrative* in Matthew's special material. His exploration of the popular levels of religious culture as represented in Matthew's source involves the reconstruction of one such source used in the infancy narrative. It builds on the repeated pattern of the angel's message followed by Joseph's compliance. The threefold repetition yields the sequence of *birth, flight,* and *return.* In the pattern that Brown has discerned, each of the three parts turn on the reciprocal formulae: (a) an angel of the Lord appeared to Joseph in a dream; (b) Joseph got up (from sleep) and (performed the task).[17] This matches rather closely the broad structure of the taxonomic studies as articulated by Alfred Nutt, apart from his nonnarrative supplementary fourth section. According to Brown, then, the basic shape of the expulsion and return pattern is already a feature of the infancy narrative that Matthew derived from his special material.

These lists are useful in helping us see what in this story formula contributes to our investigation of Matthew and violence. If, with a few adjustments, we extract from Raglan's list the features concerning the flight and the return, we arrive at six steps that clearly show the narrative

16. Lévi-Strauss, *Structural Anthropology*, I, 206–231.
17. Brown, *Birth*, 109.

matthew + violence [handwritten annotation]

symmetry of the formula.[18] The basic pattern is departure and return. Three steps describe the flight; another three steps describe the return, which occurs much later in the hero's life. In both movements, that out and that back again, the story must dislodge the hero from his current place, then move him, and then install him in the new place. So each of the triads consists of a leave-taking or relinquishment of place (1, 4), a physical change of place (2, 5), and a subsequent resettlement in a new place (3, 6). *Usurpation + revenge*

Set out for viewing, these six steps are

1. A violent usurpation leads to

2. the flight or escape of the infant prince, who

3. finds a foster home in a distant land,

   —and later, upon reaching adult state

4. experiences the discovery of his true identity, enabling

5. his victorious return against enemies, and

6. the restoration of the dynasty.

How do the themes of usurpation and revenge, emphasized in the literary studies, affect this pattern? We learn from our experience of the broader range of stories that the symmetry of flight and return is framed by the supporting symmetry of *usurpation* and *reconquest*. At this point we encounter the dictum from the laws of narrative that decrees that violence calls forth violence. In the story formula of the banished prince, this sets the expectation that the hero will reciprocate as he retrieves the kingdom. The slaughter of the Hebrew children, in the Moses story, sets the terms for the slaying of the Egyptian firstborn. The elder Hamlet's murder prompts his ghost to demand the murder of his usurping brother in response. When Scar, in *The Lion King*, takes the life of his brother and usurps his kingdom, we know his own life will be forfeit before the film is over.

This is what we want to notice about the story formula. It begins in violence and sets the stage for reciprocal violence, under the rubrics of revenge and purgation. Note that the hero is faced with two obligations

violence → reciprocal violence

18. The symmetry corresponds to the symmetry of initial lack and the repair of lack that underlies Propp's original studies of story structures. Cf. Propp, *Morphology*, 35–37. See also Patte, *What is Structural Exegesis?*, 37–39, on correlated sequences.

revenge and purgation

to be discharged before the conclusion of the story. The first of these is to exact *revenge* for the honor violated and damage done. The second is to *purge* the realm of the evil that has contaminated it.[19] Payback and purgation: *Hamlet* shows us both. The revenge dominates the play, but the rottenness in Denmark demands purging, seen in the bodies littering the stage at the conclusion.

relocations, changes in residence

MAPPING THE FORMULA STORY ONTO MATTHEW

How does this story formula affect our reading of Matthew's gospel? Let us remember, first of all, that in his reconstruction of Matthew's source for the flight and return, Raymond Brown has provided us with a Matthean social location for such a narrative. Brown saw a common pattern in the birth, flight, and return episodes found in the infancy narrative. According to Brown, then, these correspond to the main parts of the classic hero myths.

However the homecoming narrative that we want to propose for Matthew, though admittedly beginning in the early chapters of the Gospel, reaches beyond them to embrace the entire rising action of the plot. How this works can be seen in another aspect of Matthew's text—the Scripture citations in the text, seen earlier in chapter 1 to inscribe the homecoming story through the gospel text. We might recall certain features of these scripture citations. Five of them feature place names—*Bethlehem* (2:5–6), *Egypt* (2:15), and *Nazareth* (2:23); in chapter 4, *Galilee* (4:15–16); and finally, *Zion* (21:4–5). Not merely indicators of simple movement, the moves are relocations, changes in residence, stages along the way. They are the equivalent of road signs marking a progress that forms a life itinerary.

Here we find the clue to the Matthean use of the formula story. When we map one pattern onto the other, we yield a correlation: The

---

19. Insofar as the initial usurpation involved a purge of the original regime, the two impulses are combined in the narratives. But they are logically, and often enough explicitly, distinct. Cf. the discussion of the Marandas's narrative adaptation of Lévi-Strauss's formula in Beck, *Nonviolent Story,* 164–67. The payback pivots on the transformation of the hero, who at some point decides to adopt the procedures of the villain—in opposition to the villain, of course. The purgation, on the other hand, pivots on the transformation of the villain, who changes from a character with an evil trait to an evil with a character's face—noun and adjective trade places—so that the story world is purified by the simple expedient of erasing the villain.

scriptures register the hero's progress—*Bethlehem* (2:5–6) registers the usurper's violence; *Egypt* (2:15) gives us the hero's flight; *Nazareth* (2:23), the home in exile; *Galilee* (4:15–16) the announcement of the hero's return; and *Zion* (21:4–5) the victorious return itself.

To place these findings in a table:

1. Matt 2:5–6	Bethlehem	Usurpation (and Purgation)
2. Matt 2:15	Egypt	Escape and Flight
3. Matt 2:23	Nazareth	Foster Home in Distant Land
4. Matt 4:15–16	Galilee	Signs, Call to Return
5. Matt 21:4–5	Zion	Triumphal Return
6. —	—	Restoration of Dynasty

The first five steps of the story formula are sutured across the narrative by way of the scripture citations. No sixth citation corresponds to the final step of the story formula.[20] To see more clearly what is going on here, the text invites a closer look at the Old Testament passages invoke in the pattern.

The Missing Sixth Citation

Instead of a victorious ascent to the control of the kingdom, we learn of the passion and death of Jesus. Instead of a restored dynasty we have its promise—"all authority in heaven and on earth has been given to me" (28:18). From the point of view of the formula story (and not, of course, the common synoptic narrative), this gives evidence of being a failed story. And the "failure" clearly results from the ineffectuality of the hero's return, in the form of an unbloody *nostos*. No revenge is exacted, as Jesus enters as Zechariah's Prince of Peace. And the temple purgation

20. No quotation formula corresponds to the last step. However, it would seem that all the Scripture citations redactionally introduced into the text could be understood in relation to the story formula. The miraculous birth is marked by the citation in 1:22, as is the usurper's purge in 2:17, and the Merlin-like mentor figure of the Baptist at 3:3. More problematic are the citations of the Servant songs at 8:17 and 12:17–20. However, these seem to refer to the nonviolent program of the Messiah, while the citations in 13:14–15 and 13:35 seem to highlight this program's challenge to conventional understanding. As we will see later, the series culminates in the arrest scene, 26:51–56, with its sword saying (v. 52) and citation formula (v. 56) without a cited text (!). As noted later, the other scripture texts presumably reach cumulative fulfillment here. The last instance of citation, Judas's death, is marked in 27:9–10 as the contrasting confirmation of the sentiments expressed in the sword saying at Jesus' arrest, at Judas' hands.

is gestural, at best. Jesus' opponents are not eliminated, allowing them to remain in place to mount the counteroffensive that results in his death. And so he dies, but the tomb is found to be empty. This, and the interpreting angel waiting there, tell us that this story, despite appearances, is *not* a failed story.

In narrative terms the result might be described as the intertextual disruption of the formula story by the common synoptic narrative. That is, the received story of Jesus—the common synoptic narrative, that Matthew no doubt derived from Mark's Gospel—interrupts the pattern of the banished prince formula. Because Jesus' story as Matthew finds it in Mark does not allow a violent reprisal, the result is that the expected resolution of the violent formula story is replaced. The latter's symmetry is disrupted and broken, introducing an amnesty and refusing readers the bloody satisfactions of revenge.

expected resolution is replaced

Against Revenge, Forgiveness

At this point it is useful to revisit the moments of conflict resolution in Matthew, both in the plot and in the small scenarios in Jesus' teaching, that were marked at the end of the previous chapter. What happens is that Matthew's emphasis on the second moment converges with this refusal of revenge. In its place is a form of release, typically associated with the act of forgiveness. *second movement → refusal of revenge*

The law of Talion

The disruption of the expectations of revenge in the plot of the gospel finds endorsement in the sayings of Jesus embedded in the text. Three moments come to mind. The first of these is the revision of the law of Talion in Matt 5:38–42, which adapts the Q Source to Matthew's text. The dialogic interaction implied by this saying, and inverted by Jesus, is one of violation and payback. Granted, the law of Talion is intended to limit the common escalation of violence that is a feature of revenge behaviors. But Jesus' recommendation is radical. Rather than pay back the blow, he advises inviting another blow: Turn the other cheek. The saying draws a picture of behavioral dynamics that is symmetrical with the apparently "failed" ending of the plot of Matthew's banished prince. The teaching of Jesus reverses the expectation of retaliation that is invoked by the reference to the law of Talion. The reversal in turn confirms the inhibition of expected revenge exhibited in Matthew's plot.

violation + payback

Peter's question about forgiveness

A second moment is Peter's question concerning forgiveness, with Jesus' reply, in Matt 18:21–22. The injunction to unconditional forgiveness is assigned an outlandish number—seventy times seven. The text echoes Lamech's boast song of *seventy-sevenfold* revenge, in Gen 4:24. In so doing, it places forgiveness in the opposite corner from revenge. They are seen as opposed alternatives. Hannah Arendt, for one, has proposed forgiveness, a political initiative that she attributes to Jesus of Nazareth, as the only response to violence that satisfactorily serves to conclude the chain of violent, reciprocal recriminations that result from revenge.[21] Forgiveness is asymmetrical in the sense that it does not try to even the score, it does not seek to balance the account—an effort that invariably begins a new account for the other side. Instead, forgiveness concludes the cycle of reciprocities. It refuses to play the game and, instead, cancels it.

The Gethsemane Arrest

A third moment takes place at the arrest of Jesus in Gethsemane. This is a critical juncture in the action of the common synoptic narrative, as the initiative of action is handed over to Jesus, and he responds with a declaration of nonretaliation. Matthew enhances the moment, and his text deserves fuller consideration, which we will provide in chapter 7. But for the moment we can note that the sword saying is significant not only for its content, but also for the fact that it is inserted at this point in the narrative, at the moment when Jesus is invited to exact revenge. The saying underlines the implacable drive of the pattern of revenge: "*The one who lives by the sword, by the sword will perish*" (Matt 26:52). And in this way it drives home the considerable accomplishment that nonviolent response entails.

The refusal Jesus accomplishes concerning this invitation, dramatized by the disciple who cuts off the ear of the servant of the high priest—a response performed and rejected—is consonant with the nonretaliation and forgiveness in the previous examples. The episode itself dramatizes Jesus' refusal to enter the cycle of violence. The moment

---

21. Arendt, *The Human Condition*, 236–47: "Without being forgiven, released from the consequences of what we have done, our capacity to act would, as it were, be confined to one single deed from which we would never recover; we would remain the victim of its consequences forever, not unlike the sorcerer's apprentice who lacked the magic formula to break the spell." (237)

Jesus' refusal to enter the cycle of violence

concludes with the scripture formula repeated in Matt 26:56, but without a specific scripture cited. The lack of a specific scriptural text would suggest the various citations culminate in this one.

This refusal of revenge and turn to models of forgiveness sharply contrasts with the examples of the formula story that we have reviewed. That it is prescribed in the itinerary as a sequence of messages from scripture places the divine initiative in a startlingly different position as well. It is always tempting for readers to view these quotations as a divine script for Jesus' life. But if the picture I have drawn is to be believed, the "script" is better conceived as a sketch borrowed from a common cultural narrative, promoted in the culture through the formula story of the banished prince, a cultural understanding that insists on revenge as the necessary and only thinkable sequel to acts of deliberate harm. The cultural script is acted out in Matthew's Gospel only to be rewritten. The cultural story gets a new ending—a revision that is, to our surprise, divinely warranted.[22]

Again, contrast the ending of the *Odyssey*: despite Odysseus' misgivings about reciprocal violence, Athena, the divine presence in charge of the action in this case, insists on wholesale revenge. Odysseus is assured that despite the threat of igniting a cycle of violence, all recriminations will be stopped here.[23] This is, of course, one of the lies to which narrative is prone, when it is committed to rounding off a story and satisfying listeners. In human experience, by contrast, each reprisal of previous violation becomes a new violation requiring further reprisal. Realistically, the viable and revivifying alternative is the forgiveness that is proposed by Matthew's Jesus, as possibly one of those "things hidden since the foundation of the world."

refusals of revenge } turn to models of forgiveness

reciprocal violence
wholesale revenge

22. Dorothy Jean Weaver has developed a framework for Matthew's pattern of rewriting expected scripts. Cf. Weaver, "Rewriting," 376–385; "Power and Powerlessness," 454–466.

23. Homer. *Odyssey*, 20. 39–58; but cf. also 13. 426–434 and 18. 391–401.

PART TWO

Banished King; Exiled Nation

Joyce . . . worked from the awareness that the *Odyssey* and *Don Giovanni* have plots with the same shape, which means that many of the characters correspond, though Homer concentrates our attention on the avenger, Mozart and da Ponte on the usurper. And the plot of *Hamlet* has the same shape likewise, with attention concentrated on the absent avenger's son; and the plot of the *Count of Monte Cristo* also, a kind of demotic *Odyssey* on which Stephen Dedalus built fantasies once. It was a theme pertinent to nineteenth-century researches, this savoring of homomorphism.

—Hugh Kenner, *James Joyce's* Ulysses

Hugh Kenner's identification of a kinship between *Ulysses*, Joyce's master novel, and the story pattern of the banished prince does more than enlist another cluster of examples into our set of stories. He also reminds us that these stories, in addition to having "plots of the same shape," admit of a critical approach from another direction because "many of the characters correspond" as well.[1] It permits another point of entry for examining the story formula, used in this and the next two chapters.

THE CAST OF CHARACTERS

To establish the character set of the story formula, we need to sound the roster. First, the family group stands at the center of the story—the father, king of the land, the queen mother, the young prince, and the wicked uncle, the usurper. The princess, present in the story for the sake of a happy ending, can also be included in the family group, at least pro-

---

1. Kenner, "Circe," 343.

leptically. The family group contains the heart of the action. At another level, we find the exiles and commoners who are essential to the unfolding of the plot—the faithful retainers who smuggle the young prince out of the palace and off to safety, the foster parents who raise the child in obscurity, and the mentor figure who readies the future king for the fearsome task ahead.

This cast of characters can be divided into two sets in another way, along lines other than their social status. They can also be sorted according to the different values they represent for the narrative, and by implication for the society that the story projects as a part of its story world. The king certainly represents the established order, the right order as ordained by tradition and accepted by the populace, but now threatened by usurpation. As head of the family the king embodies authority. Within the terms of the narrative, he represents the social value that is felt to be lost and that the story strives to regain. The queen mother's value is closely allied to that of the king, but she contributes softer dimensions of value. Her presence allows the traditional good that the story seeks to restore to be recognized as "home." Also, without the queen the royal dominion, though prevailing, would not rise to the status of dynasty because that requires offspring. This important factor is the primary value she passes on to the princess, as future queen, crucial when the time comes to reestablish the dynasty. Although they are also members of the family set, the young prince and the wicked uncle can be set aside for the moment. They each display a degree of ambiguity that is crucial to their function in the story, but will need a closer, more careful look.

Among the secondary set of characters—retainers and foster parents—we find a set of values similar to those of the family group, but devoted to maintaining the received traditions under the unpromising conditions of exile, set in a period of lost favor. These factors help us to understand that the story of the banished prince is a shadow plot, in the sense that it takes place in lieu of the story that is unfolding in the palace, in the company of the usurper and his retainers. The banished prince is a story of a party out of favor, waiting its turn. That is why we hear of the prince only in his first years and later at his coming of age. It is at those times, and those times only, that he can be viewed in the bright lights of the palace, the arena of narrative attention.

Against this set of characters representing social stability and settled values, disturbed by usurpation, stands another set identified by a disconcerting ambiguity, a certain doubled presence. An examination of these figures and their contribution to the story plot will be the basis for chapters 4 to 6. This ambiguity, this doubleness, can be witnessed in full force in the prince. As prince and protagonist of the plot, he represents the focal point of the action. He is the carrier of accumulated value, taking us through the duration of the action. He is the figure whose individual welfare personalizes the larger well-being of his society, its social order. When the prince wins his prize, his society is restored to its place of honor and its blessed prosperity.

On the other hand, because the prince receives notice of his identification in a place of obscurity, and provided with no credentials other than remarkable signs and revelations, the threat of imposture is always there. This possibility, in fact, supplies the plot device in certain versions of the story pattern. Instances include the story of Martin Guerre, the opera of Boris Gudonov, and that other Russian story, the story of Anna Anderson, who adopted the persona of Anastasia, Tsar Nicholas's daughter. The impostor represents the threat to the social order that is feared may overcome the safeguards in place to prevent just such threats. In terms of the narrative, a primary tension in the plot is none other than this very uncertainty concerning the validity of the pretender to the throne. It will also prove to be of value in examining the gospel narrative of Matthew, in which the protagonist, Jesus, is accused of being an impostor (Matt 27:63–64), and whose arrival on the scene is felt to be a threat by the current occupant of the throne (Matt 2:1–12). The role of the impostor in Matthew's Gospel will be the focus of study in chapter 5.

The wicked uncle, who emerges early on as usurper of the throne, displays his own version of doubled significance. As the heavy, the antagonist in the plot, he clearly represents the enemy of the young prince and in social terms the disaster visiting the land. Except for the young prince, the uncle would ordinarily be next in line for the throne. Should this come about in the natural course of events, he would be acclaimed; should he force the issue, he would be considered a usurper, grabbing the reins of power falsely and illegitimately. The uncle has potential to be hero or villain. This doubleness is integral to the figure of the "wicked" uncle, who in other circumstances might be the hero.

The theme of usurpation, the question of the legitimacy of power, has special pertinence for Matthew's Gospel insofar as the account begins with an implied charge of Herod's illegitimate kingship. It unfolds further when we consider the historical role of Herod as Rome's client king in Judea and Matthew's place in the era after Rome's destruction of the Jerusalem temple. The questions raised by the confluence of these themes will necessarily be part of the discussion of the usurper, taken up in chapter 5.

The third figure in our list, the mentor, is not immediately an obvious member of the character set of the banished prince story formula. But in fact this is a character essential to the formula and always makes his appearance, from Merlin of the Arthurian cycle to the shaman, Rafiki, in *The Lion King*. The eponymous example is, of course, Pallas Athena appearing to Telemachus as "Mentor," spurring him toward the search for his father, Odysseus, and initiating the homecoming story of *The Odyssey*. The mentor figure prepares the hero for the return to power and, as such, bears the value of the regime in exile. But the mentor is not simply a passive carrier of values, like the foster parents. The mentor is also an active opponent involved in acts of sedition. The presence of the mentor implies a resistance movement that is ready to depose the present king, viewed as a usurper, and replace him with one they consider more authentic.

The ambiguity of the mentor figure derives from his public/private status. Prominent in one phase of the government, if it should prevail, he is currently working in obscurity, although continuing to apply his skills and wisdom to the task of aiding rulers. However, at the moment it is only in a covert manner. The mentor is an inherently dangerous figure, involved in seditious activity. His corresponding character in the gospel is the Baptist, whose subversive qualities are at the same time denied and recognized, as he is, in turn, praised and feared, honored and beheaded. For we are reminded that Hugh Kenner names the constituent violence of "stories of this shape" and their pivot on the interplay between the two characters he calls "the usurper" and "the avenger."

PLOTLINES

Just as the parts of speech only make full sense in grammatically structured sentences, so in stories characters require plots. And plots generate subplots. A system of plotlines can be discerned in Matthew's narrative. The following diagram served as a guide in thinking about the relationship of the conflicts described in the following chapters. Each chapter narrows its attention to a plot within the wider horizon of the previous:

The largest frame represents the conflict between colonized Judea and the Roman Empire. In the Gospel narrative this serves as the implied conflict in the background. It is the largely unremarked conflict that makes its appearance with surrogates: Herod, Archelaus, Herod Antipas, and Pilate. In Matthew's world this dimension is most conspicuously signaled by the destroyed Temple, which we can represent as the Burnt Place. This conflict is examined as we review the role of the usurper.

Within this larger conflict there is a division among the representatives of Judea. Here Jesus and his disciples are pitted against the scribes and the Pharisees in what can correctly be described as the main plot of the Gospel. The positioning of both parties in common conflict with the empire illustrates their roles as rivals in opposing the imperial power. In Matthew's world this conflict serves to dramatize for the Christian disciples a warning to avoid certain behaviors, portrayed in the drama by the opponents of Jesus. This conflict is examined in chapter 5, "Impostor."

Within the "kingdom of heaven" party identified with Jesus, a difference of opinion about the meaning of Jesus' nonviolence seems at issue. In the subplot of John and Jesus the competing values of retribution and nonretaliation are tested and compared. Does this represent a debate within Matthew's community? We do not know, but insofar as Matthew's narrative regularly reflects issues of his time and place, consistency would suggest something similar in this case. The conflict between Jesus and John is examined in chapter 6, "Mentor."

4

Usurper

But Antigonus, by way of reply to what Herod had cause to be proclaimed, and this before the Romans, and before Silo also, said that
they would not do justly if they gave the kingdom to Herod, who was
no more than a private man, and an Idumean, i.e. a half-Jew.

—Josephus, *Antiquities*, Book 14,403

The very sentence which is found to be thematic for the main plot
(1:21)—the prediction that "Jesus will save his people from their
sins"—presupposes a previous story as well. It assumes that the plot of
the gospel comes toward the end of a larger and longer plot, in which
"his people" fall victim to "their sins." And it does not take much
imagination, much reading in Matthew, or much knowledge of the
Jewish background, to see what story that is. It is the story of Israel,
more specifically the story of exile.

—N. T. Wright,
The New Testament and the People of God, 385

THE FORMULA STORY OF the banished prince begins with an act of
usurpation, frequently performed by a wicked uncle. In *Hamlet* it is
Claudius, in *The Lion King*, Scar. In Matthew's Gospel the character filling this role is Herod. However, this king is to be understood as Matthew
and his readers understood him, as the tool of Rome's imperial project.
Because, on the one hand, Matthew does not suggest that Herod is Jesus'
royal relation and because, on the other hand, neither does he overtly
link Herod to Rome, this chapter will address both of these objections.
By tracing a line from the wicked uncle figure, through the role of Herod,
to the looming presence in Judea of the imperial power of Rome, we

can see how the disruption that generates Matthew's story represents a usurpation in the largest sense. Through the figure of the usurper we can trace the story of the lost kingdom and agony of exile under alien powers, culminating in Matthew's world with the destruction of city and Temple. In this context, the story of usurpation is one of the depredations of imperial control and allows us to read Matthew's Gospel as, in some measure, a postcolonial text.

THE WICKED UNCLE

The vivid sense of déjà vu that first-time viewers of *The Lion King* may receive has its causes. The story was evolved from studies of Hamlet and Moses, among others. Hamlet's uncle, Claudius, has become Scar, the wicked uncle of Simba, the cub and prince of the animal kingdom. When Disney imposed the Lion King formula on its account of Hercules, Dis, the ruler of the underworld and brother of Zeus, Hercules' father, was pressed into service as the required uncle, despite the fact that this story is being constructed out of whole cloth. Among our animated films, even *Anastasia*, a tale turning on the overthrow of the Romanov dynasty in Russia, found an "uncle" in Rasputin, sufficiently mysterious and dark to assume the given role. The wicked uncle was needed to plot the deposition of the tsar, even though history points to the Bolshevik revolution.

King Claudius and Scar seem to have a purpose in the formula beyond the practical rhetorical need to translate social forces into manageable personal characters with which audiences can identify and with which dramatic action can work. The wicked uncle is a symptom or symbol of a weak point in the social system presupposed by the formula story of the banished prince.

The formula reflects a world of kings and dynasties. And the maintenance of dynasties requires dynastic shedding—the legal mechanism that narrows and orders the line of succession to the throne. In the primogeniture systems, such as Salix Law, daughters are automatically disqualified, as are all the sons but the eldest. But the second son is something of an anomaly. By establishing the lines of succession, an orderly transition is made possible. Of course, once that determination is made, the legitimate heir will need bodyguards because the genealogical chart that establishes his legitimacy also makes him a target for ambitious rivals. Furthermore, it also designates those next in line, whose ambition might tempt them toward eliminating the heir and taking his place.

The second son, then, is an ambiguous figure because he also doubles as the primary threat to the throne, the wicked uncle. As the first to benefit from the disqualification of the heir, he is the first suspect for possible usurpation. There is no middle ground for him. Lionized, should he come into the rule by natural means, but vilified should take matters into his own hands to achieve that result, he lives in a kind of suspended limbo, with extreme and opposite future possibilities, but a nonsignifying present. In this way, the genealogical charts that map the lines of succession identify both the target and the probable agent of usurpation. And in the stories, the Wicked Uncle, as the most probable agent, represents the possibility, and even the very act, of usurpation. He is the character that symbolizes the usurping action.

Consider also that the usurping party itself has an ambiguous value. It makes a difference which party in the tale is identified as the usurper. In the animated films we reviewed, as in *Hamlet* and similar examples from literature, the hero is the victim of a coup. In many of the classic tales studied by Dundes and others, the hero is often feared to be the perpetrator of the coup, though this is not an invariable pattern. Oedipus is removed as a child because he is suspected to be a future threat to the throne. Both Theseus and Perseus, in their separate stories, are the subjects of warnings by the Delphic oracle, telling the king to watch out for them. In these cases the hero threatens to adopt the role of the usurper, and the throne is forewarned. But in other cases, such as that of Jason or of Romulus, the infant is banished by the wicked brother of the king, the hero's father, and escapes to return later in life to regain the kingdom. Although the principle that the established order must not be violated remains a constant throughout, variation enters the picture in terms of when and where the act of usurpation occurs. In some cases it precedes the hero's story. In other cases, it is the culmination of that story.

As seen in the Moses story, particularly in the animated film version, *The Prince of Egypt*, we discover that the hero is the usurper, and the political action of which he is the leader is more akin to revolution than deposition. In another way, the Anastasia story recasts an act of revolution, the Bolshevik uprising of 1917, as usurpation, with Rasputin cast in the role of the wicked uncle. In the former case it is a matter of viewing the conflict from the revolutionary side of the struggle. In the latter case, it is a matter of rejecting the legitimacy of revolution by recasting it as usurpation. Here too, the usurper is located in a highly ambiguous situation.

Herod, Antiking

The conflict that erupts in Matthew 2 between Herod and the infant Messiah, unfolds in a story that displays all the ambiguity of the usurper role. Who is the usurper in this text? Is it Jesus? He is, after all, the provocateur. Is it Herod? He had that reputation, as Josephus, for one, reports.[1]

The case can be made that Jesus is the usurping party. The account shares those features of the classic tales in which an oracle warns the king of the looming threat to his dominion, arriving in the person of the newborn prince, who will grow up to claim the throne. The pattern seems complete. Herod, the sitting king, alerted by the "oracle" of scripture discovered by his advisors, attempts to have the life of the infant, who manages, however, to escape to a distant place. After "we learn nothing of his childhood," we witness his return as an adult, claiming to inaugurate the "kingdom of God." This would seem to satisfy, reinforced by the constant obbligato of the Moses references, for a story far from upholding the established order.

But it is clear that Herod is regarded in this text as the usurper. Among these is the reference to Ps 72:10–11, which has contributed the gifts and homage to the Matthean account, along with the pious tradition that the Magi are "kings." The psalm pictures the ideal Davidic king to reign in the golden age. The poem is taken to be a messianic psalm by both Jewish and Christian readers. But what is notable in Matthew's invocation of the psalm is not simply its identification of Jesus is the ideal Davidic king that Judeans expectantly await and which, ironically, Gentiles turn out to have the ability to discern. It also identifies Herod as the antimessiah, the opposite of the anticipated ideal ruler. In a series of stanzas, the psalm lists attributes of the prototypically just king, the Messiah to come, the implication being that Jesus fulfills this description of the future king.

At the same time, the story of Herod and the Magi dramatically underlines Herod's lack of qualifications for the role. Each stanza of the

---

1. Josephus, *Antiquities*, 14.403. Herod is characterized as both a commoner and an Idumean.

psalm stands as a vivid rebuke to the reign of Herod, as depicted by Matthew:

1. (Ps 72:1–4): The Just Ruler will defend the children and crush the oppressor. Herod does just the opposite.
2. (vv.5–7). The heavenly signs of the sun and moon are images of the endurance of the just king's reign and the fruitfulness of his dominion. Herod, however, cannot read the sign of the star and attacks the fruitfulness of the people in the slaughter of their children.
3. (vv. 8–11). The ideal king's reign is universal as well as eternal. In a chiastic arrangement we see that the kings of the earth give gifts and homage. The Magi bring gifts and present them to the child, but snub Herod and leave without notifying him.
4. (vv. 12–14). The ideal king will protect the vulnerable from molestation and violence. Herod, by contrast, exploits the vulnerable and visits violence on them.
5. (vv. 15–17). Summarizing the previous stanzas, we see that the ideal king will bring the blessing of shalom upon the land. Herod, by contrast, endows the land with a curse.

Matthew clearly presents Jesus as the true king of Israel, with the implication that Herod is a false king, illegitimately on the throne. But characterization as the antithetical of the ideal king, although it establishes Herod's place in the estimation of the evangelist, does not make him a usurper. As we've seen with Shakespeare's play, *Richard II*, incompetence doesn't justify deposition. Is Herod the usurper as well as the antiking? To answer this we need to search Matthew's text with a view to how it would read for Matthew's intended readers.

MATTHEW'S GENEALOGY (MATT 1:1–17)

In the formula story of the banished prince, the hero rises from obscurity without the benefit of pedigree. No genealogical charts are brought out to justify the claim to royal heritage. Instead, signs, omens, and unexplained powers signal not only divine favor but also the dynastic authenticity of the arriving hero. In Matthew's Gospel, however, we have a prominently positioned genealogy beginning the account. We should remember that it is for the eyes of the reader, and the reader alone. The personae in the drama must make do with signs. The Magi see a star;

Herod consults his sages, who in turn consult the ancient texts. At the baptism of Jesus we notice a heavenly voice and a mysterious dove. The genealogy is for the purpose of convincing the reader.

Son of Abraham, Son of David (Matt 1:1)

With the opening words, "The book of the genealogy of Jesus, son of Abraham, son of David," the Gospel makes a double claim for the protagonist, drawing on the language and hope of the ancient promises and spelled out in the list that follows. In the covenant with Abraham (Gen 15:7, 18) God had promised innumerable descendants and a land. In the covenant with David (2 Sam 7:11–16; Ps 89) God had promised an enduring dynastic rule over Israel. But while it is making claims for Jesus as authentically Jewish and royal, it levels an incisive critique against any claim Herod might make in competition. Here we can recall again the words of Antigonus, the last of the Hasmoneans, condemning the young Herod, who is engaged in driving him from Jerusalem, as "a commoner and an Idumean." If so, then he is accounted as neither a son of David nor a son of Abraham.

The story of Herod's rise to power is well known. Josephus hides nothing of Herod's ambition and deviations. The second son of Antipater, the Idumean convert to Judaism who was a prominent minister under the Hasmoneans, Herod learned how to acquire power while working deferentially under another power. Once Pompey took Jerusalem in 63 BCE, the Hasmoneans lost the kingship, and Judea entered the Roman Empire. By 47 BCE Herod was named governor of Galilee. After Julius Caesar's assassination in 44 BCE, Herod did Rome's work in quieting uprisings in Samaria and then marched on Jerusalem, ousting Antigonus. In 39 BCE, Herod restored the "kingdom" to Judea by agreeing to be a Roman vassal in return for the title of king. A victorious campaign though Galilee, the coast, Masada, and finally to Jerusalem, where he again ousted the last of the Hasmoneans, Antigonus, who had returned in the interim, placed the entire land under Herod's—that is, Rome's—control. It was on this occasion that Antigonus made his famous remark about Herod's lack of royal Jewish blood. Antigonus was executed, and Herod reigned from 37 to his death in 4 BCE.

The execution of Antigonus is not the only decisive action Herod performed to secure his position. The complete act of usurpation, replacing not simply a sitting king, but also an entire dynasty, required action on many fronts. In addition to deposition of the reigning king, removing his legitimate successors consolidates the move. Herod deposed Antigonus and Mattathias, but also consolidated his hold on power by removing Aristobolus, Hyrcanus II, Alexandra, and Mariamne. It is not uncommon to see an attempt to eradicate the entire bloodline, and then by marrying into the family, becoming the legal heir as well as the de facto one.

Herod was hated for many reasons. Although born a Jew, he did not practice his religion, earning the enmity of religious Jews. Building a theater and amphitheater in Jerusalem and promoting games in honor of Caesar did little to endear him with the upholders of the Jewish law. His building projects of Caesarea Maritima, the model of a Roman city, and the grand Temple in Jerusalem placed a tremendous financial burden on the people. But at the core of these, driving his success, was the allegiance to Rome that made him the local face of the empire.

Kingdom and Exile (Matt 1:2–17)

Herod was not simply a usurper on his own. His dynasty was anchored in Roman patronage, and it is to that we must tract the claims of usurpation. But Matthew's genealogy discounts more than the claims of Herod. It also makes a case for something much larger to be placed under the heading of "usurpation." In its review of the story of Israel, it brings to particular notice the history of loss and unfulfilled recovery.

The genealogy lends itself to the impulse to mine it for theological truths. The various aspects inspire this—the division into three parts, the five women named in it, the profusion of second sons—all nudge commentators toward theological explanations. But the question that remains unasked concerns its function—why is it here, leading the document? As it makes a claim for Jesus as son of Abraham and son of David, a frequent assumption is that it serves as an introductory statement of the theological themes to follow. The presumption made here is that it also sets the stage for Matthew's narrative. With that in mind, we can turn to some current views about biblical genealogies.

Recent sociological and anthropological studies of genealogies have been applied to Genesis and Chronicles, but not, to my knowledge, to Matthew's genealogy. These studies provide a helpful context of understanding Matthew's genealogy in its relation to the narrative. Linear genealogies, as opposed to segmented, or branched, make a claim of *legitimacy* concerning property or the power of authority. One might imagine it as a thread traced through the branches of a segmented geology to arrive at the conclusion with a claim of ownership or legitimacy based on the proper reading. When claims are made and promulgated, as they are in genealogies, we might assume that is because they are contested, either actually or potentially. They are an answer to an implied question. *It is this role of making a contested claim that the genealogy that heads Matthew's story finds it place.* Although the genealogy imparts information to the readers, information unavailable to the characters in story, Herod still manages to learn of the claim made for the newborn Messiah, thanks to the arrival of the Magi. In the slaughter of the Bethlehem children he clearly demonstrates his awareness that a claim is being made, and he contests it emphatically.

As support for the claim to legitimacy, linear genealogies also make a show of *continuity.* This feature too is pertinent for Matthew's list of names. Traditionally, the most important names generally are the first and last on the list. The former establishes the legitimacy of the line; the latter, when successfully defended, establishes the legitimacy of the last claimant to the inheritance. The second-last name is also important because it is assumed, by previous deliberations, that this title is legitimate, and so the current claimant need only make parentage clear to share legitimacy. Nevertheless, it is frequently thought beneficial to chart the links from ancestral founder to the present, though lists are generally reduced to no more than ten generations.[2]

Matthew's list is extraordinarily long and correspondingly complex. It is broken into three parts, which assist in establishing double founders, Abraham and David, one pressing Jewish claims, the other royal pedigree. Another way to describe this articulation is to say the list suffers two crises. From one point of view these are crises in Israel's history. One marks the beginning of the kingship (1:6) and the other marks the end of it (1:11). In each case, the history turned a significant corner, requiring that Israel's scribes and theologians negotiate the transition by way of major efforts of interpretation. If the promise to the house of David (2 Sam 7:11–16) successfully establishes monarchy in the face of traditional tribalism joined under one God, the dissolution of that kingship in the face of unending promise required equally adept efforts of interpretation.

2. Wilson, *Genealogy*, 57–68.

But the two breaks are also crises in the genealogy itself, for it seems to change its character at each of the two breaks. In the first part, between Abraham and David, the list of names follows the stories of the patriarchs. It is remarkable for the number of second (or later) sons that are included. This factor makes a prominent case for God's free election, but it also is a poor example of primogeniture legitimacy. Nevertheless, it must be conceded that the election of the second son only matters if there is already in place a presumption of primogeniture. The first break in the genealogy turns it into a king list. A king list is a record of the historical rulers, presented as a genealogy. Given the king list in the center of Matthew's genealogy, we wonder whether we are to reread the first part as preparation for the monarchy. Insofar as it traces the route leading to kingship, it assumes a new identity. This issue is even more acute with the second break. Once the kingdom is defunct, what does the continuation of names represent? Are they also royal? Presumably so. Does Matthew intend it to suggest a line of rulers in exile, persons who are carrying the royal line forward in obscurity? Presumably not. Yet what other meaning could it have?

Raymond Brown, while reminding us that this part of the genealogy embraces vast gaps with too few names for the years involved, poses the question of whether Matthew had access to a Davidic list of royal pretenders. He decides not. "There is not the slightest indication in the accounts of the ministry of Jesus that his family was of ancestral nobility or royalty. If Jesus were a dauphin, there would have been none of the wonderment about his pretensions."[3] And yet that lack of acclaim is exactly what the formula story of the banished prince serves to explain. Those in the Matthew's story are not aware of Jesus' origins. Only the narrator and the readers are privy to that information. By invoking the pattern of the banished ruler, Matthew makes possible the introduction of Jesus as the coming Son of David. In effect, he creates a space for that claim.

Knowing about Jesus' humble and obscure origins, we remain skeptical of any vision of governments in exile with Jesus as the pretender to the throne, to put it baldly as possible. But that is where the logic of the genealogy takes us. It asserts that Jesus can make a legitimate claim to the throne of David. Not everyone in the family is an heir. The principle of dynastic shedding requires paring away all but those with undisputed

3. Brown, *Birth*, 88.

right to the prize. And if this is not a line of succession, what might it be? A simple list of names that connects Joseph to Zerubbabel, the last known of the Davidic royal figures, would establish Joseph's membership in the family, but as a mark of legitimacy this is essentially trivial. It would make no claim, and could not, lacking the dynastic shedding that would strip away noncandidates from the list.

Furthermore, in I Chr 6, a documentary source for Matthew, the David genealogy does have the value of tracing a royal genealogy of succession. The royal line is held intact, ready to spring back to life given the opportunity. Continuity is an especial concern of Chronicles insofar as it makes claims of authenticity for the returning exiles that outrank those who remained in the land. It attempts to support the claim that the true Israel was the exiled group now returned, rather than the population that stayed in place. It is a difficult case to make. Those who remained were in obvious continuity with the past. The degree of anxiety in the returnees' claim to authenticity is signaled in the length to which the nine chapters of lists grow. But continuity was crucial for their claims, and so the Chroniclers labored to provide the necessary names.

In Matthew's case the crises and the claims are similar, with the exile looming as the greatest crisis. The history after that seems incomplete and partial. If we read it in terms of the covenant with Abraham (Gen 15:18–21) and David (2 Sam 7:11–16), we get a sense of the issue. It would seem that the promise to Abraham was fulfilled when they were allowed to return. But as they were still under foreign authority; the promise to David was left dangling, unfulfilled though they were back in the land.

It is difficult to calculate the precise degree of authenticity Matthew assigns to his figures and narrative patterns—not only the genealogy with its claims, but also matters such as the Bethlehem origins of the family and even the banished prince story formula itself. These patterns are found in the text and yet seem to have a value more rhetorical (or theological?) than historically factual. It seems a bit obtuse to trace them beyond surface manifestations to their fuller implications, but the text itself does not warn us off or draw limits on how far we might construe its suggestions. How far can the rhetorical use of professedly factual narration be taken? Or, to put the question otherwise, what is it that Matthew's narrative elaborations are supposed to teach? The provisional answer is to follow the thread where it leads. Then we can assess the findings.

JOSEPH'S FIRST DREAM: THE HERO'S MANDATE
(MATT 1:18–25)

Narratologists, following the pioneering work of Vladimir Propp,[4] point to an originating violation, or "lack," that generates a narrative. Something is removed or lost, and it is the business of the story to repair the lack that results. The usurpation in the story of the banished prince, for instance, introduces a lack and does so doubly. In the palace coup, the kingdom is lost; in the violent assassinations, innocence is lost, and a debt of honor is incurred, promising violent reprisals. In violent stories, we can speak of the original violence that evokes the subsequent action. When an act of usurpation is presented as the original violence in a narrative, it implies that the foundational evil is the disruption of the *status quo ante*.

The events of Matt 1:18–25, frequently referred to as "The Birth of the Messiah," is structured as an angelic communication with Joseph when he was betrothed to Mary but not yet living with her. Raymond Brown, as we saw earlier,[5] connected this to the flight to Egypt and return to Israel as belonging to a source Matthew had available to him. The "birth" was the first part of a tripartite account in which the angel gave instructions to Joseph, who then carried them out verbatim. We will also recall that this corresponded to the first segment of the similarly tripartite form of the classic hero stories as described by Von Hahn and Lord Raglan. Again we have birth, flight, and return, so we can suspect that this birth account relates directly to the coming conflict.

In this case the angel gives dual instructions, leading Joseph to do two things—put aside his hesitation and take Mary into his home and, when the child is born, name him Jesus—in Hebrew, Joshua, popularly interpreted as "Yahweh saves."[6] Crafted narratives typically have an initial moment in which the main character is given a task. In the manner to which narratives are prone, the Gospel provides a statement of its narrative program in the form of a mandate for the protagonist, found in the angel's interpretation of Jesus' name, in 1:21: "He will save his people from their sins."

---

4. Propp, *Morphology*, 35–38. See also Patte, *Structural Exegesis?* 37–44.
5. Brown, *Birth*, 109.
6. Davies and Allison, *Matthew 1–7*, 209.

Mark Allan Powell identifies this as a programmatic statement for the narrative to follow,[7] functionally equivalent, we might say, to the voice at the baptism in Mark's Gospel (Mark 1:11). Although Matthew retains the main lines of Mark's baptism account, his version no longer stands at the head of the Gospel story, and its function changes. However, the angel's message does stand at the beginning of Matthew and contributes to the plan for the narrative.

The immediate problem that narrative readings encounter with Matt 1:21, like that with the infancy narrative itself, is the confidence that we already know what this "saving" means—a meaning that is typically taken to be sacrificial. But we might want to revise this notion, in light of the quotation from Hosea that Matthew has added, twice, to his text: "I desire mercy, not sacrifice" (9:13; 12:7). I propose we put preconceived understandings aside until we can let the story speak for itself, assisted by some reorganized perspectives from recent studies. If we look for the components of the mandate, we can identify three: "his people"; "their sins"; and "save." Each of these has something to add.

"*His people*": Powell sees the larger salvation history vision of Matthew set out here.[8] Powell goes so far as to say that the main plot of Matthew is universal salvation history. The conflicts actually narrated, with the authorities and the disciples, serve as subplots to a main plot that takes place out of sight. Certain features of the text can be cited to support this view. Because the two parts of the angel's instructions would seem to be mutually interpretive, when Jesus is called "Son of God," it would seem "his people" would have a broader, if not universal, referent as well. Hence, Powell interprets the angel's dictum in terms of the final commission to the nations, in Matt 28:16–20, seeing one as the mandate for the other.

Powell follows the lead of Frank Matera,[9] who pursues the logic of the narrative backward from its point of conclusion. But Matera emphasizes the restricted scope of Jesus' mission, insisted on twice. Jesus directs the Twelve, sent on mission, to avoid the towns of pagans and Samaritans, but to "go to the lost sheep of the house of Israel" (Matt 10:6). The words are repeated in the interaction with the Canaanite woman, when Jesus describes his own mission (Matt 15:24). One might suspect

7. Powell, "Plot and Subplot," 195.

8. Powell, "Plot and Subplot," 198–200.

9. Matera, "Plot of Matthew's Gospel," 233–253.

that these interpret the angel's message in 1:21, as to the application of "his people." Of course, this broadens to the "nations" at the end of the gospel. But at that point it would seem to have the character of a new mandate, and not the fulfillment of an earlier one, as Matera insists.

Warren Carter has devoted an entire essay to Matt 1:21 in *Matthew and Empire*, the collection of deeper studies that emerged from his work on a commentary on the Gospel.[10] Reading it in the contexts supplied by the text itself and the world of Matthew's first readers, he also favors a narrower application of "his people." Both the genealogy that precedes and the conflict with Herod that follows suggest an application to the "house of Israel." He notes that the specific narrative setting for the angel's message given in chapter 1 is the past history of Israel. Jesus is situated within the context of this people, identified as a Son of David and a Son of Abraham. Although we are attracted by generalized ideas of universal salvation, it is worth noting at this point that the declared beneficiaries of his mission are the Jewish people, the House of Israel, and none other (10:6; 15:24). Although a wider mission will be opened later, particularly at the conclusion of the Gospel, the mandate given here is narrower.

"Their sins": The "sins" of Israel ("his people") are not without biblical elaboration. Daniel Smith-Christopher has carefully assembled biblical evidence of popular resistance, understandably muted and indirect, produced during the time of postexilic Persian control. Using the sociological concept developed by James Scott, the private discourse of subjected peoples as a "hidden transcript,"[11] he produces a fresh and coherent reading of the postexilic texts. In his handling of the materials, it becomes apparent that many Judeans viewed their situation as a continuation of the Babylonian exile. It was for them as if the exile had

---

10. Carter, "Save His People," 75–90.

11. Smith-Christopher, *Exile*, 23–24. The hidden transcript, as distinct from the public transcript, is a way of talking about "the significant difference between the outward declarations and language of a subordinate peoples and the private discussions." The oppressed are not likely to tell the whole story of power relations in their public transcript. Based on the studies of Asian peasants by Scott, *Domination and the Arts of Resistance*. The hidden transcript provides a hermeneutic for texts produced under political duress—"a partly sanitized, ambiguous, and coded version of the hidden transcript is always present in the public discourse of subordinate groups" (quoting Scott, 24).

never ended, except that they were now free to experience the pain of domination in their own homeland, learning a new kind of bitterness.

Smith-Christopher points to studies, from Cambodian peasants and Cree Indians in Canada to Armenian clergy in thrall to the Turks, that show how exiled, colonized, or refugee peoples pray for forgiveness for the sins that brought their plight on them.[12] One might consider the dominant nation to have the greater guilt, with little on the part of the victim peoples. Yet the pattern persists. Reasons can be conjectured. It would provide a people suddenly rendered powerless an area where they might exert some control and in that way regulate their own fate. And it may, in fact, contain some truth because the occupied or exiled people might have deferred or softened the blow by acting differently at the time. A collective examination of conscience is not beyond reason.

This pattern is represented in exiled Israel's tradition of lament. In addition to the exilic literature of Ezekiel and Lamentatations, and the Deuteronomic History, Smith-Christopher cites postexilic laments in Ezra 9, Nehemiah 9, Daniel 9, and Baruch 2–3. In the book of Nehemiah, in an otherwise rather positive account of the Persian imperial policies, we encounter a prayer rehearsing the sins of Israel, ending with an assessment of their present condition as a new experience of slavery (Neh 9:36–37). Clearly not all of those who returned from exile saw it as full liberation and interpreted the situation in terms of the sinfulness of Israel.

Similarly, the book of Daniel, set in Babylon during the exile, but written in Judea during the Hellenist imperial presence, under Antioches IV Epiphanes, delivers a prayer of repentance (Dan 9:15–18):

> "Now, O Lord, our God, who led your people
> out of the land of Egypt with a strong hand,
> and made a name for yourself even to this day,
> we have sinned, we are guilty.
> O Lord, in keeping with all your just deeds,
> let your anger and your wrath be turned away
> from your city Jerusalem, your holy mountain.
> On account of our sins and the crimes of our fathers,
> Jerusalem and your people
> have become the reproach of all our neighbors.
> Hear, therefore, O God, . . .
> let your face shine upon your desolate sanctuary.
> Give ear, O my God, and listen;
> open your eyes and see our ruins
> and the city which bears your name.

12. Smith-Christopher, *Exile*, 80–81.

The prayer equates their present condition with that of the exiles in Babylon, having found there a powerful expression of their current experience in the land, now under imperial control. We see in these prayers the themes identified by Smith-Christopher: shame, sins of the ancestors, exile or slavery as conditions they experience, and the importance of the Moses covenant.[13]

And when it is time to return, Second Isaiah provides the proclamation with divine words from the throne of God:

> Comfort, comfort my people, says your God.
> Speak tenderly to Jerusalem,
> and proclaim to her
> that her hard service has been completed,
> that her sin has been paid for,
> that she has received from the LORD's hand
> double for all her sins. (Isa 40:1–2)

These opening words of Second Isaiah are nothing less than the mandate given Israel to end the Exile and begin the trip back from Babylon, the text that inaugurates the postexilic period still thought by many in Matthew's day to be unfinished business. The command to begin the return is interpreted as a release from sins, in the same manner suggested by Matthew 1:21. Because Second Isaiah also provides the text for the arrival of John the Baptist in this Gospel (Matt 3:3; Isa 40:3), as well as the mandate for Jesus' adult mission (Matt 3:17; Isa 42:1), it is arguable that this prophet's writing lies behind this program statement for the larger narrative of the Gospel as well. When the angel informs Joseph that "he will save his people from their sins," at 1:21, the agenda for the return from exile, still unfinished, is an inescapable inference.

The homecoming of Jesus in Matthew is configured as a homecoming for Israel itself. The arrival of the Messiah is anticipated as the return of Israel to its native place. As with Ruth, the physical return has not delivered its full blessing; it is, by itself, seriously lacking as a satisfactory return home. It is unnecessary to point out that concern for the vulnerable is a defining feature of Matthew's Jesus, whose ministry is conspicuously characterized by healings and insistent attention to those in society's margins. And, in Matthew's telling of it, Jesus brought this concern with him all the way to Jerusalem, as far as the temple: "The blind and the lame came to him at the temple, and he healed them" (Matt

---

13. Smith-Christopher, *Exile,* 117.

21:14). In this Gospel, the homecoming and the plight of the vulnerable are intertwined, much as they are in the book of Ruth.

"*Save*": What does it mean to "save" Israel from its sins, in the context that we have now framed it? This too is an area in which religious ideas beyond the narrative have monopolized the meaning of the word.[14] But because the immediate context of the preceding royal genealogy is political and historical, what might a pertinent meaning be? What is Israel's need for political salvation, in this story, at this time? The most immediate answer to this question would cite the imperial hegemony of Rome and its threat to the faith community. Clues exist in postcolonial conceptions of exile.

In a set of inquiries similar to those of Smith-Christopher, but pursued in New Testament studies, N. T. Wright champions the position that a sense of incomplete return from exile continued to prevail in Jesus' time.[15] The Dead Sea Scrolls express one group's sentiments in this regard. Wright cites the *Damascus Document* of the Qumran community, which views the exile continuing until the establishment of the community that produced these texts. Although such views have long been recognized as espoused by this particular group, more and more scholars are coming to recognize that the Judean sensibility of deferred return from exile was more widespread. Commenting on Nehemiah 9:36–37, Wright writes, "The exile is not yet really over. This perception of Israel's present condition was shared by writers across the board in second-temple Judaism . . . Israel has returned to the land, but is still in the 'exile' of slavery, under the oppression of foreign overlords."[16] Because this situation still prevailed in New Testament times according to this view, the Messianic expectation was indissolubly linked to the return from exile. When the Messiah arrived, Israel would come home—in its fullest sense.

Wright is arguing a case for an awareness that pervades the New Testament world. He doesn't claim that Jesus saw himself in this role. But he does insist that the understanding was a widespread perception of the New Testament writers. Here I am only concerned with Matthew, in whose Gospel the theme of delayed homecoming seems especially

14. E.g., Davies and Allison, *Matthew*, I, 210; Hagner, *Matthew 1–13*, 19–20; Meier, *Matthew*, 8.

15. For his theory of the protracted exile, see Wright, *NTPG*, 268–72, 299–301, ch. 10 passim; *JVG*, xvi–xvii, 126, 205, 209.

16. Wright, *NTPG*, 269.

relevant to any prevailing consciousness of incomplete return from exile. The story of Jesus and the story of Israel converge. Commentators have often suggested the story of Jesus in Matthew to be the story of the New Israel, especially in relation to the Moses story. If these authors and others are correct, Judaism of the New Testament era heard the story of Moses and the Exodus as a disguised, surrogate account, for the unfinished postexilic days in which they themselves lived. For Matthew, Jesus is metaphor for Israel's return—or better, a metonymy, in which the part serves for the whole. This interpretation effectively reverses the usual trope: *Instead of seeing Israel as a type for Jesus, it understands Jesus as having become parable and instrument of Israel in its unfinished business.*

But it isn't quite enough to say that Israel is saved from its sins when the Messiah comes into his own, for in Matthew's telling, the coming of the Messiah is not welcomed. Between Matt 1:21 and Matt 28:16–20, the initial mandate and the revised, the mission miscarries. And we need to take a look, at least provisionally, at what happened. On five occasions Matthew mentions "sins" (*hamartia*). Three of these derive from his use of Mark's Gospel, whereas two are his own contribution.[17] Besides 1:21, there is the significant verse at the Supper, when Jesus says words over the cup, "This is my blood of the covenant, which is poured out for many for the forgiveness of sins" (Matt 26:28). The words inevitably evoke a sacrificial interpretation, with allusions to the covenant ceremony facilitated by Moses, in Ex 24. This is not a negligible argument, but again we need to read the text in its narrative context.

Furthermore, for many, along with the Supper saying, Matt 1:21 evokes another—the notorious response given to Pilate's protestations at the trial of Jesus: "His blood be on us and on our children" (27:25). Sometimes cited as Matthew's primary contribution to Christian anti-Semitism, this text, like that from the supper, speaks of the blood of Jesus and would seem to be one of the family of texts associated with our theme.

But this text's relation to 1:21 is troublesome. If Jesus' mission is to save his people, the saying in 27:25 seems to deny its success. If the angel's word to Joseph is the mandate for Matthew's plot, the statement in the trial would seem to assure us that the mission has failed. Although

17. Matthew follows Mark in the account of the Baptist's following (Matt 3:6), in the Paralytic story (9: 2, 5, 6), and in the "sin against the Holy Spirit" (12:31).

a failed narrative may be what Matthew is intending to give us, the situation begs for further clarification. The crucifixion seems to have ended the possibility of a fulfilled mission and narrative mandate. This will be the issue of concern in chapter 7.

Wright, as so often is the case, has provided words that vividly express the apparent failure:

> The cross, we note, already had a symbolic meaning throughout the Roman world, long before it had a new one for the Christians. It meant: we Romans run this place, and if you get in our way we'll obliterate you—and do it pretty nastily too. Crucifixion meant that the kingdom hadn't come, not that it had. Crucifixion of a would-be Messiah meant that he wasn't the Messiah, not that he was. When Jesus was crucified, every single disciple knew what it meant: we backed the wrong horse. The game is over.[18]

Any account of Matthew's narrative must take account of the apparent failure of the proclaimed mission of the Messiah and the Roman achievement in so doing. The formula story of the banished prince shares this prejudice, but the picture is again somewhat blurred.

THE MAGI COME—AND DEPART
(MATT 2:1–12)

The contents of Matthew's first chapter address the necessary preliminaries for the narrative. The genealogy establishes the identity of the protagonist, as well as that of the usurper, in a negative fashion. The account of Joseph's dream and the angel's message supplies the mandate for the ensuing narrative. Jesus is to save his people from their sins. It is not until the second chapter that the action begins. When the Magi appear on the scene, coming from outside the horizon of Matthew's story world, their arrival, in the type-scene of the Conspicuous Entry, initiates the action of Matthew's plot. This we have seen, in exploring the homecoming story. Now we see Herod responding with the slaughter of the boys of Bethlehem, like the usurper who exterminates the present regime to the limits of the clan. In observing the Magi visit the child Jesus, we learn of gifts and homage, stimulating associations with Psalm 72 and Isaiah 60. All this we have seen. Now the family must leave the town, and the circuit of the homecoming story begins. And then the Magi leave as well.

18. Wright, *Surprised*, 40.

It is the departure of the Magi that draws one's attention for what it says about the social location of Matthew's narrative.

Raymond Brown has identified Matthew's special source, commonly called the M-Source, as socially located at popular levels of the Christian movement, by which he intended to distinguish it from materials arising in liturgical or legal circles. In this way he explained certain features of Matthew's text, such as vivid imagery, seen in references to blood or dreams, or in extraordinary phenomena such as earthquakes and the dead rising to roam. While some question whether Matthew's text exhibits evidence of a separate Matthean source, the popular quality of the unique material shapes and positions this Gospel. Although Brown cites episodes such as Judas' death or Pilate's wife to make his case, this detail in the story of the Magi will do nicely for our purposes. At the end of the Magi story, as they are about the take their departure, something unexpected happens:

> And having been warned in a dream not to return to Herod, they
> departed for their country by another route. (Matt 2:12)

We are accustomed to this story, so nothing particularly remarkable seems at play here. The dream motif is likewise familiar, being a staple of the incidents in Matthew 1–2, especially in the birth, flight, and return series of Joseph's response to the angel. As with 2:22, no angel is reported at 2:12—leading to the supposition both are redactional adjustments, bringing them in line with the rest of the narrative.[19]

But who is this God, advising them to sneak out by the back route? Who is this God who does not take charge? This is not the God of the establishment, the God of the empire. That God, who takes control of events and adjusts them to fit his program, is glimpsed in the slaughter of the Bethlehem innocents. There we see the take-charge approach that characterizes the God who is in control. This shows us the God of the empire—or, in this case, the emperor's surrogate, Herod.

No, the God who advises the Magi in a dream is another God entirely, whom we recognize as the God of the gypsies, if you will, who enables them to skirt authority, avoid direct confrontation with power figures, and live life in the corners, if not the shadows. The fact that 2:12 may have been adjusted to fit the rest of the narrative simply highlights the fact that the entire infancy account adopts this social outlook and

---

19. Brown, *Birth*, 176–77.

colors the subsequent narrative. The dreams of Joseph, the flight and the delayed return, all contribute to the picture of a peasant people required by circumstances to keep watch for those in power and work around them, staying out of their way.

One way this divide between the social standing of the elites and the rest has been through the concept of the Great Tradition of the elites against the Little Tradition of the peasants. And one version of that construct that promises to be especially congenial for our uses is that version made popular by James Scott under the rubric of the hidden transcript. In particular, the departure of the Magi, and the rest of Matthew's texts, as it falls in line with this outlook, suggests that the entire Gospel can be placed under the heading of the hidden transcript: the voice of the oppressed group when by themselves.

But for now it is the God of the empire that claims our attention. This is the dominant presence, in the narrative and in the world of Matthew, in which the narrative was produced. Within the narrative Rome is represented by Archelaus, a surrogate Herod, and of course Pilate in the concluding chapters of the Gospel. And the heavy hand of the Empire, within the narrative, is found in the cross—as Wright has shown us.

But if Matthew's text as a whole can be said to be a hidden transcript in the little tradition, what can be said of the Great Tradition in the shadow of which it blooms? What can we say of the God of the empire in Matthew's text? Carter makes the case that this text names the God of the empire "Satan,"[20] seen for instance in the desert temptation, in which Satan claims control over the kingdoms of the world, with the authority to dispense them at will (Matt 4:8).

Here Matthew's attitude contrasts sharply with that of Josephus, who believed that "Israel's God has gone over to the Romans."[21] Although Josephus' views cannot be said to be consistent with other Pharisees, he does serve to illustrate a stance regarding violent power that will be on view in the next chapter, where we will explore the conflict between Jesus and the Pharisees. For the moment, we might simply note the theology Josephus' view implies—where violent power most efficiently exerts itself is where God is to be found.

The equation between divinity and violent power is exactly what Rome intended and was at pains to demonstrate. And those demonstra-

20. Carter, "Constructions," 98.
21. Wright, *NTPG*, 374, citing Josephus, *War* 2.390; 5.362–78, etc.

tions took the form of establishing the terms of reality as it was experienced. Within the frame of the gospel narrative that demonstration was the cross. "Crucifixion meant that the kingdom hadn't come, not that it had." It was the object lesson that set the terms of possible freedom and served as a constant reminder who it was that ran the world and determined one's fate. But also, in the frame of the gospel narrative, crucifixion was transformed and the sign of Roman absolute hegemony imploded.

But in Matthew's world, the world in which the gospel was written, the great object lesson of Roman control in Judea was the destroyed temple. Its absence continued as a pressure; its presence was now the "Burnt Place," positioned like a ravaged desert at the former center of the Judean world. This was absolute violence that not only threatened but also accomplished its work. The message of the Burnt Place was that the world has irrevocably changed, and Roman violence had done it. The singular strength of violence is destruction so total that life has to be built again from the ground up, presumably on the terms of the victor.

For Judeans, Rabbinic or Christian, Pharisaic or other, the only task left them was to fashion a future somehow continuous with a long but eclipsed past. For Matthew, the experienced reality was one of the dominance of violence. More than dominance, it was experienced as the very terms of reality itself. There is nothing in Matthew that promotes violence, since it is in no need of promotion; it is the fact at hand. Rather, Matthew's task is to find a way to insert an alternative reality, a reality that derives from his tradition in the Lord, a nonviolent tradition. The work of the Gospel is to find a purchasing point from that tradition to get a hearing in a climate of utter implausibility. And then, in the tale of the transformed cross, to promise the transformation of the Burnt Place, the renewal of the brutalized world.

Matthew's images of a violent God come in the parables—the parable of the Feast in which the king burns the city; the parables of the weeds and of the net, with their fire at the end of the age. Barbara Reid among others has highlighted the contrast between the present nonviolence of the disciples and the eschatological violence of God in Matthew.[22]

How can a violent God demand nonviolence of disciples? A provisional answer can be given in terms of the nature of narrative. The problem is a hole at the heart of nonviolent action—how can it be said

22. Reid, "Violent Endings," 250.

to be successful? How can it be transformative? Contemporary answers sometimes point to the superior effectiveness of nonviolence itself as a tool for resolving conflict. But theological nonviolence raises the question of vindication: How do the nonviolent disciples escape the sinking feeling that God has abandoned them, and they are washed down a bottomless hole? Where is God's vindication, and if it is pending, how is it to be framed?

An example of the difficulty can be seen in the parable of the Unforgiving Servant (Matt 18:23–25). Jesus has just recommended unconditional forgiveness ("seventy-seven times," vv. 21–22). Now he illustrates his point with a parable of a king who demands unconditional forgiveness on the part of his servant—that is, who withholds his own forgiveness on the condition of the servant's unconditional forgiveness. It seems contradictory, and of course it is. But stories have limited means to work with, and one of these is a short set of punishments and rewards to indicate approved or disapproved behavior. When the approved behavior is to abandon the demand for rewards, as in the book of Job, the rewards seem peculiar, to say the least. When the approved behavior is to relax the demand of reprisals, as in forgiveness, narrative has available only reprisals for achieving its resolution.

5

Impostor

"Sir," they said, "we have recalled that that impostor, while he was still
alive, made the claim, 'After three days I will rise.' Give orders, then,
that the grave be secured until the third day, lest his disciples come and
steal him and say to the people, 'He has been raised from the dead.'
This last imposture would be worse than the first."

— Matthew 27:63–64 (NAB)

Impostors and demagogues, under the guise of divine inspiration,
provoked revolutionary actions and impelled the masses to act like
madmen. They led them out into the wilderness so that their God
would show them signs of imminent liberation.

— Josephus, *Jewish Wars*, 2.259

A T THE END OF Matthew's Gospel the Pharisees make an unexpected
appearance. All the gospels agree that the Pharisees were not responsible for the death of Jesus, and reflecting this, Pharisees tend to dis-
appear from later chapters. But Matthew reports an encounter between
Pilate and the Pharisees concerning their desire to have a guard posted
at the tomb. During their exchange Jesus is accused of being an impostor (Matt 27:63, 64). The accusation not only echoes a tendency in the
formula story of the banished prince, but also provides a response and
countercharge to the well-known accusation of hypocrisy that Jesus, in
this Gospel, levels against them. As an expression of the formula story,
it brings forward an element of insecurity in the text concerning the
issue of Jesus' identity. As part of a system of mutual recriminations, it
provides a language for the conflict between the protagonist and antagonists of the main plotline of Matthew's Gospel. By engaging the latter,

Matthew makes a bold response to the former. The conflict addresses the insecurity.

Impostor. Hypocrite. Each of these terms suggests dramatic potential in that they imply adopted roles. It prompts us to seek the meaning of their opposition in Matthew's plot in terms of the mutual charges. But they also are roles that involve pretence and false claims. The dispute, then, is about truth and its simulation. More specifically, it concerns the truth of what it means to be "Israel" and the proper expression of God's presence in the world. Writing in the smoldering aftermath of the destruction of Jerusalem and Temple, in the shadow of imperial domination by Rome, Matthew has produced what Declan Kiberd would call a postcolonial text, following the principle that "postcolonial writing does not begin only when the occupier withdraws: rather it is initiated at the very moment when a native writer formulates a text committed to cultural resistance."[1] Disputes about authenticity and truth consequently include the meaning of resistance to the empire. The conflict between the two sets of antagonists, Jesus and his disciples versus the scribes and Pharisees, is ideological. It concerns the authenticity of their respective positions.

Claims of authenticity preoccupy postcolonial writings, and it is no different here. Commentators agree that Matthew's rather formulaic term for Jesus' opponents, "the scribes and Pharisees," is intended to suggest the proto-rabbinic movement that within Judaism provided competition with Matthew's church, however that is to be understood in detail.[2] Matthew's use of his term corresponds closely with his source in Mark, though in Mark the form of allusion varies, unlike the "scribes and Pharisees" of Matthew.[3] The conflict between Jesus and his opponents in Matthew can then be seen as representing the struggle over the meaningful future of "Israel" in the posttemple era. Rather than a primal struggle between good and evil, it is a dispute over the best form of resistance against the pressure of Roman influence. And although it is a dispute within the family of Judaism, even family quarrels may grow bitter.

1. Kiberd, *Inventing Ireland*, 6.

2. E.g., Harrington, *Matthew*, 14–16.

3. See, e.g., Saldarini, *Pharisees, Scribes and Sadducees*, 157. Also Pickup, "Matthew's and Mark's Pharisees," 108–112, and Harrington, *Matthew*, 15–16.

IMPOSTORS

"I hate that man like the Gates of Death
who says one thing but hides another in his heart."

—Achilles, of Odysseus, *Iliad* 9.378–79

In drawing on the story pattern of the banished and returning prince to shape his plot, Matthew has embedded an integral and persistent threat of imposture as part of its structure, consistent with other examples of the formula. For instance, among the animated films cited earlier, *Anastasia* tells the story of the heir of the Romanov dynasty supposedly surviving the family assassinations in 1917, a known historical event. But when the film was made, the person on whom its main character was based, a certain Anna Anderson, had already been shown through DNA sampling to be a fake. But the film played it straight, following the formula in presenting her as the authentic heir. It could have gone either way. In a certain sense, all versions of the formula story involve "impostors" because the proper way to demonstrate lineage is through a chart of heredity, a family tree, some version of official papers. Lacking these, the formula story employs a subterfuge. It doesn't demonstrate lineal descent properly, but rather makes use of substitutes, such as signs and pointers. Because no claim is verifiable, no claim is verified. All candidates are, in some sense, in the position of impostors.

Again, when Odysseus, hidden away on Calypso's Island for seven years, emerges again into the bright light of narrative action, it is to return home to Ithaca under a disguise. Presenting himself as a beggar who had known Odysseus, he wins time to get the lay of the land and develop a plan for regaining his wife and home. Such dissembling is not a problem for Odysseus, who is known as a liar and deceiver. Large among the achievements on his résumé is the deception of the Trojan horse.

But the ploy introduces a difficulty for Odysseus—if he does not return as himself, how will they believe him when ultimately he reveals his identity? After all, he has been missing for twenty years. Everyone, including his wife, fails to recognize him. The evidence comes down to four signs—his scar, his dog, his bow, and his bed. His aged nurse recognizes the scar on his leg. His faithful dog, Argos, certainly past his best years by now, detects his presence. And because Odysseus alone is capable of stringing his war bow, and he alone should know his marriage bed was shaped from a living olive tree, we also have these persuasive indicators. Signs are not as good as legal papers, but they will have to do. Of course, given a resourceful enough protagonist, they could be faked; the hero could be an impostor.

Then there are the stories. According to the tale, the fanciful adventures of Odysseus' wanderings in Books 9–12, including the episodes with the Lotus-eaters, the Cyclops, Circe, the descent to Hades, and the Sirens, are presented as factual. Meanwhile, the backstories that Odysseus invents after arriving back in Ithaka, are characterized by their greater realism and plausibility—that he escaped from Crete after an attempt to rob him, that he later went to Egypt, where he suffered mutiny and a storm, and more.[4] These, we are to understand, are lies. Why do we agree to believe the fanciful stories and deny the plausible? Not because Odysseus is a truth-teller, for we know better. Nor is it because of his claim to have come from Crete, which is, after all, home of the proverbial liar. Perhaps we recognize that plausibility is not the same as truth and in fact may substitute for it because plausibility is a virtue of fiction, rather than of fact. If it comes simply to trusting the narrator arranging the story world for us, we have the countertestimony of Erich Auerbach. In his famous opening chapter in *Mimesis*, "Odysseus' Scar," he reminds us of the "oft-repeated reproach that Homer is a liar."[5] It certainly complicates our trust in the narrator.

How then do we know that Odysseus is *not* an impostor? Obviously not because he avoids that role, as, say, Achilles might. Nor is it because we are given external evidence to the contrary, because the accounts of his adventures come from the mouth of Odysseus himself. Nor can we say it is because he has little to gain by adopting a false role, for in fact it serves him well, allowing him to prevail over Penelope's suitors. If this hero were playing a double game of pretence—pretending to be Odysseus pretending not to be—it would place him among the most successful of the usurpers! But of course, what we know of Odysseus is enough to assure us that he is the single hero of antiquity crafty enough to be capable of such a deception. Therefore, we might conclude, it must truly be him after all.

4. Odysseus' lying tales appear in the *Odyssey*: 13.290–324 (to Athena), 14.173–407 (to Eumaeus), 17.458–491 (to Antinous), 19.186–353 (to Penelope), and 24.339–53 in Fagles' translation.

5. Auerbach, *Mimesis*, 13.

This imaginative tour among less-than-reliable narrative voices, some as unlikely as those in the *Odyssey*, serves to illustrate an aspect of the story formula of the banished prince—we have no firm assurances. Because every link with the hero's past has been lost, the only possibility of picking up the thread again would be through signs and trials. But with a hero clever enough, these can be faked. By its very structure the formula is open to imposture. In fact, some versions implement that very possibility. The colorful tale of Boris Godunov, dramatized by Alexander Pushkin and converted to opera by Modest Mussorgsky, builds on events involving a usurping tsar, who becomes the target of at least three impostors posing as "Dmitri," the grandson and successor of Ivan the Terrible, the heir whom Godunov was thought to have assassinated. And although the time of troubles that followed were eventually stabilized by the Romanov imperial dynasty for three centuries, that period also ended in turmoil in the Bolshevik revolution. The Russian examples of Anastasia's story and Boris Godunov's drama show the story formula opting for imposture. The *Odyssey* instructs us that the threat of possible imposture worries every instance of its telling.

Discontinuities

The possibility of imposture is built into the formula story because of a gap, a hiatus, at its center—the hidden years when the hero grows into maturity out of sight of the reader's attention. For the pattern to work, the hero's story must contain a break, a fissure so profound that all identity is lost, typically even to the hero. No vestige of credential or status must be left because the return requires selection by sign or wonder. When Arthur pulls the sword Excalibur from the stone, it signals his identity as the "true king," the rightful heir of Uther Pendragon, his unknown father, and not an endorsement of superior capability, or even the capability to govern well. It is no more than an identifier in lieu of more proper, but unavailable, identifiers.

It would not be the same story without the hiatus at the heart of the tale. It would be some other story—for instance, the hero adventure story that takes place between the departure and return, when the adventures usually take place. By contrast, the story of the banished prince works the unused territory, spending no time at all in the period between departure and return, but paying great attention to the departure and the return, especially the latter. On the one hand, it is this loss of identity, this amnesia through which the story of the hero passes, that opens the story to the possibility of imposture, so that stories like Anastasia, or Boris Gudonov, are possible versions of the tale. On the other hand, the pattern carries promise. The story pattern sketches a way to inject fresh blood through (unintentional as well as intentional) imposture into a royal line, without claiming to do so. And with this is the matter of acquiring the common touch, from time spent among the common folk. The hero, having shared the experiences of the common populace, comes to understand their values. And so, in Shakespeare's *I Henry IV*, a drama that spends much of its time during the hiatus, Prince Hal's sojourns with Falstaff show him acquiring an education in the popular mind that will serve him well later on. And in another expression of the Russian imagination seen earlier, legend depicts the tsar traveling incognito among the peasants. It allowed the peasantry to sustain their loyalty to the tsar, despite unfavorable policies of the court. They could assign blame for unpleasant policies to the bureaucracy around him because the tsar surely understood the people and would not allow such mischief on his own.[6]

In this way, the formula story of the banished prince emphasizes the transformation that occurs in private, in the hidden time. The transformation is so complete that the identity has to be rediscovered. It is a time of hiddenness, of incognito mystery, the cocoon between the caterpillar and the butterfly, a place of silence and timelessness. It is the site of the loss of identity and the recovery of that identity—with the trust that the new identity somehow is in continuity with the old, a loss so entire that it must be rebuilt from the ground up.

The hiatus, the gap in the center of the unfolding tale between the flight and the return, the lost time when the hero is out of sight, growing toward maturity, creates its own issues. It can be seen as a crisis in the narrative's ability to continue, which otherwise threatens to come to a standstill. Odysseus' seven-year eclipse, out of sight of any who remember him, might amount to a permanent retirement, until Telemachus nudges his story back to life by initiating his search.

---

6. Scott, *Domination and the Art of Resistance*, 96–103.

Matthew

The Pharisees' charge of imposture in Matt 27:63, 64 is commonly translated into personal terms, as *deceit* or *fraud*. Like *hypocrisy*, it implies playing a part. By choosing the translation "impostor" and "imposture" in Matthew 27:63, 64, the NAB takes the position that the deception concerns a role falsely adopted—"this impostor."

> The chief priests and the Pharisees
> gathered before Pilate and said,
> "Sir, we remember
> that this impostor while still alive
> said, 'After three days I will be raised up.'
> Give orders, then, that the grave
> be secured until the third day,
> lest his disciples come and steal him
> and say to the people,
> 'He has been raised from the dead.'
> This last imposture would be worse
> than the first." (Matt 27:62–64)

Actually, two impostures are mentioned. Although the second clearly refers to the Resurrection, critics are divided on the meaning of "the first" imposture. Most point to the title of Messiah as at issue.[7] Matthew's Gospel, with its formula-story adjustments, presents the coming of the Messiah as a return. But as we have seen, invoking the story formula is not an unmixed good. More than simply establishing homecoming as a desirable outcome for the narrative, it also places the authenticity of the homecoming under dispute. The question about homecoming turns out to be the more difficult question of the authentic homecoming. Although the formula allows readers to understand and accept that the authentic descendent of the house of David can emerge from an unexpected place, it also, in making an issue of the unexpected origin, highlights the need to secure that claim to authenticity.

In the Gospel, the period of occultation of the hero occurs at the end of chapter 2, where the hidden location is identified as "Nazareth." It is to Nazareth that the child departs at the end of the infancy narrative. And it is from Nazareth that Jesus, many years later, emerges to mount a ministry that culminates in the return to Judea:

---

7. So we take it here, in convergence with the formula story of the banished prince.

He went and dwelt in a town called Nazareth (2:23). [...]
He left Nazareth and went to live
in Capernaum by the sea,
in the region of Zebulon and Naphthali (4:13).

In the interim, he disappears from the story. We know of nothing what happens in Nazareth. Time passes; memories of Bethlehem recede into the past. Jesus grows to maturity, available for the return to homeland and rightful claims. But none of this is known to the new set of characters in the story. He returns to a society that does not recognize him.

When he makes his reappearance, the Gospel text shows evidence of a certain anxiety about his identity. One indication of this is the simple fact that he is provided with an excess of identifications: Savior, Son of Man, Son of God, Emmanuel, Servant of Yahweh, Son of David. We are more familiar with these when they are examined in Christological studies, where they are read as signals of the evangelist's view of Jesus' salvific role and divinity.[8] In the present context, not only do they represent theological data distributed by Matthew throughout the text, but also the very richness of their attribution can be read as symptomatic of an uneasiness.

The flurry of titles, striving to name an identity for Jesus, reflects a predicament in the text. It is a crisis of the narrative, not in the narrative. Narrative crises are an expected and necessary feature of plots, as the main character encounters opposition that increases in intensity, until a decision is forced, and the action takes a new direction. Rather, this crisis is one that threatens the continuation of the narrative itself, insofar as it seems to lose focus and direction. Although patterns of hierarchy can be described among the list of titles and often are, these seldom are left undisputed. At the same time, in their comprehensiveness, it would seem that no attribution is rejected.

Further evidence of anxiety in the narrative appears in the genealogy with which Matthew begins his account. If the Banished Prince formula works only when the amnesiac moment is complete—that is, when the hero has no papers, no genealogical record, what do we make

---

8. In a study not uncontested, Kingsbury, *Structure, Christology, Kingdom,* has argued for the priority of the Son of God title. It is worth noting that the Son of David is also emphasized by Matthew—ten references as opposed to four each in Mark and Luke.

of that fact that Matthew conspicuously begins with a genealogy? Three considerations might cause us to hesitate to claim too much of this credential. First, it contains its own instability, its own crises, as we have seen. The two rather prominent breaks in the series, each of which cause the list to resume with a new character, even in a different genre, qualifies its helpfulness as testimony. The genealogy seems to incorporate the insecurity of discontinuity within the continuity that it promises. A second qualification is that the genealogy appears at the beginning, before the story begins, when it is actually needed later, after the hiatus in the narrative. It is then that Jesus appears to the world as an unknown quantity, ready to conduct his ministry. A third difficulty is linked to this. The genealogy is not intended to allay doubts of the personae in the narrative. Rather, it is directed to the reader, who is outside the story and outside the awareness of the characters in the story. The genealogy provides reassurances to the reader, not the characters that inhabit the story. It is positioned where it is to help the reader negotiate the leap across the division between the departure for Nazareth and the emergence. It is not there to provide Jesus with popular support by those in the story with him.

An even more explicit symptom of anxiety is found in Matthew's apologetics, particularly in the crucial passages of the birth story (1:18–25) and the guards at the tomb (27:62–66; 28:4, 11–15). The first responds to the suspected charge that Jesus was born illegitimate. We recognize here issues related to the "first imposture" of the Pharisees' accusation. The second corresponds to the "last imposture." Concerning these, Brown noted, "If that charge [of illegitimacy] were already in circulation when Matthew was writing, his narrative could be read as an effective response to it, even as the peculiarly Matthean narrative of the guard at the tomb could be read as an effective response to the Jewish charge that Jesus' disciples had stolen his body from the tomb." Brown situates these two texts within a literary framing device that we might consider the pattern of the two Josephs—Joseph of Nazareth and Joseph of Arimathea.[9] The Gospel begins with the birth, flight, and return pat-

---

9. Brown, *Birth*, 142. In Brown's reconstruction of the form, the three tomb stories alternate with reports of the guards at the tomb. The pattern of alternation between the accounts of the followers of Jesus and the more negative accounts relating the efforts of the opposition is also found in the infancy narrative, with the birth, flight, and return stories interlarded with accounts of Herod's oppositional activity.

tern, featuring Joseph, the husband of Mary. It ends with the events that begin at the tomb provided by Joseph of Arimathea.

All told, a ripple of anxiety troubles the text. It concerns the identity of Jesus, whose credentials are thrown into question by his period of lost identity. In Matthew's plot, two moments serve a narrative function of identifying and commissioning the protagonist, Jesus. The first is the mission to Israel (1:21); the second is the mission to the nations (28:16–20). Both labor under the accusation of imposture in the Pharisees' charge.

HYPOCRITES

"I hate that man like the Gates of Death, who,
ground down by poverty, stoops to peddling lies."

—Odysseus to Laertes, *Odyssey*, 14.182–83

It is well known that Matthew makes liberal use of the term *hypocrite*. It appears fifteen times in the Gospel, as opposed to one time in Mark. Of these, thirteen refer directly or implicitly to the Pharisees, usually under the formulaic combination, "the scribes and Pharisees."[10] Who is Matthew targeting here? Many consider the early rabbinic movement to be a convergence of various Judean religious movements that regrouped after the Temple disaster. Those of the scribal profession and the sectarian Pharisees, originally distinct groups, would have come together and are represented in the Gospel under the formulaic label, "scribes and Pharisees."[11] Matthew's use of this term corresponds closely with his source in Mark,[12] although in Mark the form of allusion varies, unlike the formulaic regularity of the phrase "scribes and Pharisees" in Matthew.[13]

Matthew, however, has added two prominent statements concerning the "scribes and Pharisees" to the narrative he received from Mark. They serve to provide a frame for the public ministry of Jesus (or the ris-

10. See Matt 6:2, 5, 16; 7:5; 15:7; 16:3; 22:18; 23:13, 14, 15, 23, 25, 27, 29; 24 51. The single instance in Mark is 7:6, its parallel at Matt 15:7. "Hypocrisy" is found one time in each—Matt 23:28; Mark 12:5. For a complete list of opponents and their cited texts see Carter, *Storyteller*, 231.

11. Harrington, *Matthew*, 15–16.

12. Pickup, "Matthew's and Mark's Pharisees," 108–112.

13. Saldarini, *Pharisees, Scribes and Sadducees*, 157. He adds: "In summary usually the scribes are omitted and the Pharisees added to passages where there is confrontation with Jesus. The Pharisees are seen as more active opponents of Jesus than the scribes." (164)

ing action of the plot). The first—brief, but programmatic—establishes Jesus' position in contrast to them:

I tell you, unless your righteousness surpasses that of the scribes and Pharisees, you will not enter into the kingdom of heaven" (Matt 5:20).

The second and final statement in the frame is, of course, the seven "Woes" in chapter 23, with their resounding refrain: "Woe to you, scribes and Pharisees, you hypocrites. . . ." Between these two we find the account of growing opposition and rising tension, almost always marked by the identification of the opposition as "the scribes and Pharisees." And in enough cases to make the connection permanent, they are identified as "hypocrites." This is the language of ideological contestation. It frames the time of conflict—or, in terms of the formula story, the time of return—from the opening statement of Jesus to the closing indictments. Furthermore, of course, we must add the Pharisees' surprising appearance at the end of Matthew's Gospel, at which time they make their "imposture" charge, providing the narrative with a response to Jesus' declarations of their hypocrisy. In these mutual recriminations we find the "rhetoric of blame"[14] that provides a language for the conflict between the protagonist and antagonists of the main plotline of Matthew's Gospel.

Two Roles in Opposition

The charge of hypocrisy is usually and quite naturally understood as an attack on personal integrity. It names someone as two-faced, one who says one thing while meaning another, or pretends to more saintliness than the facts warrant. This is how we use it today, as when the media name as hypocrites those politicians who publicly condemn behaviors they privately practice. But there is more to be noticed in the word. The Greek original emerged from the context of stage acting and implied a distinction between one's personal character and the public presentation—that is, pretense. Given their facility for convincingly assuming different personae, actors have at times provided a byword for insincerity. And although we frequently interpret hypocrisy as lack of personal

---

14. Said, *Culture and Imperialism*, 18, uses the phrase to name the conflicts among colonized peoples struggling to reclaim identity in the face of imperial subjugation. Postcolonial themes seem singularly appropriate in examining the post-Temple struggle within Judaism.

integrity, in the Gospel its meaning seems to include the earlier sense of play-acting, in which characters in a dramatic conflict engage each other.[15]

The interpretation in personal terms is similar to the way the accusation of imposture in Matt 27:63–64 is frequently translated as *deceit* or *fraud*. But imposture, like hypocrisy, implies playing a part, or acting out a role. Each of the two terms implies role-playing and is ready-made for use in plotted conflict. Furthermore, each term implies that the party charged as guilty is adopting a *false* role. It is this falseness that allows for ideological conflict, in the sense that each holds the other's position to be a pose. The balance of the dispute between the two parties pivots on which side is found to be authentic and which side falsely labels the other as inauthentic. Authenticity emerges as a primary theme in the conflict between Jesus and the Pharisees.

Matthew's Gospel, of course, speaks from one side of this dispute, both defending it and attacking the position of its opponents. We saw earlier the defense presented against the charge of imposture in the form of apologetics concerning the birth and resurrection of Jesus. Complementing this approach, Matthew's text also mounts an attack against the rival position of the "scribes and Pharisees." Using a strategy of binary language of *inside* and *outside,* the Gospel puts inner character and outer appearances to the test.

Three Matthean texts serve to make the point. The first gives directions for the disciples' action in the first chapter of the Sermon on the Mount, Matthew 5. The second, in the second chapter of the Sermon, Matthew 6, looks on the opposite side to list some prohibitions limiting the disciples' action. The third, the Woes of Matthew 23, completes the second set of texts by challenging the scribes and Pharisees that adopt the practices prohibited to the disciples. In each case a theme of violence or conflict surfaces. In Matthew's text, there is a connection between hypocrisy, in its separation of role and person, appearance and character, and violence. It will be our task to investigate that connection.

---

15. Greek dictionary (853) notes that in the references to "hypocrites" in Matt 6:2, 5, 16 "the mng [meaning]. 'play-actor' is strongly felt." In Matthew's time, in contrast to our own, that connotation was apparently still part of the felt meaning.

Matthew 5

Here in the Sermon on the Mount the doubleness of inside and outside finds its first major expression, immediately following 5:20—the warning that righteousness should exceed that of the scribes and Pharisees. If we consider action as outward and motivation as inward, the series of radical reinterpretations of the law that fill the bulk of chapter 5 can be read as pushing the prohibitions of certain socially detrimental actions back to their interior motivations and addressing them at that level. Reciting false oaths dissolves as a problem if lying is eliminated. So it is with adultery, lust, and so forth. The nexus between inside and outside is affirmed by dramatizing the causal effects of moving from inward to outward.

It needs to be noted that the injunctions more closely related to Matthew's views of conflict, those on anger, nonretaliation, and loving enemies (5:21–26, 38–42, 43–48), explicitly pose the question of violence in terms of interior motivation and outward action. The first advises a policy of reconciliation (5:24–25) as an outgoing action that will render the impulse of prayer more authentic. The recommendation of nonretaliation (5:39) is illustrated by examples of refusing an action that seems impossible to control. And the apparent interior impulse of love of enemies is coupled to praying for them. The entire series is anchored by the injunction of imitation: "So be perfect, just as your heavenly Father is perfect" (5:48). The prayer seals the series because no one successfully dissembles in prayer. Where is there room for imposture here?

Matthew 6

Developing this theme in the next chapter, the counsels on almsgiving, prayer, and fasting allow for the contrasting theme of "hypocrisy" to emerge (6:2, 5, 16). Avoiding hypocrisy again is illustrated by contrasts of inside and outside, but this time by way of the public arena and the private enclosure—prayer in secret, in the inner room with the door closed (6:6); almsgiving in which one hand isn't aware of the other's generosity (6:3); fasting without display (6:17–18). The lack of public display ensures authentic action. The taint of hypocrisy is not risked because no set of appearances provides a competing motivation, such as vanity, to interfere with the sincerity of the worshipful action.

Perhaps surprisingly, the conflict theme appears in the series by way of adding the Lord's Prayer as a model for the disciple. The short commentary following selects the petition about forgiveness for expansion:

> If you forgive others their transgression,
> your heavenly Father will forgive you.
> But if you do not forgive others,
> neither will your Father
> forgive your transgressions. (6:14–15)

This not only echoes the injunction of 5:48 on being perfect as your heavenly Father is perfect, but it also anticipates the fuller treatment of forgiveness in the fourth Matthean discourse of chapter 18. And with forgiveness, another model of reconciliation is presented for the willing disciple. In all cases, a transparency of motivation and action, inside and outside, prevails.

Matthew 23

The excoriating series of Woes insist on the discontinuity between inner person and outer role that is identified with hypocrisy. The tolling of the phrase, "Woe to you scribes and Pharisees, hypocrites," sets a tone of finality. Commentators, perhaps influenced by Luke's example (Luke 6:20–26), have considered Matthew's Woes in contrast with the Beatitudes[16] as part of a more general pairing of the first and last discourses of Matthew. The first Woe, accusing the hypocrites of shutting the gate of the Kingdom, establishes a direct contract with the invitation of the Beatitudes—"Yours is the Kingdom of Heaven." Other topics taken up in the Woes—oaths, tithes, and killing—echo those of the Sermon.

As the series builds to a climax, it employs images that highlight the contradiction of exterior presentation and inner reality with the metaphors of the cup and plate, clean on the outside but full of plunder and intemperance within (23:25), and of whitewashed tombs full of dead men's bones (23:27, 28). These passages that exploit the opposition of inside and outside seem to make an argument for personal integrity, but they also raise the question of the better social policy. Which is the better platform on which to mount a program of renewal for the House of Israel? Which better expresses what Israel is about? What is at issue is the character, the nature of this people, and their relationship to God.

16. Perhaps in line with the Covenant sanctions of blessings and curses (e.g., Deut 27:11—28:68).

The charge being made here is that the Pharisees party is building its house on sand. It hears, but does not do. Transparency should be the identifying mark of the Israelite, rather than an outside appearance that hides an unworthy, even violent, inner or private life. But the further charge is that the program itself is hypocritical, and not just its adherents. The program is one that promises what it does not deliver, that looks good, but stops there. Matthew calls for more, for a *metanoia*, a change of heart, a new direction, a break with the recent past to ground a fresh beginning.

Two Models of Resistance

If we accept the idea that the opposition between Jesus and the Pharisees entails two competing programs, the question follows as to how we should conceive their point of conflict. What is the nub of their differences?

One option would be to see contrasted here two views of what it means to be holy. On the one side is the Pharisees' route of ritual purity; on the other, Matthew's renewal by way of personal integrity. But both have their advantages and disadvantages. Ritual routes to purity deeply involve believers by touching all dimensions of life but risk the dangers of formalism and attenuated social responsibilities. The purity of integrity honors truth and conscience but risks self-righteousness or the kind of intolerance that Matthew's Gospel seems to exhibit at times.

We can take a clue from Marcus Borg, who points out that the various "sects" in first-century Judea shared a common commitment to resist the Roman presence in the land, though they differed dramatically in how that resistance might be pursued.[17] Borg, following Jacob Neusner, has described the purity regulations of the Pharisees, especially in meal regulations, as a policy of resistance to the invasion of the gentile Roman occupation of Judea. Extending the regulations for priestly families to the entire population, purity became a mode of resisting cultural imperialism that continued into the later period.[18]

> The Pharisaic intensification of purity laws and tithing not only flowed out of the quest for holiness, but sought to counter directly the corrosive effects of Roman political control and Gentile

---

17. Borg, *Conflict*, 55–65; Horsley, *Spiral* 15–19, 33–58.
18. Borg, *Conflict*, 43–65. See also, Harrington, *Matthew*, 14–15.

influence. . . . The conviction that the land was holy continued to
develop in the postbiblical and rabbinic periods.[19]

Borg is calling for a reassessment of the traditional view that the
Zealots represented the only real form of resistance to Rome, with the
Sadducees displaying complicity and the Pharisees, indifference. His
theory acts on the assumption that every subjected people resists in
some way, though most do not do so openly.[20] Borg's argument moves in
the direction of positing a conflict between the Pharisees and Jesus over
the meaning of holiness. The Pharisees resisted gentile contamination by
extending the purity rules originally applied to priests and their families to the entire nation, a kingdom of priests and a holy nation. Setting
themselves apart, especially by meal regulations, they proposed to maintain cultural and religious integrity and avoid gentile contamination.
While the Pharisees strove to achieve holiness by way of purity rules,
Jesus proposed a contrasting concept of holiness based on compassion.
Known for his inclusive meals, he turned the Pharisee program on its
head, in the name of reaching out to the vulnerable and dispossessed,
rather than writing them out of the holy population.

As we saw earlier in chapter 2, Mark's Gospel can be said to follow
this line of thought when it addresses the theme of ritual purity directly
by placing it as pivot of his treatment of the conflict between Jesus and
his opponents—pitting the Holy Spirit against the "unclean spirits."[21]
Here it serves the dispute concerning the nature of holiness—whether
in the model of purity, as the religious authorities would have it, or as
compassion, as Mark's Jesus, who rather consistently violates purity rules
in his healings, proposes.

But Matthew's text is doing something more, and for this we might
press Borg's notion of resistance further and see in it evidence of the
political, posttemple setting of Matthew's church. The purity discourse
that provided the language of conflict for Mark's plot is now enlisted as
metaphor for the new terms of ideological conflict in Matthew—those of
hypocrisy and imposture. Given Matthew's situation in the posttemple
world of Judaism, the resistance role of Pharisaic purity regulations
help us understand the place the theme has in this Gospel. The nub

19. Borg, *Conflict*, 74, 75.
20. See J. Scott, *Domination*, for a fuller expression of this thesis.
21. Beck, *Nonviolent Story*, 70–75.

of the dispute has shifted from the proper understanding of holiness to something else: that which constitutes an effective resistance to the Roman presence. "Hypocrisy" is a judgment on the purity program of the Pharisees as inadequate to the task and ultimately inadequate to represent the truth about "Israel."

But the Pharisees are not the only agents of resistance in this text. Matthew, for his part, offers a form of resistance in the announcement of the "Kingdom of Heaven," proposed in opposition or contrast to the imperial presumption to rule the world. Jesus' messianic claim (in Matthew, at least) is his "imposture." The scribes and Pharisees' response to this claim of the kingdom is to reject it. Warren Carter has devoted a life of scholarship to the prospect that Matthew's Gospel is "a counternarrative, a work of resistance," that "challenges the perception that Rome should rule the world."[22] Noting how scholars have examined the social benefits of the Christian movement in the impersonal world of empire, he extends the argument to include the Gospel's theological challenge to Roman ideology and its claims of sovereignty, divine presence in the world, and privilege to rule in God's name.[23]

In the last instance, he discusses three of the titles attributed to Jesus in the Gospel—Christ, King, and Son. In each of these, Jesus usurps a role Rome reserved for itself or for its emperor. Or, to speak from the perspective of Matthew's text, roles that Rome usurped. "Messiah," or "Anointed One," points to a commissioning. But because the Gospel necessarily focuses it, in 1:21, as Savior ("save his people from their sins"), and then almost immediately, "Emmanuel," that is, "God with us," the presence of God on the earth, they also are brought into tension with the Empire. They confront the emperor's claim to exclusive use of the titles of *Soter*, "savior," as well as the manifestation or presence of the divinity on earth. "King," along with the provocative proclamation of the Kingdom of God, rather obviously challenges Roman hegemony and results in the ironic *titulum* on the cross: "King of the Jews." Augustus is associated with the third title, "Son" (of God), but subsequent emperors also used the title to give theological support to the regime. The "Pax Romana" that prevailed in the New Testament times was a product of the combined influences of brutal military use of force and theological propaganda. The Gospel confronts the latter with counterclaims and the

22. Carter, *Matthew and Empire*, 53.
23. Carter, *Matthew and Empire*, 57–74.

former with nonviolence and nonretaliation. Borrowing James Scott's idea of hidden transcripts—the private discourse of subjugated peoples as opposed to their "public transcripts" of guarded accommodation—to position the Gospel in relation to the empire, Carter sees a place for Matthew's text as circulating among a faith community that contests imperial claims.[24] Here, as with the Pharisaic/rabbinic movement, we have a line of resistance to the Roman influence.

MATTHEW AS POSTCOLONIAL TEXT

Because Matthew's Gospel protests the ultimate claims of the Roman Empire, but also presents its claim as opposing the Pharisees' alternative claim to do the same, it is resistance writing of a particular kind. The recurring theme that emerges in this dispute is authenticity, both in the narrower sense of the integrity of the persons involved and in the larger sense of the better representation of true "Israel."

For reasons like these—resistance to imperial presence, rivalry with other schools of resistance, the quest for purity of origins, especially under the rubric of authenticity—we turn to those studies that deal specifically with such issues and learn to read Matthew as a postcolonial text. The work of resistance writing consists, Edward Said reminds us, "in the rediscovery and repatriation of what had been suppressed in the natives' past by the processes of imperialism."[25] This is a process full of jeopardy, false starts, and sometimes rancorous dispute.

The imperial example of the Irish experience is illustrative. As Edward Said has shown how the Orient provided Western Europe with a foil against which it defined its own character, so Declan Kiberd has shown how England in many ways "invented" Ireland as its other: "the image of Ireland as not-England."[26] A lost culture, "suppressed in the natives' past by the processes of imperialism," is submerged beneath a caricature devised by the self-serving imperial imagination—only later, in an inverse process, to be imaginatively retrieved by native writers. In the effort to retrieve a national identity, diverse theories contended among the Irish concerning what it meant to be Irish.

24. Carter, *Scott*, 91–93.

25. Said, *Culture and Imperialism*, 210.

26. Said, *Orientalism*; Kiberd, *Inventing Ireland*, 30.

> But who or what is "Irish?" What defines Irishness? Is it Irish blood
> (a tautological concept in itself)? Is it residence in Ireland (but then
> how about all the wild geese and emigrants)? What are the essen-
> tials or essences needed to qualify as "Irish"?[27]

The many answers diverge, but share a common direction, the quest for the authentic soul of the people, returning "back to a society pure and uncontaminated."[28]

But the attempted return to pure origins, to a unique character that defines a people, encounters a prohibitive difficulty. Behind the im-pulses that drive the quest is the desire to bridge a gap that separates the national revivalist from an unknown past. Here too the pattern of the hiatus looms in its ambiguous role, making possible the story of return even while bringing the return under dispute. The loss of identity that is felt to have occurred under foreign domination and cultural hegemony poses the issue of realizing any cultural identity. But because the sup-posed original identity is lost, hidden from memory, it needs to be re-constructed. The quest of the authentic "soul" of the people encounters a paradox, captured in Kiberd's title, *Inventing Ireland*. For how can au-thenticity be a matter of invention? And Vincent Cheng noted Kiberd's use of the vocabulary of authenticity, even while criticizing the efforts toward, or even the possibility of, reviving an "authentic" past.[29]

Here we encounter, in one of its many forms, the dilemma of the postcolonial writer, typically posed as the problem of using the oppres-sor's language and culture to express an opposition to cultural oppression. Kiberd writes in English, not Irish, as did Joyce and Yeats. The problem of retrieving a lost language is only one part of the daunting task of retriev-ing a lost culture. For not only does the lack of a factual record allow an expansive degree of freedom in reconstructing pure origins, but it allows a diversity of "authentic" versions contending for primacy. For Yeats it meant building a mythic prehistory of Ireland. For others, a revival of the Gaelic language. For Joyce it meant a postcolonial fiction as a critique of the empire, in a heightened version of the imperial language. Which is the "true," the most authentic, story of origins? And this leads to another, equally important, theme for the understanding postcolonial struggles—the implication of competing "authenticities." For if our story is authentic, then the others must be fake.

27. Cheng, "Authenticity," 240.
28. Bendix, *Authenticity,* 7, 16.
29. Cheng, "Authenticity," 243.

The notion of authenticity implies the existence of its opposite, the fake, and this dichotomous construct is at the heart of what make authenticity problematic. In religious discourse, identifying something as essential to a particular faith "serve to exclude other concepts, practices, even entire branches of [this religion] as inessential or even illegitimate." Similarly, identifying some cultural expression or artifacts as authentic genuine, trustworthy, or legitimate simultaneously implies that other manifestations are fake, spurious, and even illegitimate.[30]

In the wake of reified constructions of the "authentic" origins of a people, which differ from each other and are in competition, there follows a turbulent chronicle, often enough of violent reprisals, civil conflicts, and even ethnic cleansing.

Metanoia: Breaking with the Theology of Force

Edward Said organizes his book, *Culture and Imperialism*, in separate sections, so that the struggle between the native culture and the imperialist is treated in a different place than the struggle among native groups to represent the true character of the native culture, on the behalf of which the struggle is made. The two offer distinct possibilities for trouble and are wisely kept separate.[31]

Matthew's contradictory statements about violence and nonviolence owe something to the conflicting demands of these two fronts. In rejecting one source of violence, Matthew risks another. In resisting Rome's theology of force, Matthew comes into conflict with other schools of resistance that do not, and it is in this arena, depicted in the narrative plotline of conflict between Jesus and the Pharisees, that Matthew's rhetoric of harsh, even violent, retribution surfaces.

Matthew's rejection of Roman theology of force is complete. Jesus' call for conversion provides entry into "the Kingdom of heaven," that is, God's alternative rule. As an alternative reign, a thorough rejection of the Roman reality, rather than an accommodation to it, the announcement puts the ministry of Jesus in a posture of resistance. Entry is established not by purity rules, but by repentance; not by separation, but by a new identity.

---

30. Bendix, *Authenticity*, 9; referencing Jonathan Cohen, "If Rabbi Akiba were alive today . . ." or The Authenticity Argument," *American Jewish Congress* 37, 136.

31. Said, *Culture and Imperialism*, chs. 2 and 3.

It is in this context that we might understand the call to conversion and *metanoia*, repentance. In Matthew 4:17, after Jesus emerges from Nazareth and relocates in Capernaum, we hear him announce his ministry: "Repent, for the kingdom of heaven is at hand." Here repentance signifies "a radical change of heart and mind; a rebirth of sorts."[32] It is the radical break with the past that the Baptist called for (3:3) and that informs Jesus' ministry as well (4:17). Again a hiatus, a gap, is disclosed as crucial for Matthew's approach to the new. A hiatus must be experienced in the lives of the converted as well.

It is here that Matthew encounters the postcolonial dilemma—the problem of resisting the oppressor with the tools of the oppression. His solution is to break completely with the ideology of the dominating culture of empire. He implies that anything less is inadequate to renew Israel. Authentic continuity paradoxically requires discontinuity. The early rabbis project a future in continuity with what they've known. Matthew insists on a more profound break, and he risks continuity more dangerously. But in his search for authenticity, he reaches back further, to foundational texts, to origins. And here he risks the conflicts of internecine rivalry among resisters.

Matthew's complaint about the Pharisees is that they fail to complete the break with the Roman version of reality. In their use of the Roman system he detects complicity. The converse of breaking ties with a culture of violence is to remain in complicity with it. This is a charge that Matthew makes with his elaboration of the accusation, "hypocrite." They present the appearance of resistance, but fail to carry it through, to internalize it.

In the taxation story at Matt 17:24–27 the issue of paying the tax is resolved by drawing the required sum from a fish. Apart from any inherent lesson of the story,[33] the episode shows Jesus and his disciples without the coins that are necessary. This prepares us for a certain nuance in the debate story in the Temple at the end of the Gospel. When the Pharisees and Herodians question Jesus about the duty of paying Caesar, Jesus requests a coin, not having any himself. The coin produced is shown to have the image of Caesar on it. Not only is this exploiting the uses of imperialism, even while protesting it, but it also shows them

---

32. Davies and Allison, *Matthew 1–7*, 388.

33. Carter, *Matthew and Empire*, 130–144, makes the case that the story is a critique of the post-70 tax for the Temple of Jupiter Capitolinus levied by Vespasian.

carrying an image of a "god" into the Temple precincts (Matt 22:20–21). They have compromised; Jesus and his disciples have not.

Such actions also imply complicity with a theology of force and the culture of imperial violence that requires refusal. This aspect is seen clearly in the "Woes" of Matthew 23. The series peaks in intensity when it arrives at the theme of the bloody treatment of the prophets (23:30). At this point, the deliberate charge of violent behavior, already implied in the metaphor of the tombs, is explicitly directed at the "hypocrites," their pious exterior masking deadly intent. The diatribe concludes with a lament over the city of Jerusalem, "killing the prophets and stoning those who are sent to her" (23:37). For Matthew, the city, already destroyed, persists as a vivid memory. In the narrative that he writes, Jesus' words prepare the ground of his own death in that city, in the tradition of the prophets.

The phrase "innocent blood," at 23:35, anticipates later passages—the death of Judas (27:6, 7) and the protestations of Pilate (27:24, 25), along with the "blood of the covenant" proclaimed at the supper (26:28). These will need to be considered in light of the conflict resolution of Matthew's plot. For the moment, we can note that Matthew clearly links hypocrisy with violence and finds a symptom in the play of contrast between inner and outer realities.

The primary event in the given narrative that displays complicity with Roman violence is, of course, the crucifixion. What happens on the part of Jesus' Jewish opponents is not a brandishing of weapons and a personal application of violent force, but rather use made of the convenient might of the Roman military authority. It is not so much a matter of being violent as it is a matter of failing to be nonviolent. It is a revival of identity that still manages to borrow.

Risking Violence

Drawing a strict line against the imperial violence of Roman theology, Matthew risks embracing violence from another direction. We encounter in Matthew's text an unmistakable drive for authenticity. It expresses itself in a desire to return to origins, with implied contrast with the rabbinic competitors of Matthew's community. Daniel Harrington puts it this way:

Whereas the early rabbis appealed to pre-A.D. 70 teachers like Hillel and Shammai for precedents, Matthew went back to the Scriptures to show a continuity between the ancient Jewish tradition and the Christian movement. The most obvious element in this program is the use of "fulfillment" or "formula" quotations in which an OT quotation is introduced by a phrase such as "all this took place to fulfill what the Lord had spoken through the prophet."[34]

In other words, in the search for authentic origins, Matthew goes back the full distance to Abraham and Moses, David and Isaiah, while the rabbis reconstruct what they had known before. It is clearly easier to make a claim of authenticity with a demonstration of continuity than to make the same claim across a distance broken by discontinuity. And yet that is what Matthew does. For if you wish to break with the recent past while remaining in the tradition, your only recourse is the distant past of foundational origins.

So it is that "purity" takes on a new meaning. In Mark's Gospel, the ritual cleansings were exploited to give the binary language of *holy/unclean* to the narrative conflict. In Matthew the theme of purity is adopted to gauge the *authenticity* of the posttemple positions in the Woes of chapter 23. The "purity" drive toward purging evil from the world of the story that moves certain narratives, active in Mark's Gospel,[35] finds a new expression in the similar urge to purge unclean ideological influences from the society of the holy. For the quest for "pure" origins, the "pure" ideals of a people's identity, can move toward narrative strategies of violent cleansing, the purgation that ensures a happy ending, just as certainly as militant aversion to the unclean.

The critical discourse of postcolonialism repeatedly warns against the attempt to achieve a purity of origins, as necessarily projecting a failed attempt to retrieve a lost social identity and ensuring that the effort will produce a caricature of national character. Furthermore, the quest for authenticity can be, and has been, a source of deadly conflict, as the troubling phrase "ethnic cleansing" reminds us.[36] When cultural

34. Harrington, *Matthew*, 17.

35. Beck, *Nonviolent Story*, 136–37.

36. Lionel Trilling traces a penchant for violence back to the roots of the word *authenticity*: "*Authenteo*: to have full power over; also, to commit a murder. *Authentes*: not only a master and a doer, but also a perpetrator, a murderer, even a self-murderer, a suicide." Bendix adds: "Such etymological layers need not reverberate fully in the present usage of the term, although the violence caused in the name of, say, ethnic of religious

ideals become set as the pure and authentic essence of a people, in competition with other equally fixed ideals borne by other groups, troubles brew. Because the notion of authenticity implies the existence of its opposite, the fake, "absolute" truths come into conflict. Because culture wars are largely fought on the page, in imagined representations in the arena proper to culture, narrative with its conflicts and conflict resolutions is a privileged site for the waging of "absolute" truths, with absolute consequences imagined. It can be shown, as I have tried to do with the Gospel of Mark following the folk narrative analyses of Pierre Kongas and Elie Maranda, that narratives tend to resolve their conflicts with two problematic moves—(a) the attempt to achieve satisfaction, or "justice," by evening the score, and (b) the impulse to cleanse the world of the story more comprehensively by eliminating every trace of the opposition, viewed for the purpose of resolving the narrative conflict as the full incarnation of evil.[37] When acted out, the first tends toward a cycle of recrimination, even violence, whereas the second dreams of total elimination of all those who trouble us. Each is a school in unremitting violence.

If seeking the authentic origin is misguided, if claiming to have discovered a genuine identity implicitly declares all others bogus, if we can frame Matthew's accusations against the Pharisees as making this very charge, then how do we rescue Matthew's own effort to return to pure origins? Even more acutely, how do we account for Matthew's violent language in this cause? If anything has been shown so far of the tendencies in Matthew's narratives, it is the commitment to the theme of authenticity. Not only the appeal back to Abraham, Moses, David, and Isaiah, seen in the genealogy, the infancy account's recapitulation of Israel's sojourn in Egypt, or the string of scripture quotations do we find testimony to this commitment, but also in the very use of the formula story of the banished and returning prince, itself an expression of the quest to return to authenticity (as is its nineteenth-century elaboration in terms of an "Aryan" myth).[38]

---

authenticity are painful present-day realizations of such old Greek meanings." Bendix, 14. She shows how Trilling traces the "imperative of sincerity" through the sixteenth century in Europe, stimulated by the experience of theater. "Trilling observes how the fascination with theater led to an awareness of role play in life and to the realization that role play compromises sincerity. Yet if the norms of behavior required insincerity, the question arose whether, underneath these demands of civilization, Layers of uncorrupted selfhood could be found" (Bendix, *Authenticity*, 16).

37. Beck, *Nonviolent Story*, 136–37. This differs from Girard's solution, which employs the pattern of the scapegoat.

38. As in the classic studies of Von Hahn and Nutt, mentioned earlier, 71–72.

It is at this crucial point that Matthew's doctrine of nonretaliation enters the picture to inhibit the impulse toward violent altercation. Where postcolonial writings may inveigh against beliefs that "cultural purity rather than hybridity are the norm,"[39] Matthew does not take the route of abandoning the quest for authenticity. Like the Irish example we saw earlier, that vision is not to be abandoned, paradoxical though the result may be. Instead, he chooses to place a hedge around the dangers that would open up. In the teaching that one should turn the other cheek rather than indulge in retaliation (5:38–43), in the moment of return to Jerusalem and the cleansing of the Temple, a cleansing that does not involve retaliation (21:1–11, 12–17), or in the arrest in Gethsemane, with the sword saying placed precisely at the moment at which the opportunity for retaliation presents itself (26:52), the escalation toward violence is thwarted, frozen in place before it has a chance to develop. All of which raises the question of whether Matthew's understanding of nonviolence is practical and strategic or principled. That discussion will require a chapter in itself, but in the duration it is worth noting that Matthew's emphasis on transparency in the interrelation between appearances and values would argue against a strategic stance that would fall short of being principled.

CONCLUSIONS: CONFLICT IN THE NARRATIVE PLOT

The Gospel of Matthew engages as its central plotline a conflict between Jesus and the scribes and Pharisees, told from the side favorable to Jesus. This plotline has a metaphorical relation to the political and religious situation of Matthew's community, thought to be in competition with the early rabbinic movement, now projected on the narrative as the Pharisaic opponents of Jesus. The destruction of the Temple, its absence persisting as a lingering presence in the Burnt Place where the Temple once stood, sets the backdrop for the conflict in Matthew's main plotline, between Jesus and the "scribes and Pharisees." The Gospel is concerned with the proper response to this debacle and the need to recover a sense of God's movement in history.

In the inclusive plot of Matthew, the dispute figured in the Gospel plot reflects the later conflict between Matthew and his community's sectarian rivals. What we have is a contest between competing forms of

---

39. Bendix, *Authenticity*, 9.

resistance, waged at the level of Matthew's church against the proto-rabbinic movement. The struggle between these two parties has the shape of a fraternal quarrel concerning the need and character of resistance to the Roman occupation and domination of Judea, resulting in the destruction of Jerusalem and the Temple, the topographical focus of their faith. In the posttemple era, the avenues to the future are disputed, and the dispute is bitter.

The conflict at the center of Matthew's plot, then, is not so much a clash between good and evil, between heroes and villains—for the villainy is enshrined in the Burnt Place where the Temple stood. Instead, it is a dispute about how to respond to that fundamental evil, the world-altering violence inflicted by Rome as a lesson in imperialism, one that changes the reality of Judean life and worship. The struggle among the survivors for the authentic voice of Israel is a dispute grounded in deep convictions, a dispute among family members, with the disappointment and rancor such conditions can sometimes produce. [40]

Nevertheless, the harsh language of violent retribution that makes its way into this Gospel compromises its message of nonviolence and needs to be addressed. In the imperial context, the specter of violence can arise in various ways. It may be sparked by the experience of imperial domination itself, with the impulse in any form of resistance to pay it back in kind, if possible. For the "hypocrite" accused by this text, it is projected as a possibility not fully forsworn, a possibility that is still held available for practical advantage. For the suspected "impostor" at the center of the story, violence threatens to appear as a way to consolidate his position or prove one's authenticity against opponents.

In the narrative that Matthew has constructed, this harsh impulse finds its way into the words of Jesus, though not his practice, nor that of his disciples. Hedging against that impulse is the teaching of nonretaliation, the nonviolent response to harm received, presumably acting as an antidote to taking on the role of God's agents of retribution.

In an attempt to account for this harsh strand in Matthew's text, commentators have proposed that the disciples experienced persecu-

40. Harrington, *Matthew*, 17: "Matthew's Gospel should be read as one of several Jewish responses to the destruction of the Jerusalem Temple in AD 70. The Matthean community still existed within the framework of Judaism but in tension with other Jewish groups—especially the early rabbinic movement. Matthew's theological program should be viewed as an attempt to show how the Jewish tradition is best preserved in a Jewish-Christian context."

tion. They conjecture that the Matthean language ("their synagogues") reflects rough treatment of Matthew's community members at the hands of the rabbinic groups.[41] Paul's example as a Pharisee, early on, and his experience later as a disciple would seem to confirm that scenario. And yet, apart from the polemics of the New Testament, there is little evidence of the conflictual inclinations of the Pharisees. Nevertheless, while we struggle to find a basis for the opposition in Matthew's world, the narrative itself presents little motivation for the opposition to the Pharisees. Already at Matthew 3:7 we find John the Baptist excoriating the Pharisees and Sadducees as "brood of vipers." The situation seems prejudicial; even before Jesus' public ministry begins we have his opponents pointed out. However, the position that has been taken here is that the narrative conflict doesn't begin with John the Baptist. The first two chapters of Matthew need to be brought into consideration, if, as we have maintained, they are part of the narrative and not simply prologue. Because the story of Jesus' ministry continues a conflict that began earlier, in some sense the scribes and Pharisees inherit the role of opposition first elicited with the arrival of the Magi on the scene.

But if the representatives of Rome—Herod, Archelaus, Antipas— provide the narrative with antagonists in the early chapters of the Gospel, we can hardly assign a similar imperial role to "the scribes and Pharisees" in Matthew's narrative because we have already noted the resistance practices of the Pharisees. What Matthew shows us instead is a picture of Pharisaic *cooperation* with the imperial project, from carrying the images of Caesar into the Temple to contracting for a guard at the tomb. The issue is complicity with imperial violence, and it finds its central expression in the moves toward the crucifixion. The offense of the antagonists in Matthew's plot is their failure to adopt the thorough rejection of imperial processes, especially those of violence, that are expressed in Jesus' message of metanoia.

Still, this does not explain the vehemence with which Matthew describes the scribes and Pharisees. For some understanding of the development of the role of the Pharisees, we can turn to a suggestion by Sean Freyne. In a seminal article, "Vilifying the Other and Defining the Self," he noted Matthew's emphasis on teaching and proposes that in his treatment of the disputes between Jesus and his opponents, "he vin-

41. E.g., Saldarini, *Pharisees*, 172–73.

dicates not Jesus' authority but the Matthaean community rule."[42] The evangelist's concern is with the teaching of his church. In discrediting Jesus' opponents, Matthew is warning the disciples of his own day. In an illuminating appendix to his article, Freyne showed how each of the injunctions against the scribes and Pharisees in the Woes of Matt 23 find a parallel instruction to the disciples elsewhere in the Gospel.[43] Freyne's observations generate two further thoughts.

First, if we return to the Gospel narrative that stands as emblem or parable of the dispute Matthew experiences in his own church, we can say that the principle of presenting discipleship warnings as disputes between Jesus and his opponents extends to the fuller narrative itself. As a story involving conflict and its resolution, the plot of Matthew's Gospel itself depicts a warning to the disciples and members of Matthew's church. In the manner in which it pits Jesus' *metanoia* against Pharisaic imperial complicity, it is not so much judging the opposition as it is warning the followers of Jesus to make a clean break with imperial values. The scribes and Pharisees, although historical figures, primarily represent options that Matthew rejects for his community.

A second consideration is that this warning suggests a dispute existed within the community concerning the need for what we have described here as a complete dissociation from the cultural values of the empire. If the community identifies itself as one that does not espouse the practices criticized in the Pharisees, there must be a need for making this point. Given the replication within Matthew's experience of the other levels of narrative conflict in the Gospel, we can presume a dispute within the community that corresponds to this dispute. With that hint in mind, the following chapter will address the question of retribution and nonviolence in the Gospel, as figured in the depiction of the voice of retribution, John the Baptist, in his relationship to the teaching and practice of Jesus.

In this chapter and the previous one, we have considered the opposition between empire and Judea, followed by this chapter's look at the conflict in the main plotline of Matthew. In the next chapter we will consider the dispute within the Jesus movement, configured in the narrative as a shifting relation between the teaching of Jesus and that of the Baptist. In Mark's Gospel this dispute is presented as a subplot of

42. Freyne, "Vilifying," 120.
43. Freyne, "Vilifying," 143.

conflict waged between Jesus and his disciples, the latter failing to understand the meaning of his teachings on servant discipleship.[44] In this text, the Baptist's theme of retribution leveraged against the message of the Sermon on the Mount, a conflict mediated by the longer narrative of Matthew, serves that purpose for the disciples in Matthew's church. He who came before offers lessons to those who come after.

44. See Rhoads, *Mark as Story*, 90–96. Also, Beck, *Nonviolent Story*, ch. 4.

John the Baptist is
the mentor in Matthew

theme of retribution

violence/ nonviolence

6

Mentor

The exilic period represents a huge lacuna in the historical narrative of the Hebrew Bible. It stands as a murky gaping hole in the history of Yahweh and his people, illuminated only briefly by isolated beams of light.

—Rainer Albertz, *Israel in Exile*, 4

Teenaged Athena jumped up and shrieked:
"Kill! Kill for me!
Better to die than to live without killing!"

—Christopher Logue, *All Day Permanent Red*

IN THE FORMULA STORY of the banished prince a certain figure inevitably appears. Often unobtrusive, but necessary to the unfolding story, this is the guide who prepares the prince for the task regaining the lost kingdom. This is the mentor, and it is not an innocent role. The mentor represents the living memory of what was lost, along with the secret but determined resolve to see it returned. The mentor is the agent of those defeated, subjugated, or exiled under the usurping regime. But now the time has come for the rejected to make their move. The present chapter will trace this figure into Matthew's story and find its equivalent in John the Baptist, characterized here as the voice of retribution. As mentor, John introduces the idiom that Jesus adopts and extends, redirecting it in ways not anticipated by the Baptist. When the gospel narrative unfolds, a distance opens between the vision of John and that of Jesus. The space between these two visions prompts some reflection on the theme of retribution in the Gospel. This in turn raises questions about Matthew's vision of God's violence or nonviolence, which concludes the chapter.

Although Matthew's Gospel advocates nonviolence, even nonretaliation, in some of its parts, in others it contains some of the more violent imagery to be found among the Gospels. This strain of imagery begins early, with John the Baptist accusing the Sadducees and Pharisees in the vivid language of retribution (Matt 3:7). The lines of opposition appear from the start. However, this impression of entirely unmotivated opposition depends on a view that holds the baptism of Jesus as the beginning of the Gospel. In Mark's Gospel that would be true. Mark begins with the Baptist and gives him the task of setting the narrative program for the Gospel as a whole.[1] But we are already three chapters into Matthew's account. In fact, the infancy narrative is not simply prologue, as commonly considered, for it begins the plot of Matthew's story. Accordingly, John is relieved of the task of initiating the plot with a narrative program. As we've seen, Matthew has transferred that role to the angel appearing to Joseph in a dream, with a mission to the unborn child (Matt 1:21).[2] The Baptist has another role in Matthew's Gospel, as mentor of the adult Messiah in the mission of retrieving the Kingdom. At the same time, the figure of John gives Matthew a foil against which Jesus' own vision can be shown to develop.

MENTORS

Mentor, the wise friend to whom Odysseus entrusted the care and education of his son Telemachus while he was away at Troy, has given his name to represent any trustworthy older guide who helps someone at the beginning of a career. But in the formula story of the banished prince this conventional meaning obscures something more unsettling about the role, namely, its implied threat. In the story pattern that we have been using to prompt our reflection, the role has a particular focus. It identifies the character assigned to prepare the hero for the purpose of recapturing the lost kingdom. In the *Odyssey*, it is not actually Mentor who prompts the action, but Pallas Athena, appearing in the guise of Mentor, urging Telemachus to initiate the search for his father. With that ruse, the epic tale is begun.

---

1. In Mark, the narrative program, or mandate, is given in the words of the voice from heaven, which combines the messianic reference of Ps 2:7 with the Servant text of Isa 42:1. The following Gospel narrative shows Jesus working out what this would mean.

2. See Tannehill, "Narrative Christology," 61–62; Beck *Nonviolent Story*, 94–95.

According to the formula, aspects of the mentor figure must remain hidden from our sight, for there is an element of subversion built into this role. Among the aspects hidden from us is the violence implicit to the role, which occasionally emerges to reveal itself. It is the same Athena urging Telemachus to seek out his father who in the concluding books urges Odysseus onward to comprehensive revenge. The last moment is already contained in the first. Or consider "Phil," in Disney's *Hercules*. His satyrlike form and his name, Philoctetes, is borrowed from other myths, but once in the story he makes it his own. He is portrayed as a trainer of prizefighters, now concentrating his efforts on the youthful Hercules. There is a struggle ahead, and his man will be ready for it. Phil's profession is entirely consonant with his contribution to the story formula. He prepares the hero for enacting the greater violence.

The potential for violence based on the premise of the lost kingdom to be regained is typically expressed in the impulse that begins as retribution in the name of justice but ends as revenge, as Hamlet and Odysseus among so many others have taught us. In ways perhaps unexpected, that potential is concentrated in the figure of the mentor. Yet it remains obscured here, present as potential. In all these traditional stories of kingdoms lost and regained, the language of "kingdom" means that the stakes are set at the highest level. The future of an entire people is put into jeopardy, narrowly rescued at the end. But because the story pattern pictures the contest of possible regimes, an undercurrent of political intrigue inevitably inserts itself. Though the royal trappings may be taken by most readers as simply providing background color, with its celebrity world of Princesses and Princes Charming, the fact remains that a more serious world is implied. The mentor's role as a spokesperson for a party or government in exile, biding its time until the opportunity to return presents itself, remains unspoken. The hero, after all, is identified as the scion of a lost dynasty, one being equipped to lead a people that longs for its revival.

The Bible contains its own examples. We are reminded of the strong men and kingmakers of Israelite history, similar in function though perhaps not in style. Abner furthered the fortunes of King Saul. Joab dispatched him (2 Sam 3:22–39) and replaced him, performing similar services for David. This darker, more political, dimension to the mentor role is not surprising because in any account of conflicting regimes there will be the agents who represent different parties and initiate movements

entrenchment

on their behalf. In the banished prince formula, this is the mentor. In Matthew's Gospel, it is the Baptist.

Matthew's Mentor

In Matthew's Gospel, the action begins with the arrival of the Magi on the scene in the second chapter. By the time the chapter is done the conflict is well underway, with Jesus banished to a distant territory, Galilee. Already the narrative is presented with some unfinished business, a "lack" that needs to be repaired. It is the Baptist's task to initiate the events that will remove the lack. John is customarily acclaimed as precursor, the forerunner whose actions and story foreshadow that of the main character, Jesus. But that does not entirely capture his role in Matthew. He is also the mentor as threat, instrumental in initiating a restoration of the Kingdom, announced with images of an axe at the root of the tree and a winnowing fan at the ready. It is not inconsistent with this picture that John was executed for political reasons (Matt 14:3–12). However we understand the historical events behind this account, we see that John had political enemies. Matthew's use of the mentor role reflects this.

We are accustomed to discounting the political imagery in the Gospel, in lieu of a more "spiritual" meaning. But political references remain in the text and retain their latent force. The formula story tends to release them for fresh consideration. For instance, in support of his presentation of Jesus as Son of David, Matthew begins with his genealogy. Here we return to the genealogical considerations of the fourth chapter.[3] If the central section of the genealogy is a king list that traces Jesus' ancestry through Joseph, from the Babylonian exile back to King David himself, how does the final section carry this program through to Joseph? Is it also a king list, though one maintained secretly?[4] Put another way, if Matthew's claim for Jesus' ancestry is to be seen as rhetorical, it is rhetoric elaborated through an entire backstory, and not simply a

---

3. See above, p. 91–96.

4. We might compare, for instance, the genealogies of the David family in I Chronicles 3, which trace a line of succession into the postexilic era, even though these persons were no longer acting governors, as Zerubbabel had been (e.g., Knoppers, *I Chronicles 1–9*, 335). Because Matthew used the lists of I Chronicles as both pattern and source for his genealogy, seen clearly in the earlier part (Matt 1:2–6), it further urges the question of the evangelist's intent for the latter part.

matter of posting the names of famous Israelites among his ancestors. If we are to regard the genealogy as a theological statement, it is theological by way of a dramatized history, and not simply by allusive statements or direct propositions.

Voices in the Desert

With every indicator seemingly at its disposal, Matthew's text declares John the Baptist to be the true precursor of Jesus. John is a "reliable" character,[5] therefore to be trusted. He launches Jesus' public ministry, and in this text, his return from banishment. His authenticity is assured by the programmatic announcement Matthew has placed on the lips of John: "Repent, for the kingdom of heaven is at hand" (3:2). Jesus is shown to begin his ministry with John's theme, repeated verbatim (4:17). He is further certified by prophetic endorsement as "the voice of one crying in the desert, 'Prepare the way of the Lord'" (Isa 40:3; Matt 3:3). In keeping with all this, John baptizes Jesus only after negotiating the propriety of doing so (3:14–15). Finally, John's action is supported by the visitation of the Holy Spirit, along with another voice, this one from heaven: "This is my Son, my beloved, in whom I am well pleased."

Given the shape of Matthew's homecoming story, the Baptist is not simply a precursor but also a mentor, in the particular sense that role has in the formula stories of banishment and return. The proclamation of the "kingdom at hand" announces a return to the royal standard of David. But because proclaiming the impending return of a past kingdom is not a politically innocent statement, it will draw the attention of the current rulers and bring their opposition into play. And so just as John dies at the hands of a Herod (Matt 14:3–12), so Jesus will die at the hands of the empire under the words, "the King of the Jews" (27:37).

But the most certain indication of John's role as true mentor is that Jesus adopts and continues the program that the Baptist has set out for him. This is the point of the verbatim repetition of John's message at 3:2 by Jesus' opening statement at 4:17. It alerts us to other examples, such as John's strident metaphors of crisis. In a cluster of forceful images—*brood of vipers* (v.7), *fruit-bearing tree* (vv. 8, 10), and *fire* (vv. 10, 12)—John warns of the coming judgment and calls for a decision. His proper emblem is the axe at the root of the tree. The image of the barren tree,

---

5. Anderson, *Web*, 84–85.

cut down and placed in the fire (v. 10), finds a rhetorical balance in the image of the harvest. While the wheat is gathered into barns, the chaff is burnt in unquenchable fire (v. 12). Introduced by John, these reappear in the speeches of Jesus, more fully expressing the continuity shown in the equivalence of 3:2 and 4:17. In fact, the metaphors provide a convenient index to the uses of John's retributive language in the words of Jesus. Four passages in particular show Jesus echoing John's themes:

Matt 7:15–20: In the closing moments of the Sermon on the Mount, speaking to the disciples, Jesus warns against following false prophets. They will be known by their *fruits*, and every *tree* not bearing good fruit will be cut down and cast into the *fire*.

Matt 12:33–34: In response to reports of Jesus' healings, Pharisees charge him with forging an alliance with Beelzebul. Jesus counters sharply. Again we read that the *tree* is known by its *fruit*. But with the Pharisees he employs another of John's epithets: *brood of vipers*.

Matt 13:39–43, 49–50: Ending the parables unique to Matthew, Jesus issues a statement expressing divine retribution at the "close of the age." At that time, the harvest will occur, and evildoers will be gathered by the reapers and thrown in the *furnace of fire*. In addition to the Baptist's image of fire, Matthew depicts Jesus adding another of his own: *the outer darkness where there will be weeping and gnashing of teeth*.

Matt 23:33: Among the Woes uttered by Jesus against the scribes and Pharisees in his final days in Jerusalem, one of them includes language from John: *brood of vipers*.

As with the Baptist, Jesus' words are not directed against the imperium, but rather against those who fail to reject what it represents. The main conflict in the gospel narrative is not waged between Judea and its occupying forces, but between competing Judean responses to that occupation —that of the "kingdom of heaven" versus the Pharisees and others representing the rabbinic response. The dispute between these responders was examined in the preceding chapter. For the present we are interested less in the targets of invective than the producers of it, and the degree of violence presupposed in its expressions.[6]

6. In assessing these, we see that the targets of the epithets vary, with "vipers" ad-

Another Voice in the Desert

In addition to the suspicions of subversion already built into the mentor role, the specter of the false mentor adds a further complication. Consider another example of the formula story. When Buck Mulligan makes his entrance at the beginning of Joyce's novel, *Ulysses*,[7] he bears the name and apparently the function of the Baptist. Yet he is an impostor in the role. Mocking the morning milkwoman to amuse the visiting son of the empire, the Englishman Haines, Mulligan's behavior belies his proposal for a renascence of Irish writing. But Stephen recognizes her as a "messenger," presenting in her common Irishness the proper theme for his art.[8] Or consider Falstaff, who appears as mentor to Prince Hal but, ironically so, because on becoming king the prince must reject his influence. In stories, as in life, mentors are not always trustworthy.

This deceptive possibility of the mentor role also applies to Matthew's narrative. Another voice besides that of John is heard in the desert. Satan also speaks up with a narrative program for Jesus, and it also contains a vision of the kingdom to come. But this vision is one of hegemony over all nations, an explicitly imperial program. It is a vision that Jesus rejects rather than follows, in contrast to his response to John. As a representative figure in the story, Satan is the Gospel's spirit of the theology of violence as expressed through dominating power. Unlike John's humble deference to the Messiah (3:24–25), Satan demands worship (4:9). His role in representing a dominating force, or violence, is theological.

---

dressed to Pharisees, whereas the "tree" and the "fire" are in speeches addressed to disciples or Pharisees. But our concern here is with the speaker, rather than the audience, of these remarks. Prescinding provisionally from the objects of the metaphors, we are more interested here in the latent violence of the imagery, and hence of the speakers. In addition, the imputed violence of God will be a matter of concern.

7. Kenner ("Circe," 343) aligns *Ulysses* with the other stories in the banished prince formula as "another story of the same shape. . . ."

8. His full name, Malachi Roland St John Mulligan, implies the Baptist on a number of levels. Because "Malachi" means "my messenger," as in Mal 3:1, and inasmuch as Matthew along with the other Synoptics applies this verse to John the Baptist, we can safely presume that "St John" also refers to the Baptist. In the elaborate system of correspondences that Joyce constructed between the novel and Homer's epic, the milkwoman is, in the view of some commentators, the equivalent of Pallas Athena, coming to Telemachus (Stephen) disguised as Odysseus' friend, Mentor. See Benstock, "Telemachus," 3, 11. For a postcolonial reading of the opening chapter of *Ulysses*, see Cheng, *Joyce, Race, and Empire*, 151–162.

Satan as the spirit of theological violence is captured in the exchanges that take place between him and Jesus. His invitation to turn stones into bread (4:4) addresses the specific need of the desert sojourn. Satan proposes a model, a standard for dealing with obstacles—direct action by way of a display of power. If you are in charge, remove the problem. Be Alexander the Macedonian, who when faced with the problem of the Gordian knot solved it by splitting it with a sword. If you are unable to take decisive action, quit pretending to powers you do not possess. Satan's second proposal, that Jesus throw himself down from the Temple parapet (4:6), adds the theological dimension. Forceful action is a sign of divine endorsement. The theological is indicated by choosing of the Temple location, but also in Jesus' response: You shall not test God. Satan's program competes with God's and is denounced as a false theology.

Satan's third proposal (4:8–9) links his program directly to the imperial project: ruling all the nations of the world. The only requirement is to worship the spirit of violence. World domination is the essence of the imperium, and the Roman example shows it is accomplished in a violent display of power. As a recommendation for the Messiah, it would propose solving the problem of Rome by recreating it in his own image. Insofar as the ending of the gospel echoes this ideal (28:16–20), we will return to it for further attention in the final chapter.

In contrast to Satan's program, that of John is a matter of waiting on events, calling on God to bring about the dénouement that otherwise would disclose the world as a chaotic arena, throwing doubt on God's justice. From the perspective of the powerful, John's position seems one of helplessness in which a desire for reprisals encounters an inability to effect them. From this point of view, John's program seems a wistful, failed version of Satan's. Insofar as Jesus accepts John's lead and rejects that of Satan, he also would seem destined to experience a similar futility. And to the degree that Jesus also prescinds from John's demand for divine reprisals, he would seem to isolate himself further in a hopeless position where evil is not challenged even by God, thereby threatening the meaningful frame of a just world.

Whereas John's words in the desert find a continuation in the words of Jesus, Satan's proposals are firmly rejected. But the demands that surfaced in the desert do not end there, and this is true of Satan's assertions as well as John's. The "temptations" continue. The Pharisees, whom we have taken to represent the refusal to avoid complicity with the uses of violence, sustain the theme of "testing" Jesus (16:1; 19:3; 22:35). Or Peter, distracted by dreams of power, misreads the Messianic role of Jesus, earning him the title of "Satan" (16:23). In another motif that keeps the conflict from getting too far out of mind, a cluster of instances relates Satan and the kingdom with the verb, "to plunder" (*arpazo*). Not only in the Sower parable (13:19), but also in the parable of the king-dom divided against itself (12:29). Here the role of mentor is evoked by the "strong man," reminding us of John's testimony about Jesus as the stronger one (3:11). This particular motif culminates in the saying at 11:12—"from the days of John the Baptist until now the kingdom of heaven has suffered violence, and men of violence take it by force"—a matter that will require further attention.

Jesus' test in the desert has its counterpart in the garden of Gethsemane, as he approaches his final hour. Here Jesus' struggle car-ries to a conclusion. The release given in the words, "your will be done" (26:32), is immediately elaborated in the arrest that follows (26:47–56). Here is the moment of nonretaliation; here is the sword saying (v. 52); here is the definitive refusal of dominating power, first proposed by Satan.

These two "temptations," desert and garden, provide a bracket around the story of the adult Jesus. Together the two moments provide a frame for the entire adult story of Jesus, from baptism to arrest and cru-cifixion. As a narrative device it has the effect of designating the entire time as one of internal struggle for Jesus. It begins with Satan's proposals, and it ends with the arrest of Jesus and its startling moment of nonretali-ation, the moment of rejecting the sword (26:52). Between desert test and garden arrest comes the firm decision to reject violent methods of resistance. In the contrast between Satan's power and Jesus' refusal of violent retaliation we find the themes of the previous two chapters con-verging: the imperial theology of violence (chapter 4) and the firm rejec-tion of any complicity with it (chapter 5). But here they appear under the sign of struggle. Although the struggle is shown, its developing story is not. The interior struggle of Jesus can be inferred, but not observed.

But the internal struggle of the protagonist in Matthew's narrative is also, as we will see, a struggle that emerges within the text itself. It has been framed as an apparent contradiction between a demand for nonviolent discipleship by a God who otherwise favors violent retribu-

Satan's power vs Jesus' refusal

tion—as seen, for instance, in the parable endings of Matthew 13.[9] The discordance is simply increased by the injunction to "be perfect as your heavenly Father is perfect" (5:48). It is this division in the text, between the nonviolence advocated by Jesus and the violent eschatological retribution he sometimes promises that needs to be examined for signs of mediation, if not resolution.

FROM DESERT TO GARDEN

Jesus' internal struggle

As Matthew's narrative moves from the first temptation to the second, the transit from desert to garden, Jesus' internal struggle plays out in the narrative as a difference between John and Jesus. In this changing relationship between the two we find a visible, externalized image of Jesus' inner struggle. John's message, of course, begins with his initial announcement—"Repent, for the kingdom of heaven is at hand" (3:2). The radical reorientation he proposes is presented as a response and not a condition for the advent of the kingdom. The moment of crisis is near: the judgment about to be carried out. In his mentor role as readying the moment for the young king's restoration of the lost realm, it is entirely appropriate he should be announcing a kingdom and its time of revival.

Shortly thereafter, as we have seen, he elaborates on his theme (3:7–12) in language and imagery as sharp as the impending judgment of his vision. His programmatic statement sets out his themes and motifs. John is a man of the desert; his imagery favors defoliation: the axe of decision is at the root of the tree. The time has come, literally a "de-cision," a cutting-away, a dismissal of some possibilities in lieu of others. A figure of the desert ("What did you go out to the desert to see?"), with his metaphorical axe, John is calling for the moral clarity of a defoliated desert.

But something happens when this theme unfolds in the Gospel. John's message is not denied by Jesus, but in fact is repeated and intensified. At the same time a second, countervailing effect offsets it. John's message is clearly continued in the repetition of John's opening statement (3:2), at the beginning of Jesus' work in Galilee (4:17), and later in his instructions to the disciples as they are sent out on mission (10:7): "the kingdom of heaven is at hand." But in the work and company of Jesus this proclamation is modified by another phrase: "preaching the

---

9. For instance, Reid, "Violent Endings," 248–55. Also Neville, "Teleology," 131–161.

gospel of the kingdom" (4:23; 9:35; 24:14), and this new elaboration of the theme is associated with accounts of healing (4:23; 9:35; 10:7). Healings stand opposite violence, as repair does to destruction. Where John expects a judgment, Jesus speaks of healings. So John's theme of judgment continues, though it is qualified by a counter theme of healing and making whole.[10]

But it is in a juxtaposition of two scenes in particular that the drama is condensed: John's proclamation by the Jordan (Matt 3:7–12) and his query from jail (11:2–6). The two moments—the scriptures cited in each and the imagery derived from those citations—tell their own story. Analysts of Matthew commonly agree that the narrative conflict of Matthew engages in earnest in the eleventh chapter.[11] As we saw, Matthew 5–10 functions as exposition, presented earlier as the "Galilee discourse" as exposition for the reader. In Matthew 11, the conflict section of the Gospel begins with the Baptist, as did the ministry of Jesus earlier. In Matthew 11: 2–6, John sends messengers from prison to ask Jesus, "Are you the one who is to come or should we look for another?" John's expectation of the judgment at hand does not seem promising of fulfillment. More likely than making simple inquiry about Jesus' identity, John is asking, in effect, when is the axe to be put at the root of the tree? In his response, Jesus invokes two prophetic voices, one of which he applies to himself, the other to John, whom he clothes in the language and images of Malachi. This book, with its edge and its fire, suits the man of the desert.

But for himself Jesus selects text from the book of Isaiah. Passages from Isaiah 29:19, 35:5–6, and 61:1–3 ask listeners to imagine the renewal of the people of Israel as healings. "Tell John what you hear and see: the blind regain their sight, the lame walk, lepers are cleansed, the deaf hear, the dead are raised, and the poor have the good news proclaimed to them" (Matt 11:4–5). And alongside this, complementing it, the prevailing imagery, typically associated with the return from exile, is that of reforested deserts blooming with plant life (35:2–3; 61:5). We see the contrast between the two positions stated in terms of deserts and gardens. Where

10. Earlier, as we recall from chapter two, above, the text expressed the relation between nonviolence and healing as the praxis of Jesus was set out in the exposition of the Gospel, with the Sermon on the Mount of Matthew 5–7 followed by the healings of Matthew 8–9 as the Sermon's performance equivalent.

11. Kingsbury, *Story*, 72–74; Carter, "Kernels," 468, 476, *Matthew: Storyteller*, 164–67; Senior, *Matthew*, 119–123.

John would hew, Jesus plants. Again, we see the theme of healing supplementing John's initial proclamation of the kingdom coming.

Judgment to healing

Parables of Deferral

The shift from judgment to healing in the discourse of John when it is adopted by Jesus seems to promise a clear break with the policy of retribution. But when we return to look more closely at the metaphors of crisis contributed by the Baptist and picked up by Jesus—*brood of vipers, fruit-bearing tree, fire*—we are less sanguine about this. Three adjustments by Matthew complicate matters. First, the metaphors are extended dramatically in the endings of some of the parables. Jesus not only echoes John, but even adds some his own refinements. The phrase "cast into the outer darkness where there will be weeping and gnashing of teeth" appears only in the words of Matthew's Jesus. This has raised the question about Jesus' view of divine violence in this gospel. How does, for instance, the injunction to be perfect as God is perfect (5:48), advising love of enemies, align with this strong language sometimes called "retributive violence"?

A second matter that stands out in is the fact that Jesus' warnings shift from John's attention to the Pharisees and Sadducees, in John's instance (3:7), to focus attention primarily on the disciples. It is seen, for instance, in the metaphor of *fire*. Although admittedly in some key passages Jesus directs his warnings to the Pharisees as the Baptist did (12:32–42; 22:7, 13; 23:33, 37), the image of punitive fire is presented much more often as a warning to the disciples (5:22, 24; 8:12; 10:15, etc.). Obviously this only intensifies the contrast between the nonviolence and love of neighbor that Jesus requires of his disciples (5:38–48) and what he posits of God in the retribution promised in the endings of the parables. Or, to put it more trenchantly, the contradictory portrait of God, considering that the love demanded of the disciples is to bring them to "be perfect, as your heavenly Father is perfect."

A third aspect, related to this, is that the injunction against the disciples involves omissions rather than commissions. It is not some heinous crime that merits such harsh sanctions, not bad deeds committed, but rather good deeds left undone. The punishment seems wildly disproportionate, even draconian. A prominent example is the parable of the Unforgiving Servant (18:23–35), whose failure to extend forgiveness such as he received results in his abandonment, his forgiveness revoked.

Unconditional forgiveness is required of the disciple, but God's (the master's) forgiveness is conditional. Without resolving the paradox, we can note that this pattern is consistent with the demand of noncomplicity with the cultural values of the empire, and reflects the postcolonial pattern of competition among the colonized. What is opposed in the conflict with the Pharisees is prohibited to the disciples, as inimical to discipleship itself.

Although the Baptist's retribution theme is intensified in the parable endings, it is also modified in a significant way. The judgment that John proclaims as "at hand" is now deferred to the close of the age. For John, the one coming wields the (metaphorical) axe, and shortly the harvest is to be gathered in, the chaff burnt. For Jesus, not yet. The same expressions John used of the pending moment are now applied to the close of the age. Like John (3:7), Jesus announced that the kingdom was near (4:17; 10:7). But now that the "return" has begun, an interval has opened up, in which the kingdom is preached (4:23; 9:35; 24:14), but this preaching is instead associated with healing, rather than judgment (4:23; 9:35; 10:8).

For John, as for the Pharisees, the coming of Jesus and the kingdom may appear an "imposture." But here too the "first imposture" (27:64) yields to a second. In addition to the deferral of judgment from the coming of Jesus to the close of the age, that final time is itself deferred. Matthew has retained most of Mark's apocalyptic discourse (Mark 13), although he has supplemented the speech with six parables.[12] Along with the Fig Tree parable borrowed from Mark, he has constructed a sequence of seven: three parables insisting on vigilance, followed by three parables speaking of a delay, that the final judgment will arrive only after a "long time." The seventh parable, the Sheep and Goats, or the Last Judgment, presents its own problems, to be considered later in this chapter.

The language of immediacy on the one hand and deferral on the other has produced a split in the critical assessment concerning Matthew's understanding of the delay of the final judgment.[13] But when Matthew's

12. The six parables added by Matthew are the Flood (Matt 24:37–41), the Watchful Householder (24:42–44), the Wise Servant (24:45–51), the Ten Bridesmaids (25:1–13), the Talents (25:14–30), and the Last Judgment (25:31–46). The parable of the Fig Tree (Matt 24:32–36) appears in Mark 13:28–32.

13. For a review of the arguments for an immanent *eschaton* in Matthew, see Neville, "Teleology," 137–145. For a statement of the argument toward delayed *eschaton*, see Hays, *Moral Vision*, 104–106.

text refers to timing, it is either to a duration unknown or to one long past. Those who consider Matthew to have envisioned an early return do so on the basis of the vividness of imagery and the sense of urgency evoked by the text. However, that sense of urgency can be accounted for in other ways, and primary among these is the urgency imposed by the stakes involved for Matthew (i.e., in avoiding complicity with the ways of the imperium). The immediacy is that born of intensity rather than of timing. In a double move, the gospel both stresses the need for an accounting and defers it indefinitely. In terms of the gospel's stance vis-à-vis violence, this takes the form of radically prescinding from the imperial theology of violence.

On the one hand, parables of retribution are enlisted to demonstrate that God's justice is adequate to counter the absolute violence of imperial theology. On the other hand, the disciple's nonviolence and love of enemies is required to witness to something that has to do with the image of God (5:48). On the one hand, the Baptist's message is endorsed with repetition and even elaboration in the teaching of Jesus. On the other hand, it is indefinitely deferred, beyond the present experience. On the one hand, the disciples' adherence to the conditions of the kingdom is reinforced by the strictest sanctions, separating them from those who would allow themselves to cooperate with the imperial theology. On the other hand, those conditions of discipleship consist of eschewing violent measures and abandoning the impulse to retribution. In other words, justice is left to God, and the history of Christian violence in God's name is specifically forbidden by this Gospel, which has provided warrants for so much Christian violence. In the parable of the Net (Matt 13:47–50) this could not be made clearer—the militant defenders of the kingdom are advised to wait on God, at which time matters will be set aright.

Two problem parables capture Matthew's concerns. One has been mentioned—the Unforgiving Servant of Matt 18:23–35. The parable illustrates the need to keep both elements in play, accepting the forgiveness as gift and the requirement to practice it. The other parable is that of the Sheep and Goats (25:31–46), also mentioned earlier. The image of the last judgment presented here again affirms both sides of the tension, the works of compassion as well as the overwhelming consequences. And here too we see the pattern shown to be characteristic of the discipleship parables: the deeds judged under dire sanctions are not crimes committed, but virtues—acts of compassion—omitted. But there is one further aspect that demands attention—demands it because the parable is protracted to unusual length precisely to emphasize this point—and that is the way those party to the action are unaware that they are dealing with the king. That is to say, compassion being what it is, it responds to the needs and not to the command to address those needs, much as love responds spontaneously, and not by coercion.

But if this is so, what are we left with in the case of the parable of the Last Judgment? Is it about doing certain deeds, or about having a mind-set and a heart that spontaneously do them? Literally, it enjoins the disciples to perform certain acts and to perform them not from fear of punishment, but rather without regard for sanctions of punishment or reward. Like the Unforgiving Servant, a paradox sits at the heart of the story. And as also with the parables of deferral, it has the effect of qualifying the absolute dictum it seems at first to enjoin.

RETRIBUTION

Belief in retribution is an act of faith in a coherent universe. Divine retribution as a tenet of faith expresses an unwillingness to accept a world in which the guilty go unpunished and the virtuous unrecognized. It constitutes a demand for justice, and a world that is grounded in justice. Among the satisfactions of narrative is the frequent reinforcement of specifically such a vision of the just world. In the consolations of a story's imagined environment in which the wicked are thwarted and the beautiful and good rewarded, we receive a reassurance that our experiences to the contrary do not ultimately prevail. When narratives construct conflicts and manage them in such a way that they are satisfactorily resolved, our doubts are put at a distance, at least for a time.

Prominent among the limited means that narratives have at their disposal for resolution of conflict is the simple expedient of paying the evildoer back with a version of the damage caused. The satisfaction this achieves is sometimes called poetic justice. Another name for it is retribution, meaning literally to pay back (re-tribute).[14] A driving impulse

14. Another option, distinct but related, that narrative has at its disposal for resolving conflict is the drastic clearing away of all opposition, the cleansing impulse that would purge the environment of the story of any contaminating elements relating to the presence of the evildoer. Violence is a preferred tool in narratives compelled by this vision, as it promises a permanent elimination of the offending evil. Whereas payback finds a historic echo in the just war, purgation finds its corresponding historical example in holy war. This is elaborated further in the seventh chapter of this book, "Nostos."

behind retribution is a desire for symmetry, expressed in these cases as a situation of equilibrium between the harm done and its punishing consequence. Its preoccupation with balanced treatment is not simply aesthetic, though it is that. In its symmetric patterns it finds a means to configure in an accessible way within narrative the human need for a habitable and just world.

If God's justice is to be depended on, it must prove adequate to the task of establishing its sway as a final resort. It is here that the imperial demonstration of theological violence makes its demands. With the stakes raised to levels approaching the absolute, Matthew must insist on an adequate degree of divine retribution, one that will fully answer the imperial theology. At the same time, the narrative plot of the Gospel sets its opposition not simply against imperial violence, but also, and more directly, against those who oppose the imperium and yet find its program of violence suitable for their own ends. This, we have seen, is the message of the Gospel's main plotline with its portrait of the "scribes and Pharisees."

This is, of course, paradoxical. At one level it expresses itself as the problematic proposal that a violent God requires nonviolence of his followers. Requiring nonviolence of the disciple then seems an intolerable demand, especially in light of Matthew 5:48—"Be perfect as your heavenly Father is perfect." How then is justice served? If God is a God of justice, nonviolence is reduced to a temporary tactic, a convenient pose for the defeated in the time being. But that is the case, violent action retains its status as the ultimate reality, and the theology of violence wins out.

At another level, however, it would posit a nonviolent God, but a God who needs to assure us that justice is neither a chimera nor a lie. Certainly nonviolence has more than a tactical presence in this gospel, considering not only the teachings but also the practice of Jesus. But looking at the tactical angle only we can discern one of its values. Given the Christian history of violent action in God's name, much of it justified in the name of this Gospel, and supposing it to be a problem Matthew also faced in his own community, we can understand an insistence on nonviolence. If nothing more, it serves as a prophylactic against the disciple assuming the mantle of God's violent agent. Here again the intensity of the warning calibrates to the degree of need. As the Parable of the Wheat and Weeds makes quite explicit, rooting out evil in God's name is not the disciple's task (13:24–30). The injunction to nonviolence defers that action to the time of God's judgment, and not before. Retributive justice can lapse into revenge, when it turns from the social good to gaining personal advantage or redressing personal hurt. Retributive justice has rules and limits; revenge is insatiable, seeking to inflict harm that will satisfy the need to balance the hurt feeling. The lack of a sense of proportion between harm and redress that is lacking in revenge is a hallmark of retributive justice. The punishment is to fit the crime, which is not to equate proportionality with equivalence, which tends toward poetic justice and needs of satisfaction.

Sayings of Just Desserts

Matthew's text contains indications of how the problem of proportional justice and nonviolent mercy might be resolved. Certain proverbial sayings in Matthew's Gospel, supported by a tendency toward poetic parallelism, display a proportionality that is consistent with retributive justice. Some common features characterize the set. First, they are addressed exclusively to the disciples, as seen in the frequent references to "your heavenly Father." In other words, insofar as they promise retribution, they join with other discipleship texts of a similar bent, such as the parable endings of Matthew 13:40, 42, 50. A second aspect of the set is that the sayings display a formal likeness as statements of proportion. Reduced to essentials, to put their common structural features on display, the group looks like this:

Sayings of Proportion between Cause and Effect:
  a) As you would have others do to you, do to them. (7:12)
  b) Those who live by the sword perish by the sword. (26:52)

Sayings of Proportion between Heaven and Earth:
  c) Whatever you bind will be bound, whatever you loose will be loosed. (16:19; 18:18)
  d) Judge not or you will be judged. (7:1)
  e) Whoever acknowledges me I will acknowledge; whoever denies me I will deny. (10:32–33)
  f) Forgive as you are forgiven. (6:12–13; 18:33–35)
  Sayings of Disproportionate Supplement:

g) If you give good gifts to your children, how much more will your
Father in heaven give to those who ask. (7:11)

h) If you love (only) those who love you . . . (5:46)

i) Be perfect as your heavenly Father is perfect. (5:48)[15]

Some of these are unique to Matthew (b, c, f), whereas others are
borrowed, especially from the Q Source (a, d, e, g, h, i). Those borrowed have been conspicuously endorsed by Matthew with the signa-
ture phrase, "heavenly Father."[16] When Jesus speaks of "your heavenly
Father," we know he is addressing the disciples. Insofar as his words
promise retribution, these sayings belong with the parable endings that
heighten the intensity of the Baptist's language. Here again we are in the
aftermath of the mentor.

The first business of the sayings is to forge a causal link between
moral actions and their consequences. (Recall, "By their fruits you shall
know them.") That is the intent of the structure of proportionality. But
the second business is to turn the effect back onto the cause, to assist
the moral agent in making choices. To realize that those who live by the
sword also died by the sword may prove a deterrent. To anticipate what
others might do to me may help me to decide what I will do in my actions toward others. If I can put myself in the other's shoes, as they say, I
may choose to refuse certain actions.

As the segmentation of the preceding list shows, a second subset of
sayings, more characteristic of this Gospel, perhaps, draws a correspon-
dence between heaven and earth. If the Golden Rule offers a paradigm
for the entire group, the sayings on binding and loosing (16:19; 18:18)
serve a similar function for this subset. Here we find the warnings about
judging, denying, and refusing forgiveness that serve to relate these
sayings to retributive justice. It is in these also that the distinctively
Matthean expression "heavenly Father" appears. Among them the sayings involving forgiveness offer a complex picture. On the one hand, the

---

15. Stripped down in this way, the sayings show themselves to share a structure that
can be identified as a variation on the algebraic formula defining proportionality, i.e.,
a is to b as c is to d ($a/b = c/d$). However, the sayings display an extra twist, a reflexive
quality that has the second part of the formula inverting the first: $a/b = b/a$. In this
sense, the sayings can be thought of as variations on the Golden Rule (7:12). They have
their purest formal representation in the chiastic shape of 26:52: "Those who take the
sword / by the sword will perish."

16. Or "Father in heaven"; see 5:46; 6:14; 7:11; 10:32, 33; 18:35.

proportional relation between earth and heaven is made very explicit, as in commenting on the Lord's Prayer:

> For if you forgive others the wrongs they have done, your heavenly Father will also forgive you; but if you do not forgive others, the your Father will not forgive the wrongs you have done. (6:14–15)

Similarly, the parable of the Unforgiving Servant concludes with an assessment:

> And so angry was the master that he condemned the man to be tortured until he should pay the debt in full. That is how my heavenly Father will deal with you, unless you each forgive your brother from your heart. (18:34–35)

Characteristic is the requirement that forgiveness be heartfelt, and not simply performed on command. The tension between virtue motivated by commandment and that by intrinsic merit threatens to pull the saying apart.

In a countervailing impulse similar to that we have seen in other contexts, these sayings of just desserts also yield a further move that seems to cancel the formation they have established. Here the proportionality is framed, but then the frame is broken by an overflow, an excess that overcomes the strict equivalences set out by the pattern. If we are looking for a paradigmatic statement for this group, we might find it in the saying about gift-giving: "If you know how to give good gifts to your children, how much more will your heavenly Father given good things to those who ask" (7:11). Not only is the proportionality strained by "how much more," but also the concept of the gift itself, conventionally yoked in patterns of exchange though straining against those constraints, subverts the equation that contains it. The practice of giving gifts moves toward forgiveness, and the theme of forgiveness appears in this set as well. When Peter asks how many times one should forgive, and Jesus responds with his quantified answer, "seven times seventy" (18:21–22), we know he intends forgiveness to be unconditional. And with that we are in the vicinity of the parable of the Unforgiving Servant, with its struggle between debt and gift, as the servant will be forgiven on the condition he forgive unconditionally. Unconditional offering is the property of the gift. And as we know from the history of dialogue concerning justice and mercy, the free grace of the gift threatens the

frame of proportional justice. In her political analysis of the contest between power and violence, Hannah Arendt speaks to this. She privileges
forgiveness as the one certain conclusion to a pattern of reciprocal violence and credits Jesus of Nazareth with its discovery.[17] Listing revenge
and legal punishment as alternative responses to harm done, she shows
how forgiveness alone, by refusing the chance to retaliate, manages to
avoid incurring a new debt of violence. Here the functional component
is nonretaliation.

All this leads to the sayings concerning love of enemies (5:46, 48).
Love is more than mutual attraction; it also is the self-offering that invests the acts of giving and forgiving with their unconditional dimension. We return to the basic insights of the Golden Rule, insofar as our
own preference for treatment guides our behavior toward others. But
where the sayings on love of enemies take matters beyond the Golden
Rule is in the way they situate love within an arena of conflict. Thomas
Merton famously identified Gandhi's practice of nonviolence as the refusal to hate the opponent.[18] In so doing, one foregoes the pleasures of
enjoying the defeat or resenting the success of an opponent. And while
love, when associated with passion, often enough involves violence, at
heart it wishes the other well and rejoices in that eventuality should it
occur.

Of course, the most explicit rejection of the formula of retribution
is Jesus' commentary on the law of Talion (5:38–42), immediately preceding the sayings on love. If the law of Talion expresses the principle of
retributive justice, the passage on nonretaliation rejects it in principle.
In fact, nonretaliation is the essence of nonviolence in Matthew. As a
second moment, the moment of response to harm done, it gathers under its prohibition all of Matthew's second moments, whether triumphal
homecoming or retributive acts, demanding forgiveness or forswearing
the sword, requiring love of enemies or frustrating the narrative satisfactions of violent conflict resolution.

In narrative conflicts it is presupposed that the reader or listener
is included among the righteous. We are always required to take a position for one side and against another, with the presumption that ours is
the righteous side. And when the right is grievously threatened in the
unfolding of the story line, when harm is done to the righteous a debt is

17. Arendt, *Human Condition*, 238.
18. Merton, *Faith and Violence*, 19–20.

incurred that requires payment. Such payback is an essential component of the narrative economy. To ignore it in the telling of the story is not only to violate the conventions of narrative, but it is also to throw doubt on the universe as a just and habitable place. But it is just this need for symmetry of harm and requital that Matthew's Gospel questions in its particular attention to the second moment in the exchange of damaging actions. The theme of nonretaliation recurs. In the denial of the law of Talion (5:39), in the sword saying (26:52), and in the failure to complete the full complement of revenge in carrying out the formula story of the banished prince, Matthew insists on the asymmetry of a refused balance. In focusing on the moment of retaliation to deny it, Matthew jeopardizes one of the main techniques narratives employ for depicting a just world. He balances this unsettling move with another, an affirmation of retributive justice in the sayings of Jesus.

The juxtaposition of retributive justice and nonviolence might be viewed as a disturbance in the text that Matthew never satisfactorily resolves. Instead, he looks first at one side of the matter, then at the other. In its intended alignment of two divergent positions it is similar to nonviolent resistance, which attempts to confront and resist evil while avoiding the use of violence in doing so. It is a difficult balance, and many find it to be an incoherent position on the theory that all opposition, all conflict, is in some way violent. We might see Matthew struggling with the same issues, trying to insist on both values, resisting violence and acting nonviolently. If that is what we might call the near side of the problem as it appears in human practice, we can also see that Matthew is coming on a mystery at the far side, in the implied characterization of God. In some ways this is the ancient problem of God's justice and mercy, difficult to hold in mind at the same time. But again, there are suggestions in Matthew's text that he would profess a nonviolent, transcendent God.

TRANSCENDENCE

After the question John directs from prison, "Are you the one who is to come, or should we look for another?" (11:3), Jesus discusses the difference between them. The evangelist inserts at this point a verse that reflects the tension between the two apparently incompatible positions more than it resolves it: "From the days of John the Baptist till now the kingdom of heaven has suffered violence and the violent plunder it" (Matt 11:12).[19]

19. Barbara Reid's translation, as above. See her discussion of this term in "Violent Endings," 239–241.

The verse is a crux and conundrum. It is important for a number of reasons. The noun here translated as "the violent" appears only here in the New Testament. This verse then joins others such as Matthew 5: 39 (nonretaliation) in signaling the importance that Matthew invests the theme of violence and nonviolence. In addition, the verb here translated "plunder" is a Matthean term, appearing elsewhere in the Gospel in contexts including mention of Satan and kingdom. That is, he is sounding the theme of the imperial theology of violence.

Unfortunately, the obscurity of the verse is such that Davies and Allison can list in their commentary on Matthew seven distinct interpretations.[20] The ambiguity of the text in context centers on the question of whether it considers the Baptist to be part of the kingdom he announces or prior to it. Within or without? The uncertainty of position reflects the tension in Jesus' relation to John, both adhering to and revising his message. Following Barbara Reid's translation, we might ask what its message of violent plunder is for Matthew's text.

A clue can be derived from a literary interpretation of the verse—Flannery O'Connor's novel, the title of which she borrowed from Matt 11:12: *The Violent Bear It Away*. It is another homecoming story though seemingly a failed one, as the young protagonist burns the homestead down on his return. The Tarwater grandfather and grandson, who share their name with a bitter folk remedy, suggest John's baptizing water. And a baptismal act plays a pivotal role in the novel, as well. O'Connor depicts a certain kind of Christian vision inspired by the Baptist, pivoting on righteous anger. But does the Gospel verse cited by O'Connor's title consider him Christian? Again the question arises, is John in the kingdom or outside it?

The spirit of retributive violence pervades the novel and would seem to characterize young Tarwater's immolation of his home. But O'Connor makes it clear in her letters that she views young Tarwater's actions in a positive light, as a long-delayed obedient response to a call to prophesy. She concedes that many readers will not see the matter in this way, trapped in the secular mind-set that she wishes to confront. In effect, those who view the act as ironic are placed outside the novel's world of shared values. They are under judgment along with those whom the young prophet goes forth to address. O'Connor would appear to intend something other than retributive justice in her story. In this

---

20. Davies and Allison, *Matthew 8–18*, 254–55.

way it aligns with Matthew's Gospel, pointing to a supplement beyond retributive justice.

The shock of the transcendent, the Other, breaking into our neatly conventional existence, can be felt and imagined as an act of violence. O'Connor dramatically exploits that convergence in her use of narrative violence.[21] It is a powerfully effective way to dramatize the disorienting experience of encountering the divine beyond human categories. However, in using violence to describe something beyond our conventional reality, it delivers an ambiguous message, given that our conventions are quite accustomed to violence.

When we turn to the Gospel of Matthew, we might recognize that here too the text points beyond the conventions of justice, and even those of narrative—conventions that can only express sanctions within its limited means. And yet language can point beyond language. However, Matthew does not allow himself to represent the in-breaking of the transcendent by violence. For him, violent reprisal remains a page from the culture, especially the imperial theology of violence. In Matthew, the shock of the Other is represented rather by nonviolence, even nonretaliation.[22] In this case, there interposes no comforting, or confusing, endorsement of the cultural norms. There is only surprise and shock. Nonviolence is an unthinkable norm; it is unrealistic. It is consigned by disturbed critics to the messianic peace of the end-time community, where, of course, it actually would have no purpose. Matthew's words on nonresistance prompt Reinhold Niebuhr to identify Jesus' teaching on these matters as an Impossible Ideal, important to hold in mind, but impossible to place in reality. And yet it is worth noting that Matthew did not present it as an ideal, but rather as a requirement for discipleship in practice. But then the positions of the Christian Realist and the Evangelist vis-à-vis the empire differ considerably, as well.

If Matthew's God scandalizes us, it is not because of violent retribution, which is consonant with our categories of justice. Rather it is because of the insertion of nonviolence into the picture. And more specifically, that Jesus and the disciples are required to follow the nonviolent way, whereas God is not. But nonviolence prescribed as a standard, and

21. For another example, see Dillard, "Expedition", 17–52.

22. This is the import of the sayings on nonretaliation (5:38–42) and love of enemies (5:43–47), summarized by the injunction to "be perfect, just as your heavenly Father is perfect" (5:48).

not as a default posture, and as such unmotivated by the culture, points beyond to a quality of transcendence that is, in this Gospel, divine.

The false mentor differs from the true in the matter of maintaining control over the results. As a continuing reference point, the image of the false mentor provides a gauge for the quality of mentorship. John's proposal leaves things up to God, but still yearns for immediate satisfaction. Jesus removes even this. The lesson of his teaching and the example of his (seemingly failed) return is that the prophetic word is pronounced, but not for rewards. The issue becomes a matter of psychological satisfaction for those of the Kingdom. Ceding control means to postpone satisfaction or bracket it entirely. On the one hand, the disappointment at not being present for the fulfillment of the promise of justice is allayed by the assurance that overweening violence will have its comeuppance. Proportionate retributive justice assures that. This allows room for nonviolent action as the norm for the meantime. On the other hand, a standard of nonviolence prohibits premature foreclosure on the final judgment at the hands of militant Christians and establishes an image of a nonviolent God. Far from being merely a tactic, nonretaliation and love of enemies is presented as a means of being "perfect as your heavenly Father is perfect" (5:38–48).

false mentor vs real mentor

proportionate retributive justice

PART THREE

The Reckoning

THE FIRST PART OF this book, "Constructing a Narrative," establishes that Matthew's plot addresses the moment of response to harm. Nonviolent response is seen in the teachings of Jesus on forgiveness and nonretaliation. But the primary expression of the theme in the narrative itself is a homecoming story. Matthew surrounded the rising action of Mark's story with an itinerary that inscribes a circle in the plotline, from Jerusalem back to Jerusalem. In so doing, he evokes the traditional story of an infant prince, banished in a coup, who survives to return triumphant and regain his kingdom. In this image of the Gospel, Jesus' entry into the city of Jerusalem represents an agenda of resistance, displaying an unwillingness to leave earlier violations unaddressed, unprotested. But as an expression of nonviolent confrontation it finds it necessary to abandon the conventional ending of the banished prince story, replacing carnage with a symbolic gesture, the "cleansing" of the temple. In the manner of the prophets, resistance is combined with nonviolent action.

In its second part, "Banished King; Exiled Nation," the book examines more closely the narrative patterns in Matthew, elaborating the emphasis on response as a response to imperial violence. Using as an interpretive lens the homecoming story in its fuller guise as the formula of the banished prince, it searches the latent dimensions of Matthew's story for insight into the Gospel's nonviolent values.

Chapter 4, "Usurper," raises the question of the violation itself, with the implication that some adequate response to the violation will be required. In light of Matthew's social setting, it frames the story in the wider historical "usurpation" of Israel's self-rule, seen in its history of imperial subjugation, here being worked out in the conflict between Jesus' "Kingdom of Heaven" and Rome's imperium.

The fifth chapter, "Impostor," examines the conflict in the main plot as one discussing possible forms of response to the fundamental violation. It allows us to see the main plotline, the narrative between Jesus and "the scribes and Pharisees," as a conflict between different modes of resistance to the imperium. The Kingdom that Jesus proclaimed requires a complete dissociation from the violence that characterizes the imperial project. His opponents, representing for Matthew temptations of the disciple, are willing to compromise, to allow their complicity.

Chapter 6, "Mentor," examines the demands made on the disciples as viewed through the changing relation between John the Baptist and Jesus. It looks at the encouragement for nonretaliatory nonviolence required of the disciple that is given by the assurance of God's justice, stated as violent eschatological retribution, and it considers the contradictions involved. Insisting on the divine retribution that assures justice will be done in support of the disciple's resistance to injustice, the Gospel also insists on the necessity of nonviolence for the disciple. Without fully resolving the tension between these views, the text implies an ultimately nonviolent God.

At this point it seems appropriate to recall the diagram of plotlines that began the second part of this book. However, the pattern can be expanded to two diagrams, describing in this manner the two levels of the inclusive story. On the one hand, there is the presented narrative of Jesus versus the scribes and Pharisees. It finds itself positioned between a background story of imperial power versus the Judean world and a subplot of sorts contrasting Jesus and the Baptist.

Conflicts in Matthew

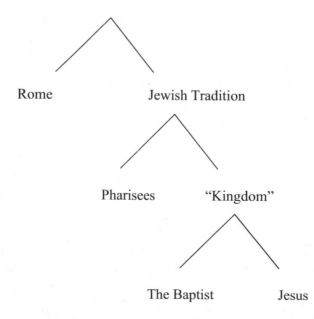

Rome   Jewish Tradition

Pharisees   "Kingdom"

The Baptist   Jesus

But this presenting story projects another meaning that is charted in the second diagram. Here the same three levels configure the world of Matthew, but now the empire has expressed itself in reducing the Temple to the Burnt Place, and the dispute, if such it is, between Jesus and the Baptist represents a putative disagreement within the community concerning the role of violence and retribution.

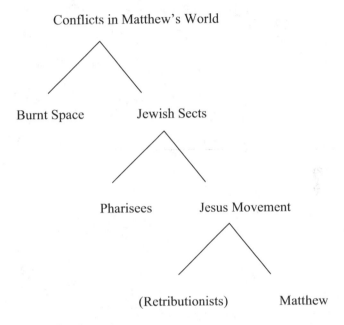

Conflicts in Matthew's World

Burnt Space   Jewish Sects

Pharisees   Jesus Movement

(Retributionists)   Matthew

This final part of the book examines the resolution of Matthew's narrative conflict, along with a look at the new, postnarrative story that is announced in the commission of the disciples in the final verses. The last week of Jesus' life corresponds, in our prevailing conceit, to the "Nostos" of the homecoming stories. These are the events that follow on the return of the banished king. We adjust our focus from the payback of retribution toward the purgation of cleansing. Although Matthew's account expresses a particular form of nonviolent response, it is also deliberate, and in this sense is not to be counted as the failed helplessness of a victim. Although the cleansing is nonviolent, the nonviolence is also purgative.

7

Nostos

WHEN JAMES JOYCE GROUPED the final chapters of his novel, Ulysses, under the title "Nostos," he had in mind Odysseus' return to Ithaca. It was to be read as precedent for Bloom's arrival back home in Eccles Street. Nostos, Greek for "homecoming," produces definite literary allusions. The classical Nostoi were tales about the Greek heroes returning from Troy, which could be treacherous. Agamemnon was famously murdered on his arrival home, which prompted an extra degree of caution for Odysseus. It also gave impetus to the hero's decision to slay the suitors who infested his residence. Agamemnon's experience is instructive of the ways of usurpation. It wants to be comprehensive to secure itself and make sure that no vestige of the former dynasty is around threatening the restoration of the now-deposed regime. So Agamemnon paid the price. As Shakespeare also reminds us with his history plays, the cycle of violence, retaliation for previous retaliation, is a threat in the case of deposing rulers as well, and civil wars may begin this way.

For biblical examples we need look no further than Jehu, king of Israel. In his campaign to rid the nation of the polluting influence of Baal worship, he provides a model of the stages through which usurpation tends to move (2 Kgs 9–10). In addition to the deposition of the ruling kings, Jehoram in the northern kingdom of Israel and Ahaziah of Judah, he completes the task through the further steps of consolidation and eradication. The need to consolidate his position persuades him to have the driving force behind the opposition, the queen mother, Jezebel, killed. Then, by assassinating some seventy princes, he eliminates any who would be likely to supply the throne with another ruler. A further stage is eradication. He zealously purges both kingdoms of family members related to Ahaz, thereby also threatening the continuation of any David family members as well. In Jerusalem, the queen mother Athaliah, daughter of Jezebel and also an adherent of Baalism, responds to her son's murder by seizing the throne and attempting to exterminate the Yahwist worshipers of the David family (2 Kgs 11:1–16). But her young grandson, Jehoash, was hidden away by the priest, Jehoiada. In a version of the banished prince story, some years later the young prince was produced to inherit the kingdom.

Although Jehu provides a vivid biblical example of the patterns of usurpation, cases closer to our story would include that of David.[1] Although the narrator of the David story in 1–2 Samuel makes sure that we understand that David is not personally responsible for the extinction of the family of Saul, and that his own remarkable ascension to the throne is written in the inscrutable moves of providence, the pattern follows the same program of effective usurpation. Not only must the sitting ruler be deposed, but also his immediate heirs. For David this service is accomplished by the Philistines in the Battle of Gilboa (I Sam 31:2, 4), which claimed the lives not only of Saul, but also his sons, Jonathan, Aminadab, and Malchishua, his immediate successors. In due order, the Saulide strongman and kingmaker, Abner, is dispatched (2 Sam 3:27), after placing a previously unreported son of Saul, Ishbaal, on the throne, who is in turn killed (2 Sam 4:7), while Jonathan's son, Meribaal, and grandson, Micah, are placed under house arrest (2 Sam 9:1–13), removing them from further action.

In the appendix to David's story (2 Sam 21:8), we read that certain loose ends were also tied up, as David dutifully hands over the five sons of Saul's daughter, Merob, to the Gibeonites, who wish to kill them to avenge an earlier outrage. Saul's illegitimate sons, Armoni and Meribaal, are dispatched in the same action. The only member of the house of Saul we know to be still extant is the clansman Shimei, left to curse David as the king himself gets a taste of usurpation at the hands of Absalom (2 Sam 16:5–8).

Usurpation tends toward massacre because it needs to cover all eventualities to secure itself against further reprisals. But there are other motivations involved other than the pragmatic. As seen with Jehu, depo-

---

1. Along with deposition, consolidation, and eradication, other measures consistently include marrying in and house arrest. The rule of Herod the Great also exhibits a complete set of these features, as chronicled in Josephus, *Ant.* 1.1, 2; 2.5; 3.1. 3, 9, 6; 2, 7. 4, 5, 6; also *War* 1.11.6; 21.12; 22.2, 5, 6.

sition of a sitting ruler and usurpation of his regime is a profoundly dis-
turbing social action and certainly cannot be attempted without serious
justifications. Shakespeare shows the pattern in Richard II, in which the
specter of uncontrolled misrule prompted the pragmatic, but also ambitious, Bolingbroke to move against the throne in an action that resulted
in civil war, the War of the Roses. The question is whether the action is
justified in light of its consequences. In his case, Jehu's attempt to purge
the land of the pollution of Baalism would provide such a reason, and it
is not exceptional in construing the threat as contagion.

Meanwhile, in response to the usurping action—the Nostos of the
deposed king—the returning prince finds himself in a position to reciprocate in kind, and for similar reasons. The pragmatic need figures here
as well. Just as the initial deposition of the regime was comprehensive
so as to be secure, so is the return movement. The returning king, by
his very existence, knows that he represents a failure in the extent of the
usurping effort, so he plans to eliminate the possibility of his counterpart escaping in the next move of the game. And this pragmatic motive
is accompanied by others. First, the demands of retribution enter the
picture, as paying back harm for harm done is required. Insofar as the
usurping event is configured as a crime against God and the social order ordained by God, it is in need of retributive justice, obviously to be
administered by the figure that God has raised up for this purpose, the
returning king.

Furthermore, a comprehensive bloodbath is urged to remove all
taint of the contaminating presence of the usurping violation of order.
And with that move, images of social pollution enter the equation.
Among narrative strategies for responding to evil forces, revenge has
dominated the discussion thus far. But there is another dynamic at work
that seeks to cleanse the world of the story from the contaminating presence of the evil against which it has been struggling. It arranges for the
happy ending by ridding the story of lingering threats of corruption. The
very image of corruption implies a need for "cleaning house." The two
needs of story—the desire for justice, expressed as revenge, and the need
to restore a moral world, seen in cleansing strategies of narratives—
might for convenience be called *payback* and *purge*. These two comprise
the main strategies of violent stories when they arrive at the final stages
of resolving the conflict. Payback is the inclination to exact revenge,
though it is promoted under the broad heading of achieving justice and

restoring order. It wants to get even for insult or injury. It wants to balance the narrative ledger. Where payback aims to redress evil by giving the perpetrator of taste of his or her own medicine, purge resolves the issue by clearing the slate entirely. Where payback envisions just war, purge favors holy war.

Among the collection of banished prince stories that constitutes our example set, Shakespeare's tragedy of Hamlet illustrates both of these patterns. On the one hand the young Hamlet is burdened with a debt of honor, requiring him to avenge his father's death. As a self-conscious example of the genre of revenge play, the play dwells on the problematics of revenge. The code of honor expresses extraordinarily well the laws of retribution and revenge. On the other hand, "something is rotten in the state of Denmark," which leads to the cathartic action that litters the stage with bodies at the final act. Although the play mounts a parodic critique of its own genre, the revenge play,[2] it frames that genre in the formula of the banished and returning prince story. Both payback and purge, revenge and corruption, emerge as explicit themes in the play.

What the code of honor illustrates well is the difficulty of breaking away from the rules of the game. One cannot simply refuse to fight because that is configured as surrender. In our terms, pacifist principle is interpreted as weakness, the principled noncombatant as a "loser." Although Shakespeare's play is a classic example of the banished prince formula revealed through the lens of the revenge genre, its quarrel with its own genre puts the demands of its conventions on display. Hamlet's homecoming turns out to become for him an unexpected task. The ghost of his father presents him with the mandate to have the murderous usurpation of his wicked uncle, Claudius, avenged. With the heightened awareness of a graduate student, Hamlet questions the requirement, and through the struggle of his leading character, Shakespeare puts the genre of the revenge play itself under examination. Not only Hamlet's persistent questioning, but also the variants of responding to an assault on honor seen in the demands made on Laertes and Fortinbras, who, like Hamlet, have a murdered father to avenge, raise doubts for the viewer. Add to

---

2. The genre of the revenge play is described by Watts (*Hamlet*, 55) as "a conspicuous plot-pattern" in which a protagonist experiences the murder of someone close being "unable to secure justice through normal legal channels . . . he pursues a scheme of private vengeance against the wrong-doer, and eventually accomplishes his revenge." We recognize features of the typical Charles Bronson movie.

this the self-conscious play-within-a-play, and we have something of a clinic on the obligations of exacting revenge. Significantly, the play, even while showing revenge to be an intolerable solution to the evils it poses, cannot find a way out other than carrying out the demands of honor, though in a drama that denies its claim to be honorable.

In terms of the story that Matthew tells, themes of obliterating entire populations by a usurping power connect to the Roman Empire. We can establish these coordinates: In Jesus' historical experience this would have taken the form of the destruction of Sepphoris in Galilee. This city, the urban center to which the village of Nazareth was satellite, was thoroughly leveled by Roman forces in 4 BCE, in response to its uprising at the death of Herod the Great. To move to Matthew's personal experience, the destruction of Jerusalem occupies this place. This campaign, designed to solve the problem of the Jews, would return the count to zero. It would be Matthew's experience of the empire's claim to total hegemony, demonstrated through elimination of its opponents. A third moment, now in the form of story, is Matthew's narrative. In this instance he presents the imperial policy of obliteration as delegated through Herod, Rome's king. In the destruction of Bethlehem the same policy is dramatized by way of the slaughter of its children. An appalling symmetry dominates all three expressions of imperial usurpation of the kingdom.

In response to these expressions of usurping presence, we have one moment asymmetrical in its refusal to adopt these measures—Jesus' entry into Jerusalem and his "cleansing" of the Temple. It is commonly called a "cleansing" for the narrative conventions already mentioned. It purges the temple area of a polluting influence, in that it resembles the totalizing actions it answers. But it is asymmetrical in its failure to balance the violations of usurpation with equivalent acts. Its asymmetry is seen on other counts as well. For one, it is directed against those complicit with the empire, rather than against the empire itself. Its thrust is oblique. For another, it declares itself on behalf of a kingship long eclipsed, the house of David, rather than the Hasmonean regime most directly affected. But primarily, its cleansing falls short of revenge, for it spares those it would accuse. Its retribution is not deadly because it takes the form of prophetic judgment, not deadly payback in kind.

TEMPLE AND GARDEN

If Homer's last eight books of the Odyssey constitute Odysseus' Nostos, so the last eight chapters of Matthew's Gospel, 21–28, represent Jesus' own "nostos." In this part of the story Matthew significantly alters and expands his narrative source, the Gospel of Mark. Perhaps more noticeable at first is the proliferation of sayings of Jesus, adding among others the parables of the Two Sons (21:28–31), the Great Feast (22:1–10), the Ten Bridesmaids (25:1–13), the Talents (25:14–30), and the Sheep and Goats (25:31–46). In addition we must include the 23rd chapter with its Woes. Certainly these changes are by no means insignificant, but the focus of this study suggests we look for alterations in the narrative. These may be less obvious for the reader, but they remain decisive. We look at five episodes here, each distinctively Matthean. The first two consist of events found in Mark, but very much altered by Matthew. They depend on and build on Mark's pattern of conflict resolution. The Temple action, intuitively called a "cleansing," is construed as the refusal of comprehensive purgation. The Garden arrest is elaborated as a refusal of payback. In addition to these, two others introduce the motif of "innocent blood." They constitute paired episodes that appear only in Matthew's text and will be considered in light of each other. Judas' suicide, following his rejection of the thirty pieces of silver, and the hand washing of Pilate at the trial of Jesus offer ironic gestures of payback and purge. Beyond their demonstration of the futility of these expedients, they also facilitate Matthew's positive image of conflict resolution. The fifth and final moment is Jesus' final commissioning of the disciples that concludes the Gospel account.

The Temple

In the second chapter of this book, Mark's conflict resolution was described as a movement shuttling between two hills, tracing out, in effect, the reciprocal challenges of Jesus and the religious authorities. With the help of Gene Sharp's theories, three moves in the gospel—the temple action, the garden arrest, and the crucifixion—were interpreted as culminating three characteristic moves in Sharp's theory of nonviolent action: nonviolent confrontation, repressive response, and nonretaliation. Mark carefully articulated the beginning and ending of each move, tagging each with the term *lestes* ("thieves"). This pattern provides Matthew with a template for making his own adjustments, reducing emphasis in some, increasing it in others. The two moments of nonviolent confrontation and nonretaliation, the first culminating in the Temple action and the second initiating in the Garden arrest, receive by far the greatest elaboration. He has reworked the entry scene considerably. Significant adjustments affect his treatment of the story line.

In the first place, the inclusion of the report at 21:10–11, telling us that the entire city was stirred by Jesus' entry, we recognize as the type-scene of the conspicuous entrance, which appears at the conclusion of the homecoming cycle, the cycle that began with the similar type-scene of the Magi's entry, at 2:1–5. This puts us on alert that the return movement is coming to completion. A second alteration adds its impact to this realization. In citing in full (Matt 21:5) the quotation from Zechariah 9:9, rather than simply alluding to it, as does Mark, Matthew brings to a conclusion the series of geographical citation formulae that charted the circle of travel in the homecoming story. In connection with this, the continuity of action integrates the entry with the cleansing. Both occur on the same day, in one movement. This assures us that the return and the cleansing are to be considered a single, though complex, moment. The moment of return is the traditional moment of purgation. So it is in Matthew, but the purgation is gestural and prophetic, not militant and violent. In another adjustment, Matthew cites the children crying "Hosanna" in the Temple during the prophetic action (21:15), reinforcing the bond between the moments of entry and cleansing. What we are to understand is that the formula story of the returning prince is in the background establishing the conventional set of expectations on the return, namely, that of thoroughgoing violent purgation of the "enemy." The narrative works itself out against this backdrop.

Matthew retains the basics of Mark's account of the judgment on the Temple, including the double quotation from Isaiah 56:7 and Jeremiah 7:11. Although Matthew omits part of the Isaian phrase, this can be accounted for by the way he unfolds his story. Where Mark has the quotation, "My house shall be a house of prayer for all nations" (Mark 11:17), Matthew leaves out the final prepositional phrase, "for all nations." It is not that Matthew is rejecting Mark's critique of limited access to the Temple, replacing a judgment about narrowness with one concerning proper prayer. Rather, he is deferring this view of the wider horizon to the end of the gospel, as fitting his plot line.

Matthew retains the Jeremiah portion of the quote intact, ". . .but you have made it a den of thieves," but he supplements it with the interpretive parable of the Great Feast, in which he has inserted an incongruous report of the rejected king retaliating against those first invited, who violently abused his messengers by killing the killers and burning their city (22:7). In this way Matthew extends Jeremiah's judgment beyond the temple to the city itself. Many commentators have noted that this verse participates in the tradition of seeing the destruction of the Jerusalem as God's punishment. It would seem that Matthew, for whom the destruction of the city was in the past, saw here a fulfillment of Jesus' judgment in its devastation by the Roman army. Although it is difficult to align this view with what we are saying of Matthew here, it should be noted that this line of thought is squarely in the tradition of Jeremiah, whose quoted warning made the same point of the first Temple's destruction. The retaliation of violence for violence provides an example of the principle of the Sword Saying: those who live by violence will perish by it.

A decisive example of redactional alterations for narrative purposes is the report of healings taking place during the account of the cleansing (21:14). In a brief notice, the blind and the lame are said to be restored to health thereby connecting the cleansing with the earlier ministry in Galilee. But in Matthew the report does more. It characterizes this moment of judgment as nonviolent. To insert mention of healing (as Luke does at the moment of Jesus' arrest), is to evoke a kind of power that stands at the opposite pole of violent destruction. As prophetic judgment, Jesus' action is a nonviolent protest against what is seen as a contaminated presence. As mentioned before, his purgation is gestural, not bloody.

As a final note, we can point out that event is given additional emphasis in Matthew. He introduces a large crowd present to the event (21:8), signaling that a public statement is being made here, one that counts as a major move in the unfolding narrative. This contrasts with the more private entry depicted in Mark.

In sum, Matthew pictures a return with a purgation of sorts, one that is nonviolent and without victims, as stressed by the inclusion of healings. Such a return enters the narrative as a sharp contrast to the expectations that the formula story has established for Matthew's readers.

The Garden

The moment of nonretaliation at the garden arrest looms much larger in Matthew's account than in Mark's. As with the entry, this is a public event with a "great crowd" attending it (Matt 21:8, 11; 26:47). Matthew notes that the bearer of the sword that afflicts the guard is with Jesus (v. 51), a connection that emphasizes the reactive impulse of the one attacked to strike back. Jesus says, "Put your sword back in its place" (v. 52).

Then there is the Sword Saying itself: "Those who live by the sword by the sword will perish" (26:52). In itself it is an expression of "natural" retribution, the notion that violence attracts violence. But in context, it constitutes the principle of nonretaliation because it inserts itself in the action at the precise moment when retribution is anticipated. The statement of confidence—"Do you not think that I cannot appeal to my Father, and he will at once send me more than twelve legions of angels?" (v. 53)—echoes the encounter with Satan in the desert (Matt 4:6) and indicates that the present event has the character of a deliberate choice, a continuation of that original rejection of Satan's violence. By insisting on this as a chosen action, it is distinguished from an act of surrender, a capitulation. The resistance continues, but not under the form of armed resistance. Matthew doubles the scripture fulfillment formulae (vv. 54, 56) adding to that already in Mark 14:49. It is interesting that, unlike the other scripture citations Matthew has contributed to the Gospel, neither of these cite a specific text. The increased emphasis seen in the doubling of reference, along with the absence of quotation, leads one to suspect that the present passage has a particular meaning for the evangelist. It is a general notice that serves as a culmination of the scripture references posted through the text, and it serves to put on record that Jesus' choice is God's will: this moment, in particular, has that meaning. Once again, we are reminded of the role that Athena played as the divine voice urging complete revenge. In this regard, Matthew's God stands in direct contrast to the Nostos tradition.

In sum, Matthew emphasizes the moment of arrest as the primary instance of nonretaliation, the refusal of payback. It is deliberate, divinely endorsed, and adopted from a position of strength rather than weakness.

Nonretaliation, Not Nonresistance

The Garden arrest is sometime seen as nonresistance, with Jesus as a helpless victim, simply submitting to his fate. But Jesus' refusal to retaliate can instead be described as a form of nonviolent resistance, a position between violent resistance and nonresistance. Unlike violent resistance the approach uses nonviolent means; unlike nonresistance, it attempts to resist evil. The Temple action is sometimes seen as violent because property is presumed destroyed, and a community's deep convictions (Temple worship, God's presence) are placed under assault. However, Jesus presents his action as a prophetic judgment, which implies a criticism of violence, and therefore (by way of a double negative) not a violent act in itself. This assertion is endorsed by the healings.

The Garden account takes pains to show Jesus is not helpless. But nonresistance is not the same as nonretaliation, as Gene Sharp has taught us.[3] Where nonresistance anticipates a degree of harm, nonretaliation has already experienced it. Nonresistance is a stance; nonretaliation is a piece of the interaction. We can see this in comparison to the interchange of actions of Mark's gospel. Although Matthew reframes the first move in the interchange, the confrontation in the Temple, he does not eliminate it. Instead, he makes explicit its character as a response to earlier violations. It retains its character as a concerted move against an opposition, a confrontation. This by itself argues against nonresistance on Jesus' part. His arrest in the Garden of Gethsemane, the moment of nonretaliation par excellence, implies the Temple action that prompted the move against Jesus. Although the sword saying uttered at his arrest (26:52) expresses a sentiment of nonviolent principle, its location here at the primary opportunity for retaliatory action adjusts its meaning. In itself a statement of principle, in context it becomes a defense of nonretaliation.

The sayings of Jesus that pertain to the theme also show this. The pertinent teachings involve scenarios, miniature dramas, rather than general statements of principle. In directing the disciples to reconcile with their accusers (5:22–26), guilt is presumed. In the teaching on the law Talion (5:38–42), provocation is not denied, simply not addressed.

---

3. Sharp's theories also are currently enjoying a revival in that they are being tested in volatile political arenas, such as Iran, where voices in the streets have been applying his ideas to their situation. See Scott Peterson, "Iran protestors: The Harvard professor behind their tactics," *Christian Science Monitor*, Dec. 29, 2009.

In fact, it corresponds nicely with the nonretaliatory moment of Jesus in the Garden. In other words, the innocence of Jesus is resituated in Matthew. His persecution was unjust, but Matthew is not saying it was unmotivated.

Refusal to retaliate in kind does not automatically imply lack of resistance. In fact, insofar as it is an unexpected response in the context of a nonviolent program, it can be assumed to imply resistance. In nonviolent protests of recent years, this is seen in the practice of "going limp" at the time of arrest. It shows resistance in that it avoids cooperation even in the moment of accepting arrest.[4] The element of asymmetry that enters the dynamic when after a violent assault the expected counterviolence is not forthcoming disturbs the rhythm of the customary interchange. It disorients and dislodges the pattern of the "game."

In Matthew's text, the moment of response is invariably a deliberate act serving to end the dynamic of reciprocating violence without actually signaling surrender. Consider how the different elements of the account of Jesus' arrest contribute to its character as both nonviolence and resistance. In the sword saying, Jesus affirms the act of nonretaliation as a purposeful, even principled, performance. On the other hand, with the announcement that ten legions of angels are available for his defense, should he choose that direction, Jesus notifies those coming to arrest him that his consent is withdrawn from their authority, for it belongs more properly to his Father. The command to put the sword aside, the scripture references, each supports the nonretaliation happening here with indications of purposeful, even divinely willed, action. Resistance is not abandoned, it simply takes a different form.

INNOCENT BLOOD

In the Temple action and the Garden arrest, Matthew shows Jesus refusing, respectively, the options of purgation and reprisal—purge and payback. But Matthew takes his plot beyond simple refusal, beyond the negative options of nonretaliation and nonviolence. In a set of deft insertions into the received Markan narrative, Matthew has introduced his own program of conflict resolution. In the theme of "innocent blood" the evangelist not only presents a parody of these false solutions to the

---

4. Sharp, *Politics*, Vol. I.

resolution of conflict, but also finds a positive solution to the original mandate of Jesus, "to save his people from their sins" (Matt 1:21).

Images of payback and purge find unique expression in two passages that appear only in Matthew's Passion. Here Judas (27:3–9) and Pilate (27:24–26) are linked in Matthew's text. Both act in response to misgivings raised by Jesus' "innocence." In throwing the coins into the Temple, Judas signals his desire to restore the situation to its previous status. The attempt is expressive, but ultimately futile, and concludes with his suicide. Ironically, he completes the attempt to return the price of Jesus' betrayal at another register, by paying a life for a life. Pilate's hand washing also signals strongly a wish to be rid of the matter. Washing his hands is a gesture of purgation that under the circumstances is a charade. For each, the gesture changes nothing; in each case the course of events holds.

The parallels between the two inserted passages are instructive:

Matt 27:3–9	Matt 27:24–26
Judas tries to be rid of guilt by saying, "I have sinned in having given over innocent blood."	Pilate tries to be rid of guilt by saying , "I am innocent of the blood of this [righteous] man."
The Jewish chief priests and elders respond, "You must see to it."	Pilate says to the priests and elders and crowds, "You must see to it."
Judas illustrates his attempt to be rid of guilt by throwing the money.	Pilate illustrates his attempt to be rid of guilt by washing his hands.
Judas' action involves the authorities with blood because they must use the blood money.	Pilate's action involves all the people with blood because they cry out, "His blood on us and on our children."

Jacques Escande describes this doublet as two expressions using the same words followed by two comparable gestures.[5] We can extend his observation by noting that the initial expression concerning innocent blood is echoed in the final gesture, with its similar language and concerns about blood. Furthermore, the word *anōos* (innocent) appears twice in the New Testament, in these two incidents featuring Judas and Pilate. The reactions of Judas and the priests receiving his money is one of abhorrent rejection. It is echoed in the scene with Pilate, the warning

5. Escande, "Judas," 96.

from his wife, and especially in the response of the people. The parallels diverge in the gestures characteristic of each—throwing money and washing one's hands, but the effect of a difference is deceptive because each gesture signals the same thing, a desire to be absolved of the action, though symbolized differently: payback on the one hand and purge on the other. We are reminded of the retributive and purity concerns in this narrative.

Judas

The episode of Judas' repentance and death acts out a pantomime of payback. It derives its terms from two antecedent passages. Together these two articulate the moves in the closing moments of Judas' story. One provides the means of exchange; the other the principle of (natural) retribution governing the exchange. The principle is given in the Sword Saying: "Those who live by the sword by the sword will perish" (26:52). At his arrest, the "handing over" that initiated the momentum toward crucifixion, Jesus utters this saying in the presence of Judas. It becomes the insignia for Judas' story. In his frustrated attempt to return the pieces of silver, a parody of Talion's "eye for an eye," we witness a bleak parallel to Jesus' refusal to pay back violence with further violence.

If the Sword Saying contributes the principle of Judas' unfolding story, the thirty pieces of silver provides a medium of exchange. Matthew has introduced the thirty pieces of silver into the account. Again he derives his vocabulary of image and motif from the Old Testament. Following the gospel pattern of citing the book of Zechariah in the final week of the narrative when Jesus is in Jerusalem, Matthew finds a precedent in that account for casting the silver pieces into the treasury (Zech 11:12–13). For Matthew, the thirty pieces of silver provide a language of exchange, not only to describe the negotiations in the resolution of the plot, but also to represent the economy of payback itself. The 30 pieces of silver in effect provide both a medium of exchange and a price for Jesus' body. More precisely, what Judas sells is his access to the company of Jesus, but in the Passion account this plays out in a system of exchanges. Later on, another system of exchange will facilitate negotiations of Barabbas for Jesus in the trial before Pilate.

But Judas' refusal is in turn refused, as the priests will not accept it. His throwing of the coins attempts to override their refusal, and in fact, the priests now have something they do not want. The money has been returned, and now it needs to be passed along. What begins in payback moves toward purge. Retribution moves toward pollution issues, as they are never far apart. Because it is blood money, the priests cannot keep it. In their attempt to escape the bloodguilt of an innocent death, they pass the money on, beyond their purview. But in so doing, they testify to the correct appraisal of the transaction as involving an unjust condemnation. Their action shows it is indeed innocent blood, and their move to escape it actually indicts them. The pattern continues.

Judas repents, but it does not save his life. His repentance is separate from his repudiation of the money, on which the balance of his life hangs. He repents of the action that participated in the process. But in casting the coins, he is not merely attempting to undo the crime by undoing the transaction. He also hopes to be ridding himself of the instruments of exchange, and in that metaphorical action repudiating the economy of violence it has come to represent. He attempts to refuse the role, but he cannot. In returning the money to the chief priests, Judas wants out of the economy of revenge. But there is no escape. He ends by paying a life for a life.

His predicament is that of one caught in the cycle of violence with no clear way out. In Escande's analysis, both Judas and Pilate are prisoners of a common system. He speaks of an inexorable movement during which Jesus, bound, is "passed hand to hand."[6] "Hand over" translates the verb, *paradidomi*. Like the toll of a bell, the repetition of this word resonates through the course of the Passion account. It forms a pattern that originally derives from Mark's account, where it is used to calibrate the increasing distance that is building between Jesus and his own (Mark 14:41–2; 15:1, 15).[7] The relentless string of instances generates an effect of inevitability.

Matthew retains this textual figure while introducing some refinements. He elaborates its connection with Judas, both in the supper account and in the episode of the coins, where it is usually translated "betray." He also sprinkles the term liberally throughout his Gospel, illustrating its possible meanings, as if to highlight its special meaning as regards Judas, as betrayal.[8] But in overloading the text in the accounts of

6. Escande, "Judas," 94. Escande speaks of a "Structure," which Brown, perhaps for American ears, renders as "system."

7. See Beck, *Nonviolent Story*, 61.

8. Items or obligations can be handed over, with the meaning of "entrust" (11:27; 25:14

the supper, arrest, and death of Judas with the term as meaning "betray," Matthew reminds his readers that Judas crucially intervenes in the pattern of supposed inevitability at those times when it threatens to stall. When the authorities begin to make their move against Jesus after the temple action, his skill in debate and the favor of the crowds prevents them from doing so. When Judas intervenes, in complicity with the Council, it restores the momentum toward crucifixion. His pact with the chief priests (Matt 26:14–16) was the move that reenergized the forward motion of the narrative that had threatened to come to a standstill.

Later, when the Council has served a guilty verdict to their own satisfaction, they still find it necessary to convince Pilate, who reserves the authority of the death penalty, to accept their accusation. Again a looming obstacle is overcome to allow the narrative to move forward. In fact, Judas' death and, later, Jesus' death at the command of Pilate testify to the instrumentality of each. Neither death would have occurred if they were not active participants in the action. So the effect of inevitability is undercut by the narrative when it draws attention to the manner in which these two figures facilitate it. Proclamations of helplessness and innocence are belied and somewhat disingenuous. Judas is thoroughly identified with the system of which he is a prisoner, the one who "hands over" the body of Jesus. And yet he is trapped by his own decision.

Judas' helplessness in the face of this "system," is of a piece with that of Hamlet in his repudiation of the conventions that require him to exact revenge while finding himself unable to escape the demand that he do so. Honor demands, in fact, serve well to articulate the "system" that traps participants in a cycle of revenge. The need for retaliation is preeminently a demand of honor maintenance, with its strict social codes of injury and retaliation, assault, and revenge. Although Matthew doesn't use the language of damaged honor, his narrative strongly evokes it. Jerome Neyrey has carefully examined Matthew's text in terms of the code of honor and articulates the "choreography" of challenge and riposte.[9] In the process, he mounts two major arguments. One has to do with Jesus' teaching to the disciples. The other concerns the death of

---

20, 22). Persons can be handed over to authorities, with the meaning of "arrest" (5:25; 10:17, 19, 21; 18:34). But in Judas' case we have a person, Jesus, handed over to authorities, violating a trust, i.e., "betray" (10:4; 26:15, 16, 21, 23, 24, 25, 45, 46, 48).

9. Neyrey, *Honor and Shame*, 20–21, 191ff. A primary goal of his study is to show that Mediterranean conventions of honor and shame apply to Judean culture as well as Greek. Matthew's Gospel is his illustration.

Jesus. Neyrey sees the pattern transcended for the disciple in three ways. In chapters called "Honoring the Dishonored," "Calling Off the Honor Game," and "Vacating the Playing Field," he shows in a series of increasingly demanding practices how disciples are enjoined to be nonviolent, from reclaiming the honor of the dishonored to simply abandoning "honor" as a determination of value.

As for Jesus' story, Neyrey makes his case in two moves. In his ministry Jesus is shown to amass a considerable fund of honor through his works. In his death, on the other hand, Matthew frames Jesus' crucifixion as a noble death, in that way inverting the Roman purpose of the practice. What was conceived as radical humiliation designed to disqualify him in the eyes of his followers and others actually becomes the basis for a new kind of leadership. For Neyrey, Jesus is not a victim of a wicked conspiracy, but rather an inaugurator of an alternative system of values, one that shows the way out of the trap of the vengeance cycle.

Although Neyrey's exposition shows decisively that Jesus does not enter into the Passion as a victim, it still leaves some questions unanswered. We see that a shameful death can be converted into an honorable way to die, but we do not understand why an honorable person should be condemned to a shameful death. Furthermore, one wonders how this honorable death differs from Mel Gibson's take on the Passion, which glorifies violence and presents Jesus as a heroic and noble figure who sustains great damage unflinchingly. Perhaps like Sisyphus or Prometheus, or Rocky Balboa? And although the disciple is enjoined to follow the example of Jesus in keeping the new code of honor, as an authoritative interpreter of God's will (Sermon on the Mount), what motivates this new code for Jesus? In sum, if Matthew prohibits "all conflictual behavior," does this allow for resistance, even if nonviolent? Does this way of framing the matter translate to simple nonresistance? Equating conflict with violence is not adequate.

Pilate

The negotiation of Barabbas for Jesus is a calculus of its own. Its objective is to move Jesus from the status of an innocent accused to one condemned and presumed guilty. The scene moves forward in distinct stages. Twice Pilate asks the crowd whom they want to have released, Jesus Barabbas or Jesus who is called Christ. After the first question, we hear about the message he received from his wife, testifying to the righteousness of Jesus. After the second posing of the question, "Which of the two do you want me to release for you?" and their response, "Barabbas," the governor asks what they want for Jesus. We hear the first of the verdicts: "Let him be crucified." Then Pilate stages the charade of hand washing, with its devastating response: "His blood be upon us and our children." One more time, "What has he done?" But no answer other than "Let him be crucified." Jesus enters the scene charged with a crime; he leaves it counted as guilty.

We are at a point in the narrative, as we were with Judas, when the onward rush of the narrative (*paradidomi*) has stalled, at least potentially. If the crucifixion is to go forward, it will require the cooperation of Pilate, who alone has the authority to mandate crucifixion. Despite the fact that he proclaims that he cannot find any reason for it, he proceeds with the command to have Jesus crucified. In other words, his gesture is empty when weighed against his actions.

As with Judas' drama, this episode begins as a calculus of exchange. Matthew has borrowed and adjusted Mark's account of the trade-off between Jesus and Barabbas. In Mark there is a pattern of incremental steps that move Jesus from accused to presumed guilty. It moves forward in distinct stages.[10] Placing Jesus' situation in the context of a rivalry for pardon already assumes guilt. The guilty are pardoned; the innocent are tried. Matthew makes three crucial changes: Pilate introduced the pardon custom himself (as noted, a decisive move), his wife's dream is reported, and his washing of hands with the crowd response brings the scene to a climax. The effect is to shift the vocabulary of guilt from exchange to contamination, from sleight of hand in the exchange of prisoners to the biblical theme of innocent blood. This is necessary for Matthew's strategy of resolving the plot.

The incident of hand washing also has two antecedent episodes that provide it with a language—Judas' statement about innocent blood and Pilate's wife's dream. Judas' fear that he incur the stain of "innocent

10. In Mark's Gospel, Jesus slides from innocent to condemned by a series of moves. The custom of releasing a prisoner already presupposes a level of guilt, as noted. But then in three moves, (a) Barabbas is declared free (= innocent), (b) Jesus is declared condemned, and (c) the lack of adequate charges is ignored. In response to Pilate's question, the crowd proposes releasing Barabbas. Pilate's first response is to ask what he should do with Jesus. On hearing "Crucify him!" he then asks for what crime? Upon hearing the call for crucifixion repeated, he then moves ahead. With each exchange, Jesus edges closer to condemnation.

blood" introduces this motif, first encountered in the "Woes" (23:35), to the Passion account. The priests' reaction in having to deal with the discarded money illustrates its function. It is a contaminant, insofar as it implicates by contact, and it is a threat of pollution that can invade the community. His wife's dream sets the stage for Pilate's vignette. Just as the sword saying provides a language for the episode of Judas' tossing of the coins, so her dream prepares for the cleansing of Pilate's hands. The language of contamination by contact shapes her message—"Have nothing to do with that righteous man" (27:15). Have no contact with that person. It suggests the conditions for which Pilate's gesture attempts a solution. To rid oneself of polluting contact, the answer is a cleansing.[11]

As with the thirty pieces of silver, Matthew draws on scriptural precedents for the language of "innocent blood." In the Old Testament ritual blood generally has a purifying role. It serves as a purifying agent for the altar (Ezek 43:20) and the Temple (Lev 16:15–16; Ezek 45:18–20). Lepers are cleansed to return from the unclean to normal life (Lev 14), whereas priests are cleansed to leave normal life and enter the holy (Exod 29:9–21; Lev 8:24). Among the few exceptions to this rule was the case of killing an innocent. In that case blood became a polluting force, which, according to the rules of purity, affected the full community. In Deut 21:1–9, we find the procedure for dealing with homicide by an unknown assailant. The community would be threatened with bloodguilt should the community not be ritually cleared of the pollution of bloodguilt.[12] By his succession of disclaimers, Judas, the priests, and then Pilate, Matthew recreates the situation in which no particular individual is assigned guilt. What interests Matthew is the quality of response to unmerited assault. But in presenting their disclaimers of innocence, Matthew is also assigning responsibility.[13]

If we take the scenarios of Judas and Pilate straight, without irony, it would seem that the only agents of the death of Jesus left standing are the Jewish people. Escande, for instance, draws the conclusion by his own

11. Brown (*Death*, 807) suggests that her suffering "may be that she is sharing some of the anguish brought on by innocent blood."

12. A deep obscurity is found here in the bias against killing, as seen in the violation it represents in unjustified homicide, in tension with the need to slaughter to procure ritual blood. This irresolvable problem is handled ritually by discriminating between good and bad killing. In Matthew it serves the narrative in the work of assigning responsibility for the death of Jesus.

13. Brown develops this idea, *Death*, 641–42, 832.

structural analysis that the Gospel puts the blame squarely on the Jews. Further intensifying this reading is that each of the figures in the paired passages contributes something to that reading. Because "Judas" can be read simply as "Jew," and given the response that Pilate elicits, "his blood be upon us and on our children" (Matt 27:25), we would seem to have all the evidence necessary to blame the Jewish people for the crucifixion of Jesus, and thereby justify whatever animus we might muster against them. However, that is a misreading of what Matthew is up to.

As the innocent blood motif plays out, Judas, then the priests, and finally Pilate all are shown making efforts to escape contamination. Whether we are to understand these disclaimers as successful is debatable. Nevertheless, in this exercise in assigning responsibility, it becomes clear that "all the people" are left with the blame. Various readings have been proposed that would mitigate the inclusiveness of the charge that seems implied here. For instance, Amy-Jill Levine in a careful study proposes that it focuses on Jerusalem and specifies the leadership rather than the whole people. Warren Carter speaks of the "elites" that direct the crowd and serves as the antagonist party in his reading of the Gospel. Nevertheless, because Judas, the priests, and Pilate each work concertedly to avoid the stain of bloodguilt, while the people explicitly accept it, we can only conclude, despite the machinations of the characters involved, that Brown is correct in asserting that Matthew intends to indicate that only the people as a whole accept responsibility. [14]

Furthermore, the biblical category of "innocent blood" indicates communal guilt. In identifying themselves as being the responsible agents of Jesus' death, the people claim to be guilty of the blood of the innocent. Shed blood becomes a polluting force; the influence of pollution invades the group. Deut 21:1–9, seen by some as pivotal,[15] gives the procedure to follow when one does not know who committed a murder. "Let not (the guilt for) innocent blood be deposited in the midst of your people Israel" (Deut 21:7). In this example the guilt threatens to contaminate the whole people. That is, it works as pollution proper. This is the concept operative in Matthew's account. However, in Deuteronomy it envisions a local situation, with the nearest settlement at risk. For the situation in which the pollution is total rather than local there is a ritual

---

14. Levine, *Social Dimensions*, esp. 193–239, 261–71; Carter, *Margins*, 528; Brown, *Death*, 832.

15. H. Frankemölle, *Jahwebunde*, 208–9.

in place: the Day of Atonement, and the banishing of the scapegoat. And with this move, Matthew's narrative moves from nonviolent conflict resolution conceived negatively as simply avoiding violence to nonviolence conceived as a positive action.

The Scapegoat

In the Israelite tradition, communal guilt of the whole people is removed in terms of the imagery field of pollution. It is the work of the scapegoat on the Day of Atonement. Leviticus 14 describes the ritual. Two goats were chosen, one to be sacrificed with its blood anointing the sacred objects in the temple, the other to be driven into the wilderness taking with it the sins of the people. The concept is not sacrificial, but rather absorbent. The sins are placed on the goat, which takes the pollution far from the settlement. The Mishnah (Yoma 6:6) describes a ritual in which the route to the wilderness is marked with booths or stations that formalize the departure. Along the way some would calumniate the goat, pull on its hairs, and cry, "Bear (our sins) and begone." The goat was led to a high precipice, a rock was tied to its horns, and it was cast over the cliff to its death. In this way the pollution was drawn off and away from the people.

When we consider the arc of Matthew's plot in terms of the mandate at 1:21, we see a gospel that carefully restricts Jesus' mission to the "lost sheep of the house of Israel." Given that the postresurrection commission goes out to all nations, it would seem that something decisive has happened between the ministry and the resurrection to alter directions. The simplest (though incorrect) reading is that Jesus' mission to Israel failed because he was rejected, and that is the significance of 27:25. He was rejected; his mission to Israel failed.

However, Matthew's theme of innocent blood would suggest something else. Despite the lack of explicit reference to the scapegoat ritual, the narrative evokes its presence. Matthew's additions to the Passion account largely concern the theme of innocent blood and exploit this motif to organize the resolution of the plot. This resolution of the pollution thematic is nothing more (and nothing less) than Jesus absorbing violence rather than pushing it back. In this case, the ironic reality of the narrative is that Jesus does in fact save his people from their sins (1:21). Insofar as all Israel is involved in the pollution of innocent blood, deliverance is accomplished by the death of Jesus, achieved without reprisal.

In Matthew's narrative Jesus suffers, but not for the sake of suffering itself. Rather, it is suffering instead. In the narrative context it is an alternative to the cultural norm. Jesus is not the culture hero. He does not return violence in the attempt to save the day. Instead, he absorbs it so that it stops there. No reprisals. One might compare Hannah Arendt's notion of forgiveness. In her reading, forgiveness, seen as a theme that enters political discourse through the teachings and practice of Jesus, interrupts a strand of violent reprisals by refusing to pay it back, despite justifications to do so. The options of vengeance or punishment attempt to achieve closure on cycles of violence, but fail to do so. Only letting go of the pattern of reciprocity will accomplish that. And we have seen the prominence that the theme of forgiveness takes in Matthew's account. So what remains necessary is to adopt the model Jesus provides, as spelled out in his instructions to his disciples in the Sermon on the Mount, and elsewhere.

In Matthew's narrative, then, these redactional effects converge:

1. An emphasis on "all the people," seen for instance in Matthew's preference for the term "Israel8," as in "all Israel" (2 Sam 5:5; Matt 2:6).

2. A process of elimination involving Judas, the priests, and Pilate, that would simulate the situation envisioned in Deuteronomy 21—a crime without an identifiable perpetrator.

3. The scapegoat ritual as a nonsacrificial model for drawing off the guilt of the whole people (Lev 16:10).

4. The nonviolent pattern of being willing to absorb evil and violence rather than paying them back, thereby ending real or potential strands of reprisal.

5. The practice of Jesus as a nonviolent model for the disciple in situations of conflict (Matt 5:38–43).

Of course, invoking the image of the scapegoat is scarcely possible today without some consideration of the thesis of René Girard, who brought that theme to current prominence in critical theory. Although Girard's insight of the scapegoat is suggestive, it might be anchored more securely in the text if we heed Brown's caveat that the story and gesture in Matthew are Jewish. This is a Jewish story, and the key to their meaning is in the scriptures.[16]

Girard sees in the trial of Jesus an example of the scapegoat according to his theory. That would posit a pattern in which two feuding parties, trapped in a cycle of revenge and counterrevenge, stop the cycle by identifying a third party, the scapegoat, as the putative cause. The scapegoat, a victim too weak to continue the cycle of violence, becomes its end point. The feud is concluded so long as the parties at odds can continue to convince themselves that the scapegoat, weak as it is, is still capable of being the cause of the dispute and reservoir of its violence. Girard holds that the Christian story has the reader identify with the sacrificial victim and see the operation for what it is, a psychological mind game. In this case the reader is deprived of the pleasure of believing in the guilt of the scapegoat. By identifying with the victim, the reader understands the helplessness of the scapegoat. The Christian reader finds the mechanism of the scapegoat no longer believable and therefore bankrupt as a useful stratagem for dispersing the social reservoir of violence. Pilate's hand washing then would prepare his decision that Jesus replace Barabbas and therefore bear the brunt of displaced guilt.

But as Neyrey has insisted, Jesus is no victim in this story. His is a deliberate choice. His resistance continues. In his dialogue with Judas at the arrest, and in his dialogue with Pilate at the trial, we witness his sense of purpose. His nonviolence remains a form of resistance. Rather, it seems to me, something else is happening here. Instead of being the victim, Jesus is refusing to blame a victim, to play the card of accusing the scapegoat. It is Jesus' story, and he remains an actor in the Passion. His action consists in refusing the conventional solaces, the usual easy attributions. Pilate is Jesus' foil here, just as Judas is at the arrest. Pilate plays the pollution scenario, from the cleansing ceremony to the negotiation of Jesus and Barabbas, at which point he smuggles in Jesus as the substitute who will now bear the guilt. But Jesus, in his silence and refusals, remains in charge of the action and accomplishes what Pilate cannot.

A common mechanism of stories, in their quest for a happy ending, is to cleanse the story world of all evil by equating that evil with

16. Brown, *Death*, I, 834–35. Girard is not as close a reader of the biblical text as he is an advocate for the concept of the scapegoat. For instance, he attributes Matthew's vignette of Pilate's wife to John's Gospel.

the antagonist of the piece, the villain, and then permanently removing the villain from the scene. At this point the character is no longer a human being with bad habits but in fact the pure personification of badness—evil with a human face. So it is that violent dispatching of the villain is counted as a virtuous act. Of course, pulling this off requires a mental trick, particularly when the evil being removed is itself violence. Employing violence to purge a domain of its violence is no closer to peace than the "poetic justice" of revenge is true justice. Each seeks satisfaction, rather than truth. Insofar as he accepts the violence without returning it, Jesus reverses the common narrative pattern.

In sum: In all the stories, the moment of return is the time of purging the realm, whether it is delayed as in Hamlet, or protracted as in the Odyssey and the Moses story. In Matthew's gospel it is, however, immediate. When Jesus arrives in Jerusalem he enters the Temple without delay. There is no pondering the move overnight as in Mark's account, in which Jesus returns the next day for the confrontation that we instinctively call the Temple "cleansing." But in Jesus' return there is no bloodshed, no thorough liquidation of the enemy, no casualties, unless we count, eventually, himself. In terms of the story formula with its need for comprehensive slaughter, Jesus' Temple action is prophetically accusatory, even while being nonretaliatory. As a protest it is a gesture; as a gesture it is nonviolent.

At the subsequent moment of his arrest, Jesus rejects the violent mode of resistance, though he continues to resist in another register. Still in control, he has ten legions of angels at his disposal should he choose that form of defense. But the point of nonretaliation is the refusal to regard the opponent as enemy. In submitting without surrendering, two things happen in their relationship between Jesus and his opponents. He refuses to dehumanize them. In not demonizing them, in respecting them and not allow them to be cast as the embodiment of evil, they retain their human faces and persona dignity. The gesture interrupts their prepared response, which is to act just in that manner, the role expected of them. But another dynamic is at work as well. Jesus, though surrendering, is not intimidated. In the remarkable decision to oppose without fighting his own personality is asserted to the extent that they must acknowledge him and recognize in turn a different quality of relationship.

GO FORTH TO ALL NATIONS

"Nostos" finds a sentimental surrogate in "Nostalgia," designating a futile, sometimes pathological, need to return to an unavailable past. Miriam Pestowitz suggests a definition as "a wistful desire to return in thought or in fact to a former time in one's life, to one's home or home-land, or to one's family or friends."[17] As a compound of two Greek words, representing the "ache" (*algos*) of "returning home" (*nostos*), it names a sentimental dream of homecoming and can also describe a medical condition, known in English as homesickness. Pestowitz considers the theme in a postcolonial context, thinking about ways in which colonists recall a home they construct in their minds, either as homeland or even as the colony itself, as for instance in picturing America as the "New Jerusalem." In the course of her reflection she considers the role of the "Holy Land" as a "true" home for many pious Christians. In fact, it would seem that "return" to the Holy Land may be another version to reading the gospel as a return to origins.

With the pull of homecoming in mind, along with Matthew's theme of homecoming, it is striking to see Matthew's Gospel end with a move away from the land, as if the first return, the entry in chapter 21, would be sufficient to honor any claims of return. Perhaps it is paradoxical that all through the text, guided by the Old Testament references, the Gospel draws on past memories to project a future. The final verses of the Gospel have the character of a new beginning:

> Then the eleven disciples went to Galilee,
> to the mountain where Jesus had told them to go.
> When they saw him, they worshiped him;
> but some doubted.
> Then Jesus came to them and said,
> "All authority in heaven and on earth has been given to me.
> Therefore go and make disciples of all nations,
> baptizing them in the name of the Father and of the Son
> and of the Holy Spirit,
> and teaching them to obey everything I have commanded you.
> And surely I am with you always,
> to the very end of the age." (Matt 28:16–20)

17. Pestowitz. "Tropes," 83–84.

The new story that begins here is the story of the church that produced this gospel, Matthew's church. Its emblem is the missionary discourse of Matthew 10. We saw how that chapter superimposes the later story of Matthew's church on the story of Jesus. The Gospel does not enact a return to the former story, the story of Jesus, but rather appropriates Jesus' story for a possible future, a future that contains the church of Matthew.

A clue is found in the promise, "I am with you always, to the very end of the age" (v. 20). We recall the title "Emmanuel" ("God with us") with which the story of Jesus began (Matt 1:23), and we realize that this final commissioning reworks the original mandate that set out the narrative project of this Gospel: Jesus is to "save his people from their sins" (Matt 1:21). As we determined earlier in chapter 1, the "people" consists of "the lost sheep of the house of Israel." And so Jesus insists, first with the disciples that he is sending out on mission, and then with the "Canaanite" woman whose daughter Jesus rid of demonic possession (Matt 10:6; 15:24).

But now we discover that mandate has moved to "all nations." Something has happened in the meantime to alter the program—or perhaps, more accurately, to initiate another. And what has happened is that "all the people" have rejected his mission (27:25), a rejection taking the form of crucifixion. And in the resurrection, on the other side of crucifixion, another story begins.

So we are left with two social identifications, and a tightly tensed contrast between them: "all the people" (27:25); "all nations" (28:19). The first identifies those who have rejected Jesus; the second those who have yet to hear of him. Both terms are vigorously disputed as to the content and extent of their range of implication.[18] Together they frame a traditional interpretation that "all the people" points to the Jews while "all nations" points to the Gentiles, and together they represent the rejection of the former in favor of the latter. Today, in light of the unspeakable damage inflicted through history on Jews by Christians and Christian regimes, culminating in the holocaust, efforts are being made to reconsider this reading.

On the one hand, scholars dispute the thesis that Matt 27:25, the response to Pilate, refers to the Jewish people in general. But certainly

18. See, e.g., Grayston, "Translation," 105–109; Hare, "Disciples," 359–369; Meier, "Nations," 94–102.

Raymond Brown is correct in saying that the dramatic effect of the narrative depends on the generalized reading, despite our wish that it be otherwise. On the other hand, we've seen that scholars have also disputed the reading of Matt 28:14 that would exclude Jews from its reference and envision it to include Gentiles only. In this regard, certainly we are correct to see the "new Israel" as a Jewish vision, and therefore a Jewish future. And if Bruce Malina's assertion is correct, that the concept of universalism is unavailable at this time in history, that humanness was conceived only within tribal limits, it would seem that Matthew's new Israel is not devoid of Jewish traces, but is in fact framed in terms of Judaism.[19] The New Israel is for Matthew a Judaism-beyond-Judaism.

But if it isn't a form of universalism, where does Matthew's vision acquire its expansive scope? At this point we again encounter ambivalence in the Gospel's relation to empire. For the imperial vision proposed by Satan on the mountain of 4:8 is now reprised as the vision of Jesus' new mandate from the mountain of 28:16. This would seem to be the last temptation, the temptation of the church, to replicate the career of empire with its own mission. And we know that in the history of Christianity it has often understood its missionary mandate to be partnered with the imperial drive of Christian Europe. But this new mandate at the need of the written gospel imitates empire only to counter it. It is an anti-imperial program presented as an alternative to empire. When Jesus instructs his disciples to be apostles, to go forth baptizing and teaching, we are to remember that the baptism seals a metanoia, a hiatus, a break with the cultural standards, and the teaching includes a prohibition of violence, with a command to love one's enemies. The mandate is given to defuse empire, not to extend it.

19. Malina, *Social Gospel*, 10.

Bibliography

Aichele, George, Peter Miscall, and Richard Walsh. "An Elephant in the Room: Historical-Critical and Postmodern Interpretations of the Bible." *Journal of Biblical Literature (JBL)* 128, no. 2 (2009) 383–404.

Albertz, Rainer. *Israel in Exile: The History and Literature of the Sixth Century B.C.E.* Atlanta, GA: Society of Biblical Literature, 2002.

Alter, Robert, and Frank Kermode, eds. *The Literary Guide to the Bible.* Cambridge, MA: Belknap, Harvard Press, 1987.

Alter, Robert. *The Art of Biblical Narrative.* San Francisco: Basic Books, 1981.

Anderson, Janice Capel. *Matthew's Narrative Web: Over, and Over, and Over Again.* Sheffield, UK: Sheffield Academic Press, 1994.

Arendt, Hannah. *Between Past and Future: Eight Essays in Political Thought.* New York: Viking Press, 1954.

———. *On Violence.* New York: Harcourt, Brace, and World, 1969.

———. *The Human Condition.* Chicago: University of Chicago Press, 1958.

Auerbach, Erich. *Mimesis.* Translated by Willard Trask. Princeton, NJ: Princeton University Press, 1956.

Balabanski, Vicky. *Eschatology in the Making: Mark, Matthew and the Didache.* Cambridge, UK: University of Cambridge, 1997.

Bauer, David R. "The Kingship of Jesus in the Matthean Infancy Narrative: A Literary Analysis." *Catholic Biblical Quarterly* 57 (1995) 306–23.

Beck, Robert R. *Nonviolent Story: Narrative Conflict Resolution in the Gospel of Mark.* Maryknoll, NY: Orbis, 1996. Reprint: Eugene, OR: Wipf and Stock, 2009.

Bendix, Regina. *In Search of Authenticity: The Formation of Folklore Studies.* Madison: The University of Wisconsin Press, 1997.

Benstock, Bernard. "Telemachus." In *James Joyce's Ulysses,* edited by Clive Hart and David Hayman. Berkeley: University of California Press, 1974.

Berger, Peter L., and Thomas Luckmann. *The Social Construction of Reality: A Treatise in the Sociology of Knowledge.* Garden City, NY: Doubleday, 1966.

Bevington, David, ed. *Richard II.* The Bantam Shakespeare. New York: Bantam Books, 1980.

Bondurant, Joan V. *Conflict: Violence and Non-Violence.* Chicago: Aldine-Atherton, 1971.

———. *The Conquest of Violence: The Gandhian Philosophy of Conflict.* Princeton, N J: Princeton University Press, 1988.

Borg, Marcus. *Conflict, Holiness, and Politics in the Teachings of Jesus.* 2nd ed. Harrisburg, PA: Trinity Press International, 1998.

Brown, Raymond. *The Birth of the Messiah: A Commentary on the Infancy Narratives in the Gospels of Matthew and Luke.* New York: Doubleday, 1979.

———. *The Death of the Messiah: From Gethsemane to the Grave.* 2 Volumes. New York: Doubleday, 1994.

Brueggemann, Walter. "A Shattered Transcendence? Exile and Restoration," In *Old Testament Theology: Essays on Structure, Theme, and Text,* edited by Patrick Miller. Minneapolis: Fortress, 1992.

———. *Cadences of Home: Preaching Among Exiles.* Louisville: Westminster John Knox, 1997.

———. *Theology of the Old Testament.* Minneapolis: Fortress, 1997.

Campbell, Joseph. *The Hero with a Thousand Faces.* Princeton, NJ: Princeton University Press, 1972.

Carter, Warren. "Constructions of Violence and Identities in Matthew's Gospel." In *Violence in the New Testament.* Shelly Matthews and E. Leigh Gibson, eds. New York and London: T&T Clark. 2005, 81–108.

———. "James C. Scott and New Testament Studies: A Response to Allen Callahan, William Herzog, and Richard Horsley." In *Hidden Transcripts and the Arts of Resistance: Applying the Work of James C. Scott to Jesus and Paul,* edited by Richard A. Horsley, 81–94. Semeia Studies, No. 48. Atlanta, GA: Society of Biblical Literature, 2004.

———. "Kernels and Narrative Blocks: The Structure of Matthew's Gospel." *Catholic Biblical Quarterly* 54 (1992) 463–81.

———. "Resisting and Imitating the Empire: Imperial Paradigms in Two Matthean Parables." *Interpretation* 56, no. 3 (2002) 260–72.

———. *Matthew and Empire: Initial Explorations.* Harrisburg, PA: Trinity Press International, 2001.

———. *Matthew and the Margins: A Socio-Political and Religious Reading.* Maryknoll, NY: Orbis, 2000.

———. *Matthew: Storyteller, Interpreter, Evangelist.* Revised edition. Peabody, MA: Hendrickson, 2004.

Cheng, Vincent J. "Authenticity and Identity: Catching the Irish Spirit." In *Semicolonial Joyce,* edited by Derek Attridge and Marjorie Howes, 240–59. Cambridge, UK: Cambridge University Press, 2000.

———. *Joyce, Race, and Empire.* Cambridge, UK: Cambridge University Press, 1995.

Cope, O. Lamar. "'To the Close of the Age': The Role of Apocalyptic Thought in the Gospel of Matthew." In *Apocalyptic and the New Testament: Essays in Honor of J. Louis Martyn,* edited by J. Marcus and M. L. Soards, 113–23. JNTS Supplement, 24. Sheffield, UK: JSOT Press, 1989.

Crossan, John Dominic. *God and Empire: Jesus Against Rome, Then and Now.* San Francisco: HarperSanFrancisco, 2007.

Davies, W. D., and Dale C. Allison. *A Critical and Exegetical Commentary on the Gospel According to Saint Matthew,* 3 vols. Edinburgh: T. & T. Clark, 1988.

Dillard, Annie. "An Expedition to the Pole." In *Teaching a Stone to Talk: Expeditions and Encounters,* 17–52. San Francisco: Harper and Row, 1982.

Doniger, Wendy "Female Bandits? What next!"—review of *Robin Hood: A Mythic Biography,* by Stephen Knight. *London Review of Books* 20, no. 14 (2004).

Drury, John. "Mark." In *The Literary Guide to the Bible,* edited by Robert Alter and Frank Kermode. Cambridge, MA: Belknap, Harvard Press, 1987.

Dundes, Alan. *The Study of Folklore.* Englewood Cliffs, NJ: Prentice Hall, 1965.

———. *The Hero Pattern and the Life of Jesus.* Edited by W. Wuellner. Berkeley, CA: Center for Hermeneutical Studies, 1977.

Dunn, James D. G. "The Significance of Matthew's Eschatology for Biblical Theology." *SBL 1996 Seminar Papers.* Society of Biblical Literature, 150–62.

Eagleton, Terry. "Discourse and Ideology." In *Ideology: An Introduction*, 193–220. London, New York: Verso, 1991.

Escande, Jacques. "Judas et Pilate prisonniers d'une même structure (Mt 27,1–26)." *Foi et Vie* 78 (June 3, 1979) 92–100.

Evans, Craig A. *Word Biblical Commentary. Mark 8:27—16:20.* Vol. 34b. Nashville, TN: Thomas Nelson, 2001.

Fitzgerald, Sally, ed. *Flannery O'Connor, The Habit of Being: Letters edited and with an Introduction.* New York: Farrar, Straus, Giroux, 1979.

Flanagan, James W. "Succession and Genealogy in the Davidic Dynasty." In *The Quest for the Kingdom of God": Studies in honor of George E. Mendenhall*, 35–55. Winona Lake, IN: Eisenbrauns, 1983.

———. *David's Social Drama: A Hologram of Israel's Early Iron Age.* The Social World of Biblical Antiquity Series, 7. Sheffield: Almond Press, 1988.

Flavius Josephus. *The New Complete Works of Josephus.* Translated by William Whiston. Grand Rapids, MI: Kergel, 1999.

Forker, Charles R. *King Richard II.* The Arden Shakespeare. London: Thomson Learning, 2002.

Foucault, Michel. *The Archaeology of Knowledge and the Discourse on Language.* Translated by A. M. Sheridan Smith. New York: Pantheon Books. 1971, 1972.

———. *The Order of Things: An Archaeology of the Human Sciences.* New York: Random House, 1970, 1994.

Frankemölle, Hubert. *Jahwebunde und Kirche Christi. Studien zur Form- und Traditionsgeschichte des 'Evangeliums' nach Matthäus.* Münster: Aschendorf, 1984.

Fredriksen, Paula. "Did Jesus Oppose the Purity Laws?" *Bible Review* 11/ 3 (1995) 18–25, 42–47.

Freud, Sigmund. "Family Romances." In *Collected Papers,* Vol. V. Translated by James Strachey, 74–78. New York: Basic Books, 1959.

Freyne, Sean. *Galilee, Jesus and the Gospels: Literary Approaches and Historical Investigations* Philadelphia: Fortress, 1988.

———. "Vilifying the Other and Defining the Self: Matthew's and John's Anti-Jewish Polemic in Focus." In *"To See Ourselves a Others See Us": Christians, Jews, and "Others" in Late Antiquity*, edited by Jacob Neusner and Ernest S. Frerichs, 117–43. Chico, CA: Scholars Press, 1985.

Girard, René. *Job, the Victim of His People.* Translated by Yvonne Freccero. Stanford CA: Stanford University Press, 1987.

———. *The Scapegoat.* Translated by Yvonne Freccero. Baltimore: Johns Hopkins University Press, 1986.

———. *Violence and the Sacred.* Translated by Patrick Gregory. Baltimore: Johns Hopkins University Press, 1972.

Grayston, K. "The Translation of Matthew 28.17." *Journal for the Study of the New Testament* 21 (1984) 105–9.

Hagner, Donald A. "The *Sitz im Leben* of the Gospel of Matthew." In *Treasures New and Old: Contributions to Matthean Studies*, edited by David Bauer and Mark Allan Powell. Atlanta, GA: Scholars Press 1996.

———. "Matthew's Eschatology." *SBL 1996 Seminar Papers*. Society of Biblical Literature. 163–81.

Hare, Douglas R. A., and Daniel J. Harrington. "'Make Disciples of All the Gentiles' (Mt 28:19)" *Catholic Biblical Quarterly* 37 (1975) 359–69.

Harrington, Daniel J. *The Gospel of Matthew*. Sacra Pagina Series. Vol. 1. Collegeville, MN: Liturgical Press, 1991.

———. *The Gospel of Matthew*. Sacra Pagina Series, Vol. I. Collegeville, MN: Liturgical Press, 1991.

Hathaway, Michael, ed. *The Cambridge Companion to Shakespeare's History Plays*. Cambridge, UK: Cambridge University Press, 2002.

Hays, Richard B. *The Moral Vision of the New Testament: Community, Cross, New Creation; A Contemporary Introduction to New Testament Ethics*. San Francisco: HarperSanFrancisco, 1996.

Hertig, Paul. "Geographical Marginality in the Matthean Journeys of Jesus." *SBL 1999 Seminar Papers*. Society of Biblical Literature. 472–89.

Homer. *The Odyssey*. Translated by Robert Fagles. New York: Penguin, 1996.

Horsley, Richard A. "The Politics of Disguise and Public Declaration of the Hidden Transcript: Broadening Our Approach to the Historical Jesus with Scott's 'Arts of Resistance' Theory." In *Hidden Transcripts and the Arts of Resistance: Applying the Work of James C. Scott to Jesus and Paul*, edited by Richard A. Horsley, 61–80. Semeia Studies, No. 48. Atlanta, GA: Society of Biblical Literature, 2004.

———. *Telling the Whole Story: The Politics of Plot in Mark's Gospel*. Louisville, KY: Westminster John Knox, 2001.

———. *The Liberation of Christmas: The Infancy Narratives in Social Context*. London: Continuum International Publishing Group, 1989. Reprint: Eugene, OR: Wipf & Stock, 2004.

———, ed. *Hidden transcripts and the Arts of Resistance: Applying the Work of James C. Scott to Jesus and Paul*. Semeia Studies, 48. Atlanta, GA: Society of Biblical Literature, 2004.

Howell, David B. *Matthew's Inclusive Story: A Study in the Narrative Rhetoric of the First Gospel*. Sheffield, UK: University of Sheffield Press, 1990.

Hugh Kenner, "Circe." In *James Joyce's Ulysses*, edited by Clive Hart and David Hayman, 341–62. Berkeley: University of California Press, 1977.

Jenkins, Harold. *Hamlet*. The Arden Shakespeare. London: Thomson Learning, 1982.

Johnson, Marshall D. *The Purpose of the Biblical Genealogies: With Special Reference to the Setting of the Genealogies of Jesus*. Cambridge, UK: Cambridge University Press, 1969.

Joyce, James. *Ulysses*. Edited by Hans Walter Gabler. London: Bodley Head, 1986.

Kiberd, Declan. *Inventing Ireland: The Literature of the Modern Nation*. Cambridge, MA: Harvard University Press, 1995.

Kingsbury, Jack Dean. *Matthew: Structure, Christology, Kingdom*. Philadelphia: Fortress, 1975.

———. *Matthew as Story*. 2nd ed. Philadelphia: Fortress, 1988.

Knoppers, Gary. *I Chronicles 1–9*. Yale Anchor Bible Series. New Haven, CT: Yale University Press, 2004.

Lévi-Strauss, Claude. *Structural Anthropology*. Vol. I. Translated by Claire Jacobson and Brooke Grundfest Schoepf. New York: Basic Books, 1963.

Levine, Amy-Jill. *The Social and Ethnic Dimensions of Matthean Salvation History.* Studies in the Bible and Early Christianity. Vol. 14. Lewiston, NY: Edwin Mellen \, 1988.

Logue, Christopher. *All Day Permanent Red: The First Battle Scenes of Homer's Iliad, Rewritten.* New York: Farrar, Straus and Giroux, 2003.

Malina, Bruce J. *The Social Gospel of Jesus: The Kingdom of God in Mediterranean Perspective.* Minneapolis: Fortress, 2001.

Matera, Frank J. "The Plot of Matthew's Gospel." *Catholic Biblical Quarterly* 49 (1987) 233–53.

Matthews, Shelly, and E. Leigh Gibson, eds. *Violence in the New Testament.* New York and London: T&T Clark. 2005.

McKenzie, Steven L. *King David: A Biography.* Oxford, UK: Oxford University Press, 2000.

Meier, John P. "Nations or Gentiles in Matthew 28:19?" *Catholic Biblical Quarterly* 39 (1977) 94–102.

———. *Matthew.* New Testament Message 3. Collegeville, MN: Liturgical Press, 1980, 1990.

Merton, Thomas, ed. *Gandhi on Non-violence: Selected Texts from Mohandas K. Gandhi's "Non-violence in Peace and War."* New York: Scribner's, 1940.

———. *Faith and Violence: Christian Teaching and Christian Practice.* Notre Dame, IN: University of Notre Dame Press, 1968.

Mills, Sara "Discourse and Ideology." In *Discourse.* London and New York: Routledge: 1997, 29–47.

Neusner, Jacob, and Bruce D. Chilton, eds. *In Quest of the Historical Pharisees.* Waco, TX: Baylor University Press, 2007.

Neville, David J. "Toward a Teleology of Peace: Contesting Matthew's Violent Eschatology." *Journal for the Study of the New Testament* 30, no. 2 (2007) 131–61.

Neyrey, Jerome H. *Honor and Shame in the Gospel of Matthew.* Louisville, KY: Westminster John Knox, 1998.

———. "The Idea of Purity in Mark's Gospel." *Semeia* 35 (1986) 91–128.

Niebuhr, Reinhold. *Moral Man and Immoral Society.* Louisville, KY: Westminster John Knox Press, 2002.

———. "Why the Church Is Not Pacifist." In *Christianity and Power Politics.* New York: Scribner's, 1940. Reprint: North Haven, CT: Archon, 1969.

———. *An Interpretation of Christian Ethics.* New York: Seabury, 1979.

Norwich, John Julius. *Shakespeare's Kings: The Great Plays and the History of England in the Middle Ages, 1337–1485.* New York: Simon and Schuster, 1999.

Nutt, Alfred. "The Aryan Expulsion and Return Formula in the Folk- and Hero-Tales of the Celts." In *The Folk-lore Record.* Vol. IV. London: Folk-lore Society, 1881, 1–44.

O'Connor, Flannery. *The Violent Bear It Away.* New York: Farrar, Straus and Giroux, 2007.

Otto, Rudolf, *The Idea of the Holy: An Inquiry into the Non-Rational Factor in the Idea of the Divine and Its Relation to the Rational.* Translated by John W. Harvey. London: Oxford University Press, 1926.

Patte, Daniel. *What Is Structural Exegesis?* Philadelphia: Fortress, 1976.

Pestowitz, Miriam. "Tropes of Travel." In *Semeia 75: Postcolonialism and Scriptural Reading,* edited by Laura A. Donaldson, 83–84. Atlanta, GA: Scholars Press, 1996.

Pickup, Martin. "Matthew's and Mark's Pharisees." In *In Quest of the Historical Pharisees*, edited by Jacob Neusner and Bruce Chilton, 108–12. Waco, TX: Baylor University Press, 2007.

Pilch, John. *Healing in the New Testament: Insights from Medical and Mediterranean Anthropology*. Minneapolis: Fortress, 2000.

Poster, Mark. *Foucault, Marxism and History*. Cambridge, UK: Polity Press, 1984.

Powell, Mark Allan. "Plot and Subplot of Matthew's Gospel." *New Testament Studies*, 38 (1992) 187–204.

———. "Toward a Narrative-Critical Understanding of Matthew." *Interpretation*, 46/4 (1992) 341–46.

Propp, Vladimir. *The Morphology of the Folktale*. Translated by Laurence Scott. Austin, TX: University of Texas Press, 1968.

Prosser, Eleanor. *Hamlet and Revenge*. Stanford, CA: Stanford University Press, 1967.

Rank, Otto. *The Myth of the Birth of the Hero*. Translated by F. Robbins and Smith Ely Jelliffe, NY: Knopf, 1959.

Reid, Barbara E. "Violent Endings in Matthew's Parables and Christian Nonviolence." *Catholic Biblical Quarterly* 66 (2004) 237–55.

Rhoads, David, Joanna Dewey, and Donald Michie. *Mark as Story: An Introduction to the Narrative of a Gospel*. 2nd ed. Minneapolis: Fortress, 1999.

Riches, John K. *Conflicting Mythologies: Identity Formation in the Gospels of Mark and Matthew*. Edinburgh: T&T Clark, 2000.

Ricoeur, Paul. "Biblical Hermeneutics," *Semeia* 4 (1975) 75–106.

Said, Edward W. *Culture and Imperialism*. New York: Random House, 1994.

Saldarini, Anthony J. *Pharisees, Scribes and Sadducees in Palestinian Society*. 2nd ed. Grand Rapids, MI: Eerdmans, 2001.

Scholes, Robert. *Textual Power: Literary Theory and the Teaching of English*. New Haven, CT: Yale University Press, 1985.

Scott, Bernard Brandon. *Hear Then the Parable: A Commentary on the Parables of Jesus*. Minneapolis: Augsburg, 1989.

Scott, James C. *Domination and the Arts of Resistance: Hidden Transcripts*. New Haven, CT: Yale University Press, 1990.

Senior, Donald. *The Gospel of Matthew*. Nashville: Abingdon, 1997.

———. *What Are They saying about Matthew?*, Rev. ed. Mahwah, NJ: Paulist, 1996.

Sharp, Gene. *The Politics of Nonviolent Action. Vol. I: Power and Struggle*. Boston: Porter Sargent Publishers, 1973.

———. *The Poligics of Nonviolent Action, Vol. 3: The Dynamics of Nonviolent Action*. Boston: Porter Sargent Publishers, 1973.

Smith-Christopher, Daniel. *A Biblical Theology of Exile*. Minneapolis: Fortress, 2002.

———. *The Religion of the Landless: The Social Context of the Babylonian Exile*. Bloomington, IN: Meyer-Stone, 1989.

Sperling, S. David, "Blood." In *Anchor Bible Dictionary*, I, 762.

Stendahl, Krister. "Quis et Unde? An Analysis of Matthew 1–2. (1960)." In *The Interpretation of Matthew*, edited by Graham Stanton. Philadelphia: Fortress, 1983.

———. *The School of St. Matthew and Its Use of the New Testament*. Philadelphia: Fortress, 1968,

Swartley, Willard M. *Covenant of Peace: The Missing Peace in New Testament Theology and Ethics*. Grand Rapids, MI: Eerdmans, 2006.

Tannehill, Robert. "The Gospel of Mark as Narrative Christology," *Perspectives on Mark's Gospel, Semeia 16*, edited by Norman R. Petersen. Missoula, MT: SBL, 1980.

Theissen, Gerd, and Annette Merz. *The Historical Jesus: A Comprehensive Guide.* Minneapolis: Fortress, 1996.

Trilling, Lionel. *Sincerity and Authenticity.* Cambridge, MA: Harvard University Press, 1971.

Viviano, Benedict. "Matthew." *New Jerome Biblical Commentary.* 3rd ed. Edited by Raymond Brown, Joseph A. Fitzmyer, and Roland E. Murphy. Englewood Cliffs, NJ: Prentice Hall, 1999.

Von Rad, Gerhard. *Wisdom in Israel.* Translated by James D. Martin. Nashville and New York: Abingdon, 1972.

Watts, Cedric. *Hamlet.* Boston: Twayne, 1988.

Weaver, Dorothy Jean. "Power and Powerlessness: Matthew's Use of Irony in the Portrayal of Political Leaders," In *Treasures New and Old: Recent Contributions to Matthew Studies*, edited by David R. Bauer and Mark Allan Powell, 454–66. Society of Biblical Literature Seminar, 31. Atlanta, GA: Scholar's Press, 1992.

———. "Rewriting the Messianic Script: Matthew's Account of the Birth of Jesus," *Interpretation* (2000) 376–85.

Weber, Kathleen. "Plot and Matthew." *SBL 1996 Seminar Papers.* Society of Biblical Literature. 400–31.

Whybray, R. N. *The Succession Narrative: A Study of II Samuel 9–20; I Kings 1 and 2.* London: SCM, 1968.

Wilson, Robert R. *Genealogy and History in the Biblical World.* New Haven, CT: Yale University Press, 1977.

Wright, N. T. *Jesus and the Victory of God.* Minneapolis: Fortress, 1996.

———. *Surprised by Hope.* New York: HarperCollins, 2008.

———. *The New Testament and the People of God.* Minneapolis: Fortress, 1992.

Subject/Name Index

44; hiatus, 13, 115–17, 129;
hometown, 9, 23, 26–28;
rejection at, 38; narrative
site, 13, 14, 18–26, 75–76;
theological site, 9, 23; in Luke's
account, 21, 23
Nehemiah, 100, 102
Neusner, Jacob, 123
Neville, David J., 148, 151
Neyrey, Jerome, SJ, 40, 181–182, 188
Niebuhr, Reinhold, xiii, 161
nonviolence, xi–xvi, 31, 54–56, 86, 108,
126, 128, 133–136, 139, 148–
150, 152, 154, 158–162, 164–
165, 177, 186, 188; definitions,
xiii, xv; nonresistance, xiii,
47, 48, 54, 161, 167, 176, 182;
nonretaliation, 1, 47, 48, 53,
78, 86, 121, 126, 133, 134, 140,
147, 158–162, 163, 172, 173,
175–177, 189; nonretaliation as
prophylactic, 133–34. See also
nonviolent conflict resolution
nonviolent conflict resolution, 33, 186
nonviolent resistance, xiv, 47–48, 159,
176
nostalgia, 190
nostos, xiv, 5, 76, 153, 165, 167, 169,
172, 175, 190
Nutt, Alfred, 71, 73, 132

O'Connor, Flannery, 5, 160
Odyssey, 5, 58, 59, 67–69, 79, 81, 84,
112, 113, 118, 140, 172, 189
outer darkness, 144, 150

parables: Great Feast (Matt 22:1–14)
172, 174; Sheep and Goats (Last
Judgment; Matt 25:31-46), 151–
153, 172; Sower (Matt 13:3–9;
18-23), 35–37, 147; Talents
(Matt 25:14–30), 151, 172; Ten
Bridesmaids (Matt 25:1–13),
151, 172 ; Two Sons (Matt
21:28–32), 172; Unforgiving
Servant (Matt 18:23–35), 108,
150, 152–153, 157

parable endings, 1, 148, 150–151, 155,
156, 164
payback (retribution), 69, 75, 77, 153,
159, 169–172, 175, 177–180
Perseus, 89
Pestowitz, Miriam, 190
Pharisees, 31, 38, 42, 43, 51–52, 85, 106,
107, 109–110, 115, 117–126,
128–129, 132136, 140, 144–146,
150–151, 154, 164, 165
Philoctetes, 63, 141
Pickup, Martin, 110, 118
Pilate's wife, 105, 179, 182, 183, 184, 188
Pilch, John, 39, 41
plotlines, nested diagram, 85, 164, 165
poetic justice, 153, 155, 189
Pontius Pilate, 85, 103, 106, 109, 115,
130, 172, 178–185, 187–188,
191
postcolonial criticism, xvi, 88, 102,
110, 119, 126–129, 131, 133,
145, 151, 190; authenticity,
110, 115, 120, 126–134; faked
authenticity, 127–28; hybridity,
133
Poster, Mark, 38
Powell, Mark Allan, 98
praxis (discourse), 35, 38, 41, 43, 50,
51, 149
Prince of Egypt, The (film), 60, 66–67,
70, 89
proportion (justice), 155–158, 162
Propp, Vladimir, 60, 74, 97
Psalm 72, 90–91, 105
purge (narrative cleansing), 75, 76, 131,
153, 167, 169–172, 177–180,
189
purity: as ritual holiness (Mark), 38–43;
as resistance, 42, 123–124; as
authenticity, 124–125

Q-Source, 39, 77

rabbinic movement, 11, 12, 40, 107,
110, 118, 124, 126, 130, 133,
134, 135, 144
Rachel's tomb, 25